BALANCING ACTS

JAMES CONKLIN

Balancing

Acts

A HUMAN SYSTEMS
APPROACH TO
ORGANIZATIONAL
CHANGE

UNIVERSITY OF TORONTO PRESS
Toronto Buffalo London

© James Conklin 2021
Rotman-UTP Publishing
An imprint of University of Toronto Press
Toronto Buffalo London
utorontopress.com

ISBN 978-1-4875-4027-2 (cloth)   ISBN 978-1-4875-4029-6 (EPUB)
                                  ISBN 978-1-4875-4028-9 (PDF)

Library and Archives Canada Cataloguing in Publication

Title: Balancing acts : a human systems approach to organizational
   change / James Conklin.
Names: Conklin, James (Lecturer in applied human sciences), author.
Description: Includes bibliographical references and index.
Identifiers: Canadiana (print) 2021021869X | Canadiana (ebook)
   20210219114 | ISBN 9781487540272 (cloth) | ISBN 9781487540296
   (EPUB) | ISBN 9781487540289 (PDF)
Subjects: LCSH: Organizational change. | LCSH: Organizational
   change – Planning.
Classification: LCC HD58.8.C69 2021 | DDC 658.4/06–dc23

We acknowledge the financial support of the Government of Canada, the Canada Council for the Arts, and the Ontario Arts Council, an agency of the Government of Ontario, for our publishing activities.

ONTARIO ARTS COUNCIL
CONSEIL DES ARTS DE L'ONTARIO
an Ontario government agency
un organisme du gouvernement de l'Ontario

Canada Council   Conseil des Arts
for the Arts   du Canada

Funded by the   Financé par le
Government   gouvernement
of Canada   du Canada

For Susan

Contents

Preface   ix

Acknowledgments   xiii

PART ONE: THINKING ABOUT CHANGE   3

1 Terms of Art   10

2 Doing Things *to* People and Doing Things *with* People   33

3 Searching for Answers   57

PART TWO: THE DOING OF CHANGE   83

4 Creating a Contract with Your Client   91

5 Exploring the Client System   134

6 Making Sense of Things   171

7 Implementing and Evaluating the Intervention   217

8 The Ethics of Intervention   260

9 Changing the Future of Planned Change   294

Notes   313

References   333

Index   347

Preface

This book is about planning and implementing interventions into human systems.

The approach to change that I present on these pages derives from the following assertion: when you help a group of people to change, you are performing a balancing act.

All human groups that stay together and do things together over time function as systems, and interventions into human systems meet with similar opportunities and challenges and follow similar courses. The intervener must balance four critical concerns while helping the group to change.

I believe that it is essential that you recognize these balancing acts and that you regulate your own thoughts and actions to maintain a balance that allows you to fulfill your commitments to your client.

You will engage in four critical balancing acts:

1. You must balance the need to challenge and at times push your client toward success with the need to create safety and to show compassion for your client. You are confrontational *and* you are compassionate.
2. You must balance the need to become part of the client system, so you can form relationships and gather information, with the need to remain distinct and apart, so you can avoid being

absorbed into the client's characteristic ways of thinking and acting. You participate *and* you observe.
3. You must balance your inclination to tell your client the answer
with the need to create the conditions in which members of your
client system can discover the answers for themselves. You assert
and you inquire.
4. You must balance the need to engage in planned and intentional
activity with the need to be open to the emergent and unexpected. You stay the course *and* you change course.

Notice that the choice here is not a choice of one or the other. The
choice is a matter of finding the appropriate balance for this client in
this situation. One of my friends and mentors often urged upon me
the idea that when we are dealing with human beings there are no
categorical variables. There are only continuous variables. Human
traits, preferences, inclinations, and skills do not reside inside hard
and impenetrable boundaries. They reside on continua, on spec-
trums, that range from the lesser to the greater. I am always acting
on the basis of some intention, and I am always in a stance of discovery. Recognizing and using that complexity is one of the hallmarks
of the skilled interventionist.

A host of complex interpersonal skills lurks beneath that assertion. You must be present with and attentive to your client and the
patterns of thought and behavior that bring coherence to the social milieu. You must participate without becoming immersed. You
must be brave enough to display your own ignorance and helplessness. You must endure prolonged periods of client resistance. You
must be prepared to tell the truth, and to admit that you are wrong.

You must also, over time, become a skilled observer of the interaction patterns that create the living reality of your client's system.
You must be able to see human behavior as a series of moves in an
unfolding game, and to recognize how certain moves open up the

system to creativity and innovation while others close it down to protect it from perceived threats.

You must be able to see how these moves arise from mindsets and give rise to social structures that in turn reinforce the group's patterns of thought and action. You must develop the capacity to gauge your own capacity and the client's capacity, and to devise and implement interventions that help you and the client to develop, to solve problems, and to create more congenial and productive worlds.

This book is about all of these things.

How This Book Works

Part 1 of the book consists of three chapters dealing with ways of thinking about change. These chapters provide definitions, and consider some generative stances, approaches, and conceptual frameworks. Part 1 concludes by presenting a simple, powerful model that an interventionist can use to organize her thinking about the human system that she is helping.

The book then moves into part 2 with six chapters that show how you might apply these concepts and frameworks in practice. This is where we will delve into the four balancing acts that the interventionist must master. What do you need to do, and what does your team need to do? How should you interact with the people who will be most affected by the change? What sort of plan is needed, and how rigid or flexible should you be as you implement the plan? What sorts of challenges, problems, and ethical dilemmas can you anticipate? What does success look like as you pursue improvements in complex social environments?

The book concludes with a chapter that offers some final thoughts about the science and art of social change, and about how you might think productively about the four critical balancing acts as you test these ideas in the context of your own life.

I often illustrate the ideas presented in the book by providing an example or telling a story. All of the examples and stories are taken from my own experiences and those of a few colleagues. To protect the privacy of people who play a part in these examples, I have used fictitious names and have altered some details.

This book is written for anybody who is interested in understanding the affordances and constraints of change processes. If you are a student taking a course in organizational behavior, organization development, change management, or community development, this book is for you. If you lead or intend to lead change initiatives, the book should be of value. The book will provide you with a useful way to think about social change. It will offer a simple, pragmatic framework for conceptualizing the functioning of a human system and for designing interventions that could alter that functioning. It takes you through the steps that often arise during a change process, and it will help you to anticipate some surprises that may occur. It focuses on the four critical balancing acts because they provide the leverage you need to do good work. This book is about you, the agent of change, and the people who ultimately have to make the change work, and about the relationship between you and those people.

The book can be read in a conventional manner, from beginning to end. If you are more interested in conceptual material, then part 1 may be of most interest to you. If you are more interested in practical matters, then part 2 will be more interesting.

Acknowledgments

I wrote this book while sitting alone at my desk in my basement office, facing my computer screen, dredging up memories of past experiences, pulling books down from my shelves, and searching out articles on scholarly databases around the world. The writing was a solitary activity, but the planning and editing of the manuscript was also a social enterprise. My interest in organizational change and whatever knowledge and skill I have of this subject derive from interactions I have had with others that go back some forty-five years. I have been lucky to spend time with excellent leaders, peers, practitioners, scholars, and students. These many friends and colleagues nourished me with many experiences, ideas, and suggestions.

Dr. Frank Dumont read several chapters of the manuscript and stimulated me with his lively conversation on the mysteries of behavior change. Drs. Edgar Schein and Gervase Bushe both obliged me by reading chapters and offering their estimates and suggestions. My former students Emma Sobel, Riham Ahmed, and Colin Robertson read and commented helpfully on chapters.

I also benefited from exchanges with and assistance from several colleagues in the Department of Applied Human Sciences at Concordia University. I am grateful to Drs. Varda Mann-Feder, Rosemary Reilly, Ghislaine Guérard, Bluma Litner, and Peter Morden. I also owe a debt to scientists and research colleagues who helped me to delve into the dynamics of social learning, in particular Drs. Barbara Farrell, Paul Stolee, Anita Kothari, Larry Chambers, Bill Hogg, Hillary Hart, Saul Carliner, Kevin Pottie, and Ken LeClair.

Over the years I participated in many organizational change efforts. What I remember the most about those days are the struggles, and the great people who stood with me as we worked through them. Those who remain vivid in my mind include Gino Braha, Elaine Phillips, Keith Wilson, Trish Wainnika, David Baker, J.P. Parenty, Dean Wilmot, Debbie Reindeau, Barb Spurway, Caroline Ben-Ari, Wolfgang Baun, Bob Knight, Judy Glick-Smith, Mary Wise, Ken Rainey, and Henry Willms.

I have also been lucky to work with many fine graduate students, some of whom have stayed in contact as they have gone forth to change the world. In addition to those I mentioned earlier, I want to offer thanks to Judith Newland, Rhonda deBeaupre, Andrew Beckett, Sabrina Bonfini, Emma Legault, Kit Malo, Lynda Gerty, Catherine Somrani, Rene Felipe Garcia, Gabrielle Beaulieu, Nadia Plummer, Tejaswinee Jhunjhunwala, Amina Bombiata, Theresa Humphreys, Kate Woolhouse, James Lapalme, Rhonda Schwartz, Ann-Louise Howard, and Vanessa Cortes.

The men and women who developed and who are involved with the ontological leadership program had considerable influence on me, some of which is evident in this book. I want to thank them for their thought-provoking work – in particular, Werner Erhard, Michael Jensen, Kari Granger, Jeri Echeverria, Steve Zaffron, and Chip Souba.

And I want to recognize my dear friend and conversational combatant, the late Adrian DiCastri, with whom I had so many enjoyable sparring matches, and whose keen intelligence and wide reading were a tonic.

I am delighted to be able to thank, in print, Jennifer DiDomenico, my editor at the Rotman-UTP imprint of the University of Toronto

Press. Her patience and persistence are legendary now in my household, and I am grateful for her belief in this book and for her clear, incisive guidance as we prepared the final manuscript during the pandemic lockdown of late 2020.

Finally, I recognize that I do not know how to describe the debt I owe to Susan, my brilliant wife. She lived many of the moments with me that are presented in this book and sat with me through mornings and evenings as we discussed the experiences and ideas presented here. Susan understands and practices process consultation better than anyone I have ever met. Not only did she create the conditions in which I was able to write all of this down, but she also walked with me on the intellectual and experiential journey that culminates here.

All of these people contributed to whatever is of worth in this book. Its shortcomings, of course, belong entirely to me.

BALANCING ACTS

PART ONE

Thinking about Change

In their book *Breaking the Code of Change*, Michael Beer and Nitin Nohria suggest that there are two broad approaches to changing organizations.[1] On the one hand, Theory E focuses exclusively on the financial performance and economic value of the organization. Beer and Nohria tell us that Theory E change is led by top-down leaders who set the agenda for the change and who issue orders to corporate and line staff about what and how to change. These leaders focus attention entirely on altering organizational strategies, systems, and structures that can be manhandled like so many parts of a machine. The change process is conceived of as a carefully designed program, with a detailed plan that is executed with discipline. Often, external consultants are brought on board to shore up gaps in knowledge and to devise and implement solutions.

Theory O, on the other hand, focuses on developing new organizational capability, largely by helping managers and employees to become better at diagnosing and solving workplace problems. Beer and Nohria believe that leaders of Theory O change are collaborative and participative, allowing the change effort to be informed by the intelligence and experiences of people at all levels and locations in the organization. Often, the focus is on altering organizational culture, because these change leaders believe that culture provides a coherent and pervasive foundation for the way that organizational members behave. If we get the right culture in place, we will release behaviors that assure success. The change process is thought of as flexible and emergent, and frequently is not based on a roadmap whose details have been worked out by corporate staff. Instead, leaders provide a framework, and managers and staff figure out how to implement it. When consultants are brought in, they usually offer processes rather than solutions. Organizational members themselves diagnose the key issues, develop proposed solutions, try things out, and then regroup and adapt when needed.

Beer and Nohria suggest that a synthesis of these two theories will often provide the best approach to change, and they designed their book to mirror the sort of synthesis they anticipate. This work is an admirable effort to distill some essential meaning out of the mountain of discourse on organizational change. As I was writing this paragraph, I googled the words "books about organizational change" and received 23,500,000 hits. I then performed a keyword search for books on Amazon with the words "change management" and received 106,215 results. I then did a Boolean keyword search for "change management" on Google Scholar and received 338,000 results; a search for "organizational change" yielded 777,000 results; and a search for "social change" brought 2,380,000 results.

With this growing mountain of discourse about social change, I can well understand Beer and Nohria's effort to boil things down to a single, fundamental distinction: cash or capability. Other authors have also attempted to arrive at basic distinctions or frameworks that allow us to think clearly about leadership and change. In the 1960s Douglas McGregor, an eminent scholar at the MIT's Sloan School, concluded that managers tended to hold a particular set of beliefs, which he labeled Theory X and Theory Y, about the causes of human behavior.[2] Those who subscribed to Theory X assumed that people tend to respond largely to financial incentives and often need to be managed through careful supervision and control, while those who subscribed to Theory Y assumed that people are usually self-motivated, especially when they are given opportunities to participate in organizational decision making. As you might expect, Beer and Nohria acknowledge the similarities between their Theories E and O and McGregor's Theories X and Y.

A few years later, Rensis Likert, director of the Institute for Social Research at the University of Michigan and the man who gave his name to the popular Likert scale used in survey research, suggested that there are four types of management systems: system 1 is exploitative and authoritative; system 2 is benevolent and authoritative; system 3 is consultative; and system 4 is participative.[3] Much of his work was intended to assist leaders who were interested in moving their organizations away from system 1 structures and approaches and toward system 4. Chris Argyris, the Harvard scholar and consultant who helped to develop the concept of organizational learning, wrote many books and articles about two opposing theories of action, Model I and Model II, which roughly correspond to more controlling versus more collaborative approaches to leadership and change.[4] Similarly, Heifetz and Linsky argue that organizational leaders tend to be faced with two types of change which they term technical and adaptive.[5] Technical change is needed when the problems we face have known solutions, and the leader's task is to call on the experts who know how to solve the problem. Adaptive change is a foray into the unknown, a search for solutions to novel problems that are not fully understood and that require experimentation, exploration, and the mobilization of numerous points of view.

Wherever we look in the copious literature on social and organizational change, we find distinctions of this sort. On the one hand there is the desire to control and predict; on the other hand there is the desire to collaborate and explore. Some authors suggest that one is better than the other, while others claim that we should seek

Table P1. The two contrasting approaches to change

	Predictive Change	Adaptive Change
The basic idea is	Orderly, controlled change in pursuit of targets established by leaders.	Flexible, adaptive change in pursuit of targets negotiated by system members.
Actions tend to be	Planned, sequential, moving toward a known target. Monitoring is used to measure progress.	Emergent, exploratory, moving toward a flexible target. Monitoring is used to allow for reflection and adaptation.
Support is provided by	A detailed implementation plan carried out by program staff.	Broad goals and a communication strategy that includes most (or all) system members, with work done by teams whose membership may change.
A motto might be	First control yourself, and then control your environment.	Everything changes, even change.

to balance the two. Within the field of action science, authors claim that change leaders profess to value collaborative approaches, but their actions belie these claims and suggest that deep down they prefer to be in control of things. Table P1 summarizes some of the key points of these two perspectives.

As I read through this material, it is clear that most authors have a preference for the adaptive approach. Sometimes they are scornful of the desire to control and predict. The argument often takes the following form:

We live in a complex world made up of almost countless components and forces. It is impossible to control and predict what might happen later today let alone later this year or later in the decade. What's more, the people who are in the best position to exert control over others and over the environment are those who currently monopolize power, and this means that control and prediction are the instruments of the politically powerful and the rich. To endorse approaches that value control and prediction is to endorse a status quo that sometimes can be unfair and oppressive. Therefore, I will side with the collaborative and participative approach, which sounds more consistent with democratic principles.

I am a product of a democratic, Western nation, and I like to be consulted when those who have power over me decide to pursue a change that will affect my standing in the community or my work. I like the collaborative, adaptive approach.

But I also like things to be relatively orderly and coherent. I understand that for us to work together, some give and take will be needed, and this means that we need to rely on processes to consolidate and aggregate opinions and beliefs, to coordinate plans, to make decisions and get things done. Many historians have said that the motto of my country, Canada, is *"peace, order, and good government."* I like this motto. When I am part of a group that is seeking to change something, I like to set a goal, to "begin with the end in mind," and then I like to consider the steps that are needed to achieve that goal.

We can anticipate some things that will happen in the future, but we cannot anticipate everything. It is good to set out on a definite course and to exert some control over things, and it is good to be prepared when the need arises to change course. I want an approach that holds this tension.

It makes sense to me that when a human collective is preparing to embark upon a change, no single leader and no small leadership group, regardless of their intelligence, are able to fully grasp all of the issues and problems that will arise on the change journey. To access as much information as possible about what might happen, and what might be done to mitigate risk and keep moving forward, it is necessary to mobilize the knowledge of the people who are going to live through the change process. This means creating ways for frontline staff, suppliers, customers, and other stakeholders to influence and contribute to the change process. We need to create a temporary social structure to contain all of these aspirations and activities.

A simple dichotomy that separates prediction and control from adaptation and flexibility is not enough. As we go about changing a social system, we will likely need to balance the need for coherence and control with the need for adaptability and flexibility. We won't abandon the one for the other. We will be performing a balancing act, the result of which will be that we may achieve something close to our original intentions, and we will not be stymied when we encounter unexpected problems along the way. This is one of the balancing acts that you will encounter later in this book: an interventionist must balance the need to engage in planned and intentional activity with the need to be open to the emergent and unexpected. You stay the course *and* you change course.

In the next three chapters we will consider ways to think about change. In these chapters we will consider *what needs to be done*. Then in part 2 of the book we will consider the doing of change. In part 2, we consider *how to do* what needs to be done.

I am approaching the topic this way for a reason. Several years ago, I participated in several large information technology outsourcing projects. My participation took place at the start of the projects, when the relationships and interfaces were being designed and the transition to the outsourcer was getting underway. At the very start of these processes, I noticed that the complexity of the undertaking, the myriad details that needed to be attended to, often left people discouraged and exhausted. I found that it was sometimes useful to create a simple conceptual framework to hold the overall endeavor that would allow us to frame our thinking and our actions within a shared vocabulary and system of thought. The framework consisted of two parts. One part was a vision of the end state to which we were journeying. This would be some sort of representation of the result, the conclusion, the relationship between client and outsourcer once it was up and running and in a stable condition. The other part was a roadmap showing the journey to arrive at this destination. You might think of this as a project plan, a pathway, or a navigation chart. Together, these two ideas showed us our yellow brick road and the grand city of Oz, and allowed us to find coherence in the maze of details and activities that engulfed us during the busy transition process.

In the next three chapters I will describe the solution – the destination – that an intervener is concerned with as she begins to plan the intervention that is intended to bring about change. What are we acting upon as we try to change a human social and technical system? What is the target of our intervention? Later, in part 2, I will discuss the process for bringing about the change.

CHAPTER ONE

Terms of Art

Over the past three decades I have had many conversations with students, consultants, and organizational leaders about organizational change. I have learned that different people think differently about social change. We use terms in different ways, we work from different assumptions, and we rely on different concepts.

I experienced a dramatic illustration of this in July 2013 at a meeting of research scientists in Ottawa. A colleague and I had designed a research project that was intended to produce behavior changes among clinicians who worked in long-term care homes and primary care practices. This meeting provided an orientation to the project and the team, and was attended by seven scientists and four research staff. During the meeting I talked about organizational change. Since all of the other researchers were clinicians (either pharmacists or family physicians), I thought they would enjoy seeing some data gathered from the social sciences and management science. Health researchers tend to be familiar with the literature in their own field, which in this case was the design and delivery of health services, and less familiar with the scientific literature that lies outside of their domain.

I wanted to make the point that our attempt to bring about sustainable change to health practices was likely to be difficult, and so I had created a slide that summarized the findings from recent research about the success and failure rates of organizational change. As I showed the slide, I talked about how organizational scholars were fascinated by the poor success rates evident in these studies, and I drew my colleagues' attention to the data point indicating that the overall median success rate for these initiatives was 33 per cent.[1]

At this point a family physician who is also a distinguished research scientist raised his hand. He said that he was surprised to hear me refer to these numbers as indicating failures. He explained that in his professional world, success rates ranging from 20 per cent to 60 per cent would be considered extremely positive. "If I developed an intervention that benefitted 20 per cent or 30 per cent of my patients, I would be delighted, and I would recommend that they give it a try."

I was astonished. Among the organizational leaders and consultants with whom I had worked for most of my career, these numbers would be seen as disappointing. But as I reflected on his comment in the days following the meeting, I realized that his was a perfectly reasonable outlook on the success and failure of change initiatives. We were approaching the matter from different professional worlds, and this influenced our attitudes.

My colleague is a doctor. He provides medical treatments to individual patients. When he is appraising a new treatment that has just become available, he wants to know how often this treatment is successful. If scientific tests have been conducted on the benefits produced by the new treatment, these tests will likely have yielded a prediction about how often the treatment produces positive results among certain categories of patients. Depending on the medical condition that the patient is experiencing, a treatment that is beneficial for 20 per cent of patients might be a big step forward (if, let's say, the previous best treatment was helpful for only 8 per cent of patients). As he looked at the data on my slide, my colleague was imagining how great it would be to see those sorts of numbers in relation to the treatment of individual patients with complex medical conditions. He was not thinking about organizational change but instead was supposing that the way he thought about patients could be transferred intact to his thinking about organizational change.

But this is not the way that organizational leaders or consultants typically think about organizational change. The leader is not concerned with a population of organizations. He is concerned with his own organization and with the need to solve the pressing problems of the moment in order to remain viable and effective. A failed change initiative could have dire consequences for the organization, and there may not be time to try something else. Whereas a doctor may look upon a 33 per cent success rate as positive, and may unhesitatingly recommend that a patient give the new treatment a try, an organizational leader may look upon this statistic as discouraging, and may suggest to peers that they try to find something that provides a greater chance of success.

My colleague's stance represents good thinking for a doctor. The doctor writes a prescription for a medication and sends the patient home. An organizational change initiative may require an investment of millions of dollars and may take three years to complete. The organizational leader remains inside the organization, interacting with people and experiencing the results of change initiatives along with his colleagues. The doctor will be disappointed but will not personally suffer if the treatment fails. The organizational leader suffers, along with everyone else.

Nonetheless, the way that doctors and organizational leaders think about change are similar in one important way. A good doctor knows that evidence-based treatments often need to be individualized, depending on the health and social circumstances of the patient. Every patient is different. Some have allergies, some have multiple medical conditions and are taking several medications, and some are not able to easily visit a physiotherapist or a pharmacist.

A good doctor will take all of this into consideration when prescribing a treatment.[2] The treatment will often be tailored to the unique circumstances of the person who is seated on the examining table.

An organizational leader faces the same dilemma. Each organization, each human collective, is unique. Undoubtedly some organizations resemble each other in important ways, but invariably there are also important differences. The administrative, clinical, and occupational hierarchies in a big urban teaching hospital differ from the hierarchy that exists in an automobile factory – and the culture of this hospital will also differ from the culture of a small rural hospital. An intervention that works well in one social milieu might be transferred to a different social milieu where it is then implemented with *fidelity* – that is, in precisely the same way that it was implemented in the first milieu – and yet the second implementation may fail.[3] A good idea in one place may be a bad idea in another, and thus interventions must almost always be adapted as they move from one social milieu to another.

To understand this, it can be helpful to distinguish between the *content* of a change intervention (*what* we are going to do) and the *process* of implementing the intervention (*how* we are going to do it). If I have successfully implemented a new continuous improvement process in a plant in New Mexico and now I have been asked to replicate my success in a plant in Ontario, I may need to consider whether the continuous improvement mechanisms need to be adjusted for the Ontario situation, and whether the implementation process might also need to be tweaked.

So far, we have encountered two important ideas about change. First, change is always a local phenomenon. A new approach to teaching mathematics that is devised and tested in Boston may have to be adapted before it can be successfully used in Whitehorse. A water re-use strategy that wins awards in Galveston may be a disaster in Saskatoon, unless it undergoes significant adaptation to local circumstances.

Second, an intervener into human systems is always interested primarily in *this* system, the client system with which the intervener is currently working. The fact that a given intervention has been successful in 20 per cent of the organizations that have tried it is not good enough. The intervener's responsibility is to assist *this* client to bring about change. If success rates are low, then the intervener needs to find a way to maximize the client's chance of success. The intervener does not just prescribe a treatment; instead, the intervener also helps to design and apply a process for implementing the treatment with this client.

We have seen that different people think about change in different ways. How should a skilled intervener into human systems think about change?

To increase the likelihood that we ascribe the same meaning to the terms of art that are used in this book, I begin with some definitions. This book offers a human systems approach to organizational change, and it does so by discussing the planning and implementing of interventions in human systems. To put in place the shared vocabulary we need for a coherent discussion of this subject, I will define three important terms: planned change, human systems, and intervention. With this terminology in place, we will then set about creating a larger conceptual framework in the next two chapters.

What Is Planned Change?

This is a book about planned change. For our purposes, a planned change is a conscious intervention into a human system with the intention of bringing about a premeditated result.

But wait a minute. Edgar Schein has claimed that the fourth principle of process consultation is that "everything you do is an intervention."[4] He explains:

Just as every interaction reveals diagnostic information, so does every interaction have consequences both for the client and for me. I therefore have to own everything I do and assess the consequences to be sure that they fit my goals of creating a helping relationship.

And I agree. Everything that a change agent says, every action that he undertakes, will produce consequences for the client, and the client's actions will produce consequences for the change agent. When I enter into a human system, I enter into and necessarily influence the pattern of interaction that is characteristic of that system, and I cannot possibly predict the precise consequences of my actions – especially when I am a newcomer in the system.

I am talking here about *planned* change, and that means that I am thinking about an action that was preceded by the creation of a plan. The plan does not have to be a formal plan with a Gantt chart that spells out timelines, deliverables, and roles and responsibilities. It can be an intention that I form in my mind as I observe what is happening in the room and that I consciously decide to take action on.

For our purposes, then, a planned intervention will always be based on an intention that takes the form of a *theory of action*.

The term *theory of action* is often associated with the work of Chris Argyris and with the field of program evaluation.[5] Put simply, a theory of action is a theory that a human being has, or that a group of human beings share, about the relationship between actions and consequences. I may believe that if I am participating in a discussion and I raise my hand, the meeting chair will recognize me and invite me to speak. My theory of action is that raising my hand will produce an opportunity to say something. When I want to cross a street without the benefit of a crosswalk or a traffic light, I might hesitate at the curb, look both ways, and then cross the street when I see no oncoming vehicles. My theory of action is that by looking both ways before crossing the street I will avoid being hit by a vehicle.

We all navigate our way through our lives on the basis of our theories of action. Over time, as we have more and more experiences, we create a rich and varied repertoire that makes up our theories of action. When we encounter new circumstances that we have not faced before, we can nonetheless usually find past experiences that are sufficiently similar to the novel situation that we can devise tests that will allow us to learn as we move into the unknown. The first time that I attend the meeting of a board of directors for a nonprofit charity, I might reasonably draw upon my experience of attending other meetings to devise a theory of action that is appropriate and effective for this new situation. When I get behind the wheel of a new automobile that I have never driven before, my past experiences of driving other automobiles will help me to identify actions that might produce the desired results in this new vehicle.

Let's get back to our topic – planned change. When I am preparing to intervene in a client system and I form a theory of action that helps me to anticipate what action will produce a desirable result, and then I take that action, I am engaging in planned change. This is true regardless of whether I planned a series of intricate actions while pondering the data I have accumulated about a client system in my office, or whether I am in the midst of the action in a client factory or meeting room, observing what people are doing and then consciously devising and implementing an action strategy that might help to move the client in the direction that they wish to move. In the one case I seem to be acting with more deliberation, and in the other case I am acting with more spontaneity, but in both cases I have consciously formed a theory of action before doing anything.

Here, then, is our first definition:

An intervener into a human system is engaged in planned change when s/he forms an intention, has a theory of action that suggests how the intention might be achieved, and then takes action to bring about the intended result.

What Is a Human System?

I have noticed that some people use the term *human system* as though it were synonymous with the term *human group*. This is a mistake. A human system is indeed a human group, but the use of the word *system* is intended to add some important meaning to the earlier conceptualization.

We have learned a great deal about the behavior and development of human groups over the past 100 years. At one point many people believed that having a job and working on a task was an entirely individual activity, and that a good manager would ensure that workers were not distracted by social interaction or relationships.[6] However, since the Hawthorne Experiments that were carried out in the 1920s and 1930s at the Western Electric Hawthorne Works near Chicago, we have learned that any human group that works together can best be understood in relation to both its social and its task dimension.[7] We now know that a group's social dimension can either impede or facilitate the group's productivity, and thus researchers and organizational leaders have spent considerable time and energy trying to understand how to develop and sustain a social and task environment that enhances worker productivity.

This exploration of human groups has resulted in theories of group development (think of the familiar forming-storming-norming-performing theory that almost everybody has encountered in a workshop or classroom)[8] and organizational culture[9] and an understanding of how a group's implicit norms can shape and govern behavior.[10] Sometimes a group's norms can result in higher levels of productivity, and sometimes norms can impede productivity.[11] We also know that human groups are characterized by ongoing action, and hence we use the term *group dynamics* to refer to the recurring intra-group and boundary-spanning processes that are characteristic of a particular group.[12] We often think that the way a group makes decisions, allocates and manages power, handles conflict, manages time, and is oriented to reflection and action are important aspects of its dynamic.

All of this tells us that human groups think and act in ways that produce patterns. These patterns remain relatively stable over time. For example, I recently worked with a cohort of graduate students that demonstrated a recurring pattern that remained with them for most of their first year in their master's program. Their pattern had two key elements: first, any individual group member who experienced and communicated distress was deserving of immediate and intense attention and support from other group members; and second, although task requirements were important, they were not as important as responding to the distress of individual group members. The resulting pattern of behavior could be observed week after week, inside and outside of the classroom. Students worked hard to keep up with the demands of their rigorous MA curriculum. Some students occasionally found these demands to be overwhelming, and they experienced and communicated their distress to others. Other students then set aside their work to provide support to their overwhelmed classmates. People felt better and calmed down, and everyone returned to work. However, some people had now fallen behind with their work, and so the demands quickly ratcheted up again. The pattern then repeated.

This is the first sense in which a human group can be said to be a system. The group produces patterns of thought, action, and structuring (where a structure can be a group norm that is produced by the shared pattern of thought or action, or a policy that is imposed on the group by an external agency – such as the assignments that a professor imposes upon graduate students, or patient safety targets that a health authority imposes upon health care providers). These patterns remain in a state of more-or-less equilibrium. In other words, the patterns are not perfectly stable, but they tend toward stability. External influences, the arrival of new people, or the intro-duction of a new idea or an innovative new practice can disrupt the existing pattern and lead to the creation of a new pattern.

The term *human system* has some other connotations that are worth considering. Some people, such as Peter Senge in his influ-ential book *The Fifth Discipline*, urge us to use "systems thinking" when we consider organizational problems and to look upon organ-izations and groups as having system-like qualities.[13] For some this means that we need to pay attention to context. When a criminal commits a crime, his action occurs within the context of a particular social milieu and in the context of his life experiences. To think sys-temically about the crime that has been committed may therefore mean to consider the peer pressures that exist within that milieu or the circumstances (such as poverty, neglect, or abuse) that contrib-uted to an individual's taking up a life of crime.

This of course can be a very useful way to think about the origins of problems, but it does not really get at the meaning of the word *system*. Thinking about root causes does not necessarily lead one to think about systems.

We use the word *system* to describe all sorts of things that exist in the natural and social world. We talk about planetary systems, river systems, respiratory systems, ecological systems, production systems, and distribution systems. We talk about the health system and the economic system. It sometimes seems as though the natural and social worlds are awash in overlapping systems. Fortunately, an intervener into human systems needs to master only a handful of key ideas about systems. Our goal is to be able to think and act effectively when intervening in a human system. We are looking for the sort of pragmatic understanding that Kurt Lewin had in mind when he said, "There is nothing so practical as a good theory."[14]

I have already explained that a human system will produce pat-terns that can be understood in terms of the thinking, acting, and structuring that are produced by system members. We should also note that a system is made up of parts. Those parts exist in relationship with each other, and they interact in ways that maintain a more-or-less equilibrium or a status quo. A system usually has a boundary around it, so one can distinguish between the system and its external environment. Usually, the boundary is open or porous. This means that the system is able to influence its environment, and in turn is influenced by its environment. A system is often characterized by the interrelated phenomena of input, throughput, and output and achieves some degree of self-regulation via a mechanism known as a feedback loop. For example, energy may enter into a system and undergo a process that converts the energy into useful products and also waste products. The system receives information from its environment that allows it to assess its continued viability and that may allow it to adapt to changing circumstances.

I operated a small organizational consultancy for more than twenty years. This small company was undoubtedly a human system that can be thought of in the terms that I just described. Figure 1.1 is a simplified illustration of how my company functioned as a system. Inputs entered into the system in the form of employees and subcontractors who would perform the client work, along with Requests for Proposals (RFPs) and client opportunities to take on new assignments. Of course, there were other inputs as well, including such things as supplies and equipment, payments from clients after work was completed, and professional development activities to help the team remain sharp and focused on client needs. Within the company there were a number of internal throughput processes, which allowed us to carry out our work with our clients, to handle administrative, marketing, and sales tasks, and to continuously add to our knowledge and skill. All of this produced a number of outputs, including first and foremost the deliverables

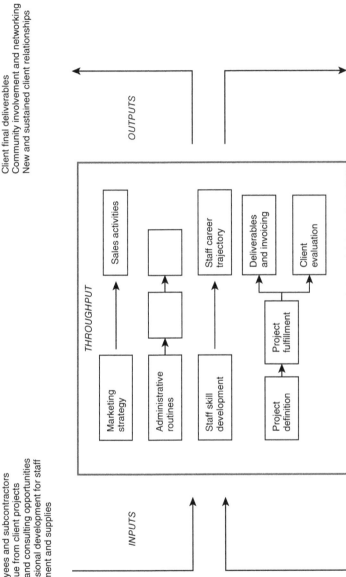

Figure 1.1. Consultancy as a simple system with feedback loop

that we provided to clients, and also various community activities (such as sitting on volunteer boards, or attending meetings of the Chamber of Commerce), as well as new relationships that could eventually lead to new client opportunities. At the same time, a feedback loop allowed us to remain aware of emerging opportunities and markets, and also of areas where we needed to improve our own competencies. The result was a more-or-less equilibrium state for the consultancy, allowing us to operate successfully for two decades.

The trouble with this drawing is that it depicts this human system, the consultancy that I once operated, as a rational, logical, linear entity. I can assure you that that was not at all how I experienced my company. I can say that the experience of operating the company, like the company itself, was *somewhat* rational, logical, and linear, and that the experience was also emotional, intuitive, uncertain, and given to sudden disruptions. As some theorists today would say, this human system was complex.

It is not necessary for our purposes for us to arrive at a thorough and complete conceptualization of a human system as, for example, a complex adaptive system. We have the more pragmatic goal of creating definitions and concepts that will help us to be effective interveners into human systems. To meet that goal, we merely need to tease out a few of the main implications of the assertion that human systems are complex.

When we think about intervening in a human system, or of designing and implementing some sort of change in an organization, we usually are thinking in cause-and-effect terms. The intervention is conceptualized as a cause that will bring into being some sort of effect in the target human system.

There is nothing inherently wrong with cause-and-effect conceptualizations. This kind of thinking serves human beings very well in many instances. Much of our medical science is based on a search for causes (usually thought of as treatments) that will mitigate or resolve vexing health issues. It is this sort of thinking that allows us to say that thirty minutes of exercise every day can yield a longer, healthier life; that eliminating tobacco use can reduce your risk of developing certain forms of cancer; that taking a proven blood pressure medication can reduce your risk of developing heart disease; or that vaccinating children for measles and whooping cough will virtually eliminate the likelihood of their contracting these diseases. The treatment causes the effect.

In fact, there is a growing body of science suggesting that human beings have an innate tendency to interpret the world in terms of causes and effects.[15] We notice correlations between phenomena, and we posit the correlation as a cause-and-effect relationship – when Bob is the project lead we always meet our milestones, and therefore I conclude that Bob causes us to meet our deadlines. This is a simple and powerful way to think about social phenomena, and it allows us to devise our action strategies for realizing our intentions.

However, cause-and-effect thinking is more problematic when we are thinking about an intervention to bring about change in a human system. This is because of some of the characteristics of human systems that we have already discussed. An intervention into a human system will produce an effect upon the existing pattern of thinking, acting, and structuring. That pattern is held in place through the formal and informal relationships that exist among all system components. It is also held in place by pressures that are exerted upon the system by external forces. If I do not consider these complex patterns and relationships when I devise my intervention, I may find that all of my effort is wasted.

Suppose you are attempting to improve the customer service provided by a municipal government department that issues licenses to developers and carries out inspections of development projects. You do some digging around to understand the existing situation, and you discover that most frontline staff are not aware that their customer service ratings are poor, that they have never had customer service training, and that most staff like their jobs but find it tiresome to deal with grumpy developers. Based on this information, you create a three-part intervention. First, you plan to hold forty-five-minute meetings with staff during which you will show them the customer service data that have been gathered that indicate their performance in this area is somewhat low. Then you will offer customer service workshops to develop new competencies, and workshops on proven strategies for dealing with difficult people.

This intervention sounds sensible, and it may indeed produce the desired result. However, what if it turns out that the developers who provide the low customer service ratings are compelled to interact with several state and municipal agencies to get their permits and to have their work evaluated, and they are frustrated by all of these interactions, not just by the interactions with your department? What if employees in your department know that their annual pay increases depend on whether they achieve certain productivity targets, and this leads them to value fast and efficient transactions rather than fostering congenial relationships with customers? And what if within the office there are three long-time employees who over time have developed contemptuous attitudes toward the developers they serve, who often express these attitudes to fellow employees, and who deride employees who appear to be trying to be nice to developers?

The result might be the situation depicted in figure 1.2.

Even though your plan makes sense, there are a number of factors at work within this human system that could reduce its impact. In fact, it is even possible that your plan could backfire. Employees may experience the awareness raising and the training

The Intervention Promotes a Beneficial Change	Hidden Forces in the System Block the Change

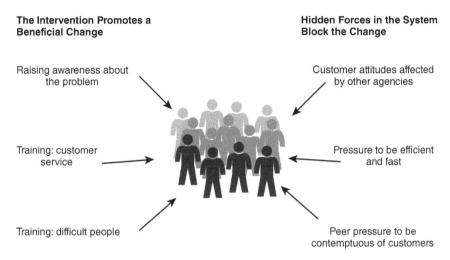

Raising awareness about the problem

Customer attitudes affected by other agencies

Training: customer service

Pressure to be efficient and fast

Training: difficult people

Peer pressure to be contemptuous of customers

Figure 1.2. Forces promoting and opposing a planned change

workshops as evidence that management doesn't understand their reality. They may become cynical or disillusioned. It is even possible that customer service ratings could fall during the next round of measurements.

The field of realistic evaluation provides a useful explanation for this phenomenon, which is expressed with the following formula: mechanism + context = outcome.[16] This formula suggests that it would be a mistake to think of an intervention (the mechanism) as being a cause that acts upon a target (the context) to bring about an outcome. Instead, it suggests that we think of an interaction between intervention and target that yields the outcome. Given that each intervention will be somewhat different and each target group will have unique characteristics, each interaction is going to be different, and will thus produce different outcomes.

I am not saying that your actions do not produce effects, or that a planned intervention will not produce an effect. I am saying that we often cannot accurately predict the effect of an action taken in a complex human system. Any parent who has attempted to change the behavior of a child has encountered this slippery fact of life. We are probably never fully aware of all of the forces and factors at work within a social field, and thus we cannot possibly know how a novel action will affect the patterns at work in the field.

This means that a human system possesses the quality of *emergence*. Emergence means that it is not possible to fully predict (and thus it is impossible to fully control) the future behavior of a human system.

What, then, is a human system? Here is my suggestion:

For our purposes, a human system is a human collective that exists to perform a function (or functions); that is characterized by a more-or-less stable pattern of thinking, acting, and structuring; that acts upon and is acted upon by its external environment; and that possesses the quality of emergence in that it is impossible to reliably predict how the system will respond to new stimuli.

What Is an Intervention?

With our definitions of *planned change* and *human systems* in hand, we can now seek greater precision in understanding the meaning of the term *intervention*. As we do so, we will begin to perform the *balancing act* that is the metaphor I have chosen to convey the single most important idea described in this book. An intervention is a kind of balancing act that is necessitated by the human need to plan a change and by the nature of emergence in human systems. We conceive of change in terms of cause-and-effect relations, and we make our plans based on our existing theory of action. We hypothesize that certain actions (which can of course include human behavior, conversations, more explicit communications such as documents and manuals, or the introduction of new policies, roles, or rules, and even the introduction of new technologies and work processes) will produce specific results. We create a plan that packages these actions into an intervention, and then we implement the plan. For the remainder of this book, I will refer to this as the *formal plan*, and I will sometimes talk about the implementation of the formal plan.

However, when we implement the plan in a living, breathing human system, we encounter emergence. The system does not respond quite as we had expected. If we ignore the signals that things are going wrong, our change initiative will almost certainly fail.

The quality of emergence in human systems does not mean that our formal intervention plans are ill-considered or stupid. I suggest that we think of the formal plan as a starting point or as a hypothesis about how the change process might unfold. As we take action and gain a better understanding of the system, it is almost certain that we will need to revise this plan.

No single human being can possibly have a full and complete understanding of the functioning of a complex human system. Moreover, a complex human system is constantly in flux – its internal components evolve, and its external environment is constantly changing. A human system possesses some integrity, and it is also always changing. In fact, in most of the large organizations that I have consulted with, when we are planning a new intervention it usually comes to light that not only is the system experiencing the usual changes expected through employee turnover, technological innovation, changes in customer expectations, and so on, but there are often three or four other major organizational changes underway.

This means that as we implement the formal intervention plan, the intervener must be open to continuous learning. Despite the fact that the plan is based on extensive information gathering and analysis and presents a convincing picture of how a desirable change might be wrought, the plan may have missed some important information, or the situation being acted upon by the intervention may change unexpectedly during the intervention process.

The intervener is alert, opportunistic, and adaptive. I like to say that the intervener enacts an *emergent plan* for the intervention, and this enactment is always evident in the intervener's demeanor. A good intervener is frequently asking questions and is often reconsidering the theory of action on which the formal plan is based. The intervener is always watching for what teachers call *teachable moments* – moments when something new and unexpected happens, and when it makes sense to set aside the formal plan and inquire into what is happening in the here and now.

An intervention, then, is a process that consists of two parts. The first part is the intervention conceived of as an object: a plan that is to be implemented. Images that might come to mind when thinking of this part of the intervention could include that of a seed (the intervention) that is being planted in a garden (the target), or of a new character (the intervention) who is being introduced into a TV soap opera (the target), or of a new department (the intervention) that is being introduced into a bureaucratic organization (the target). In all of these cases, the intervention has become objectified. It is like a thing, an object that is being introduced into another thing. The thing-like intervention is being pushed into the thing-like human system, and the result will be an outcome that is anticipated in the formal intervention plan. In fact, I tend to equate this part of the intervention with the formal intervention plan that is based on our initial theory of action (that specific actions will produce specific outcomes in the target system), and with the implementation of that plan.

However, as von Moltke is often quoted as saying, "No plan survives contact with the enemy."[17] Soon after we begin to implement the formal intervention plan, we usually learn new things about the system and its environment that bring to light shortcomings in our original plan. We can press ahead regardless – and I have seen many organizational change efforts that do just that, and end in failure – or we can adapt.

And this brings us to the second part of the intervention process, and to the reason why it is vital that we conceive of an intervention as a process consisting of many actions. As the intervener attempts to implement the intervention plan – whether it is a quality assurance plan for a factory, or a patient safety protocol in an acute care hospital, or a new curriculum component in a school, or a knowledge translation strategy in a national health charity – unexpected situations will be encountered. New information about the organizational context will come to light. Constraining pressures from the external environment will be identified.

Rather than simply continuing with the implementation and in effect trying to force-fit the intervention into a recalcitrant social environment, a skilled intervener will take in this new information, will revise the theory of action on which the intervention is based, and will engage in a process of learning, of testing ideas, and of being open to alternative explanations and suggestions. The intervention is no longer an object that is being imposed upon a human system. Instead, the intervention is now an active search for the desired outcome.

Here is my proposed definition:

An intervention into a human system consists of two parts. First, there is the formal intervention plan that conceives of specific actions (broadly understood as including behavior and the introduction or alteration of structure) that are intended to produce the desired changes. Second, there is the emergent plan that consists of an adaptable process of actions that evolve over time as the intervener learns more about the functioning of the human system. Conceived of in this way, an intervention is a search for a desired outcome rather than the imposition of a predetermined outcome.

This is a radical reconceptualization of the idea of an intervention. How radical it is can be seen by the emphasis placed on the concept of *fidelity* by program planners and many scholars working in the area of implementation science, and by the relatively low investments made in evaluations of the impact and process of interventions.[18] Traditionally, implementation science has emphasized the importance of ensuring that when an intervention is "scaled up," or is moved from an initial pilot test site to numerous other sites (for example, from three schools in New Jersey where it was first developed to many schools across the United States), it is implemented with fidelity (that is, the original program remains identical in all sites where it is implemented). Implementation scientists then hold conferences to puzzle over the fact that the intervention never seems to work in quite the same way in the different implementation sites. Similarly, program evaluators often comment on how difficult it is to clearly establish the benefits delivered by interventions and on how the processes used to implement an intervention and the precise nature of the social context in which the intervention is implemented appear to influence program outcomes. This is probably why we have seen two important innovations in the field of program evaluation over the past two decades, the first being the advent of realistic evaluation and the second being the growing popularity of developmental evaluation, which focuses less on measuring impact and more on assuring that there is impact.[19]

The notion of emergent planning recognizes that we cannot predict all of the outcomes of a change process. Some people will be uncomfortable with this apparent lack of control. It may seem to imply that the interveners don't know what they are doing. And if that is the case, why should people trust them? In reality, emergent planning is simply a pragmatic approach, given the nature of human systems. Rather than subscribing to the delusion that a small group can anticipate everything and can have answers to all possible questions, emergent planning places its bet on the possibility of creating a strong and adaptive intervention process. The rest of this book will describe how this is done.

Summary

Different people think differently about change. Some people think about change in relation to specific problems and groups. Others think about change in relation to large populations. If I am thinking about a specific group, then my ideas about the success of a change will depend on whether this specific group succeeded in implementing the change. If I am thinking about a population or a large number of people or organizations, then my ideas about success will depend on the percentage of population members who successfully implement the change. How, then, should someone who intends to intervene in a human system think about change?

Change is always local. It always involves this person who is part of this group which is located in this place and works under these circumstances with these opportunities and constraints. We might want to keep the content of a change (what we are going to do) constant as we consider using the same intervention on several occasions, but the process of implementing the intervention (how we are going to do it) is likely going to need to be adapted to fit each unique situation.

In this book our subject is planned change. An intervener into a human system is engaged in planned change when she forms an intention, has a theory of action that suggests how the intention might be achieved, and then takes action to bring about the intended result.

For our purposes, a human system is a human collective that exists to perform a function (or functions); that is characterized by a more-or-less stable pattern of thinking, acting, and structuring; that acts upon and is acted upon by its external environment; and that possesses the quality of emergence in that it is impossible to reliably predict how the system will respond to the intervention.

An intervention into a human system consists of two parts. First, there is the formal intervention plan that conceives of specific actions (broadly understood as including behavior and the introduction or alteration of structure) as producing the desired changes. Second, there is the emergent plan, which consists of an adaptable process of actions that evolve over time as the intervener learns more about the functioning of the human system. Conceived of in this way, an intervention is a search for a desired outcome rather than the imposition of a predetermined outcome.

CHAPTER TWO

Doing Things *to* People and Doing Things *with* People

In the early 2000s I conducted some research in partnership with Dr. Hillary Hart, a distinguished lecturer in the engineering school at the University of Texas at Austin.[1] Hillary and I were interested in the changes experienced by communications professionals who supported the work of engineers and scientists. It seemed to us that in the 1980s these professionals had been largely concerned with the design and production of texts, but that recently their work had begun to focus more on two-way interactions among those who created scientific and technical products and those who used the products. As we gathered data and made sense of what we were learning, we used a model proposed by Dr. Craig Waddell to conceptualize the ways in which people could participate in scientific and environmental decisions.[2]

Waddell conceived of a flow of information between scientists and the public that might be highly restricted and controlled, or that might be more fluid and open. I draw on Waddell's model, and especially on the framework that Hillary and I devised, to illustrate the different ways in which we can conceive of social change (see figure 2.1).

The top of the framework illustrates a hierarchical, top-down approach to change. Those with power and influence in a social milieu invent or select the content and process to be used in a change

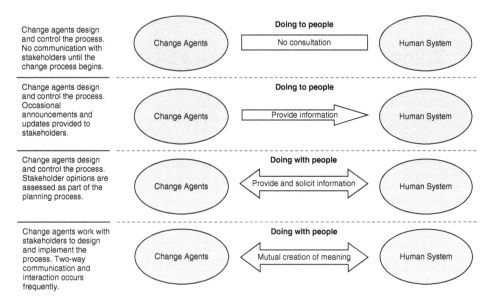

Figure 2.1. A framework for change through interaction

initiative, and then they impose the change on the human system that they have targeted. This is an example of change as something that is *done to people*. The human system is a target. It is expected to cooperate by accepting and absorbing the change and to produce the benefits that the leaders expect the change to provide.

As you move down the framework, you see a gradual shift from doing things *to* people (some prefer to say doing things *for* people) to doing things *with* people.

Communication channels open up. Change leaders begin to provide information to stakeholders. Town halls might be held. People can ask questions. Sometimes they are invited to provide "input."

When we arrive at the bottom of the framework, we are in a different world. Here the change leaders do not work out all of the details of the change in advance. They may take a preliminary stab at defining the problems that need to be solved and at outlining broad goals that must be achieved. However, to create the detailed plan for the change initiative, to identify the barriers that must be overcome and the timelines and objectives that will be pursued, the change leaders share perspectives and information with stakeholders. Facilitated discussions are held, results are shared, and targets are negotiated.

Many of us prefer this participative approach to change because it seems more democratic and inclusive. It is an approach that treats people as human beings, not as objects to be manipulated so management can make their bonus targets. However, although doing things *with* (rather than *to*) people may appeal to our values, this is not the only reason to prefer the process depicted at the bottom of the framework.

A plan to solve problems and implement improvements through a change initiative is the product of human thought. We need to gather information about what is going on in the human system and its environment. We need to consider what is feasible, what resources are available, and what capacity we have on hand. We then need to consider what actions are likely to produce the desired results and how to ensure that the new way of being that we create will be sustained over time. All of this requires data and analysis. It requires thinking, and it requires access to relevant knowledge.

But who will do the thinking, and where will this knowledge be sought?

A human system is made up of numerous individual people, each with their own experiences and perspectives, each with some capacity and ability to carry out their responsibilities and to create new solutions. Each system member knows something about the functioning of the system, about the way problems are manifesting themselves in the social world, and about the opportunities and constraints that are present. A small group of organizational leaders and consultants cannot possibly have access to all of this knowledge. It is spread amongst the living minds throughout the system.

If a small group of change leaders works in secret to create detailed plans for a change initiative, without accessing the knowledge that is spread throughout system members, they will often experience bitter disappointment as they try to implement their plan. People will point to numerous circumstances and situations that exist on the frontlines and in the back offices that give rise to conditions that make it impossible to implement aspects of the plan. Moreover, many people will feel ignored or slighted or even betrayed. Why didn't you consult us? Do you think we are stupid? Don't you trust us? Aren't we supposed to be part of the team?

When thinking about change, it is useful to consider this distinction: is it your intention to do things *to* people, or do you want to do things *with* people? Are you implementing a secret plan concocted by experts, or are you mobilizing the intelligence and knowledge and commitment that exist throughout the system?

It may sometimes make sense to do things to people. A surgeon does not consult with the patient as he makes his incisions and repairs a damaged body. A boss who faces the necessity of laying off workers may believe that it is more compassionate to get the severance packages and counseling services in place before making the grim announcement.

More often, however, when we are developing new strategies, or seeking to transform a moribund organization by infusing it with new innovations and productivity, we need to engage the hearts and minds of those who bring the organization to life. We do this by working *with* them.

What Causes Human Behavior?

I use the framework in figure 2.1 to consider the extent to which and the ways in which members of a human system might participate in the overall change process. I now want to consider the motivations that are at work when people pursue or resist change.

From the early 1960s to the mid-1980s, Warren Bennis, Robert Chin, and Kenneth Benne, professors at Boston University who were also associated with the National Training Laboratories and Boston's Human Relations Center, published a series of influential books about planned change. In the final edition, published in 1985, they explained that their purpose was to use the knowledge generated through social science to resolve or alleviate human conflicts and problems.[3] They said that their intention was to pursue the "planful application of valid and appropriate knowledge in human affairs for the purpose of creating intelligent action and change."

The book includes an essay by Chin and Benne suggesting that there are three basic strategies for introducing new knowledge and technology into human systems.[4] The empirical-rational strategy assumes that human beings are rational creatures who generally try to act in their own self-interest or in the interest of the groups to which they belong. According to this strategy, to bring about change one must explain to people how and why the change is in their best interests. I used to hear people involved in change projects talk about the WIIFM (pronounced "wi-fem") phenomenon – "What's in it for me?" This question assumes that people are primarily motivated by self-interest.

Chin and Benne suggested that the second strategy, the normative-reeducative strategy, recognizes that human beings do indeed often act in rational ways, and their behavior is also shaped by cultural norms that arise from the values and attitudes of people in a system. This strategy suggests that a change initiative must persuade people to give up their commitment to the previous norms by changing attitudes, skills, values, and relationships. To implement this strategy, the leader must find ways to involve people in the change process and must be prepared to encounter hidden obstacles to the change. The recent emphasis on change initiatives that target organizational culture is an outgrowth of this normative perspective on change. Over time, human groups create a shared culture that acts as a repository for collective knowledge and that shapes and influences the behavior of members of the group. To change behavior, and to ensure that the change is sustained over time, one must change the culture.

The third strategy identified by Chin and Benne has to do with compulsion and force. The power-coercive strategy relies on the application of power to compel people to change their behavior. This can involve the use of economic and political incentives or sanctions to encourage change and can also involve the coercive use of moral power by inducing uncooperative people to feel shame or guilt. Chin and Benne acknowledge that power is evident in all planned efforts to intervene in and change human systems. However, a power-coercive strategy relies on power as the primary means for bringing about change. Here is an example. In the early 2000s a tragedy occurred in a nursing home in the province of Ontario. A confused resident who suffered from dementia murdered another resident. Citizens of the province were appalled to learn that such a thing could happen in what was supposed to be a sanctuary for the frail elderly, and the provincial government scrambled to put in place measures to ensure that this sort of incident would not re-occur. Initially, the government's response involved the creation of an inspection and compliance regime that would compel administrators to curb any future violence in nursing homes. The provincial government used its considerable power to coerce nursing homes into complying with strict rules.

Chin and Benne are not suggesting that a change will always be based on a pure form of one of these three strategies. Instead, it is likely that a change will include all three, and will emphasize one over the other two. A change strategy might be largely based on rational appeals to the good sense of employees and be accompanied by some training that focuses on raising awareness and changing attitudes, and also by a latent threat of sanctions for those who do not cooperate. Alternatively, a change might be largely coercive (all employees must adopt the new desktop technology standards before year end) but also include a rational explanation communicated in a newsletter and a series of meetings where timetables and expectations are communicated and concerns are noted.

A few years after Chin and Benne published their framework, two educational scholars, Tom Daniels and Sue DeWine of Ohio University, proposed adding a fourth strategy to the framework.[5] They pointed out that a human collective such as a factory, government department, or insurance company is a constructed social reality.[6] What they mean is that human beings work and cooperate together to create a shared social reality that is fundamentally different from the physical reality that we all inhabit. A standard operating procedure in a call center certainly exists, but it does not exist in the same way that a slab of granite on a mountainside exists. The granite is real in a physical, tangible way. If I thump my fist on it, I am likely to exclaim "Ouch!" The procedure does not have this sort of tangible, physical existence. The procedure exists because a group of people say it exists and act as though it exists. We construct this bit of social reality, just as we construct rules and laws (the rules of tennis, say, or the Constitution of the United States) and norms that shape our behavior as we go about our daily lives.

The point is that changing physical reality is different from changing social reality. If we want to bring about a change to the physical reality of that piece of granite, we need a piece of equipment or a tool to bring about the change that we desire – maybe a hammer to break off a chip, or a hoist to lever it into a new position. If we want to change the way people are organized and work is carried out in a call center, we need a different kind of tool.

Daniels and DeWine suggest that human beings think and talk their social reality into existence, and this means that the primary tool for changing an organization is human communication. They agree that the normative-reeducative approach is valuable, but they complain that it tends to move our attention away from the ways in which culture is constructed (through human interaction and communication) to concepts such as roles, norms, and culture. This means that with a normative-reeducative strategy the target of a change will have a thing-like quality: we are going to change a thing called "culture," or a thing called "middle-management attitudes." And this takes our attention away from the ways in which culture and attitudes are created and sustained – through the interactions, communications, and conversations that are forever occurring within an organization.

Daniels and DeWine thus propose that we add an interpretive-communicative strategy to this framework for motivation and change. The change must be talked into existence, and then the ensuing pattern of talk within the organization must sustain the change. Change is in part a hermeneutic or interpretive process, where we communicate with each other about what is going on, who we are, what we do and how we do it, and what is important and valuable to us. Through interaction and conversation, we construct a coherent sense of our shared reality along with a sense of our individual place within that reality. We may also construct a sense of purpose for our individual and collective activities, and by interacting with the environment and each other as we perform our jobs, we create the skill and competence needed to ground us in the work of the group. A change leader must be skilled at forming relationships with the people who are expected to create the change within the organization, and skilled at talking with stakeholders to collaboratively define and make sense of the emerging reality.

Figure 2.2 illustrates a framework for intervention derived from Chin and Benne's three strategies and Daniels's and DeWine's fourth strategy.

Over the past fifteen years, the add-on proposed by Daniels and DeWine has grown into a new perspective on organization development and transformational change that is commonly referred to as *dialogic organization development* (or dialogic OD). Proponents of dialogic OD say that they are setting aside the old command-and-control approaches in favor of approaches that embrace the insights of complexity science.[7] Bushe and Marshak, for example, claim that looking for the environmental determinants of human behavior has been a waste of time: "What happens in organizations is influenced more by how people interact and make meaning than how presumably objective external factors and forces impact the system."[8]

This is similar to Argyris's notion of pattern causality, which suggests that existing patterns of group interaction and communication influence the behavior of individuals, giving them a role and a set of moves within the pattern.[9] Though it might appear as though the actions of individuals add up to or aggregate into the pattern, the view here is that once the pattern is in place it exerts a force on system members to continue producing the pattern. According to dialogic OD, human interaction often involves verbal communication in the form of conversations by which participants create meaning. Through conversation, we create a shared understanding of our social experiences. To change a social experience, such as our

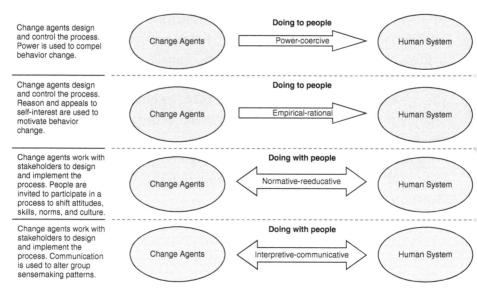

Figure 2.2. A framework for intervention

experience of an organization where we are employed, we must change these conversations.

The proponents of dialogic OD argue that they have discovered more fruitful ways to bring about transformational change, and they also imply that it is impossible to plan and control change. Instead of creating formal plans, Bushe and Marshak tell us, the change agent must be opportunistic and curious: "Transformational change cannot be planned toward some predetermined future state. Rather, transformation requires holding an intention while moving into the unknown. Disrupting current patterns in a way that engages people in uncovering collective intentions and shared motivations is required."[10] According to Bushe and Marshak, transformative change will occur (1) when the prevailing pattern of co-constructing social reality is disrupted (and the dialogic response is to create "containers" where system members can make sense of the disruptions);

(2) when a core narrative (an oft-repeated story that makes sense of collective experience) of the organization is changed; and (3) when a new image (in the form of statements, metaphors, pictures, etc.) is created that opens up new ways of thinking and acting in the organizational context. Transformational change in organizations is always emergent, never planned.

So far, we have established that when a leader intends to introduce change into a human system, it will be necessary to create some sort of relationship with the system members. We might think of this relationship as lying on a spectrum, where at one end the leader is doing things to (or for) people and at the other end the leader is doing things with people. We have also considered the human motivations that are at work during a change process. These motivations may have to do with power and compulsion, with reason and logic, with social norms and cultures, and with patterns of sensemaking that yield coherence, identity, and purpose.

There is a relationship between the theories that a person holds about what causes or motivates human behavior and the kinds of strategies that people are likely to use when designing and leading change. If I believe that people respond mostly to force, I am likely to rely largely on a power-coercive change strategy. If I believe that most people are rational creatures whose motivations are logical and who are usually concerned with their self-interest, then I will be inclined to use an empirical-rational change strategy. If I believe that people inhabit social worlds in which behavior is influenced by cultural rules and implicit and explicit behavioral norms, then I will probably opt for a normative-reeducative change strategy. And finally, if I believe that human beings are constantly constructing their cultural rules and norms through patterns of communication, then I will be inclined toward an interpretive-communicative change strategy.

Many of the change efforts I have witnessed or worked on over the past few decades have recognized that human beings act as they do for a variety of reasons, and that different people are probably motivated by slightly different factors at different times.[11] In a change initiative involving a school system we will probably find that some administrators and teachers are mostly concerned with job security and salary levels, while others are primarily concerned with working conditions, and still others are mostly interested in having a rich and stimulating experience of work or in the welfare and success of students. It is also usually the case that most organizations (whether they are public sector, private sector, or nonprofit organizations) are organized in a hierarchy wherein the most powerful people are at the top of the organizational pyramid and less powerful people are at the bottom. Power, in other words, is almost always at play in organizational change, and it would be naive to think that a collaborative change process is completely free from coercive forces and tendencies.

This means that when we are planning an intervention into a human system, we are usually not thinking in terms of a pure approach that relies exclusively on (for example) cultural considerations. It is usually the case that at least some hierarchical power is brought to bear, especially at the start of the process, and then sometimes later if momentum becomes stalled. This use of power sometimes takes rather benign forms – how often have you heard people talk about the importance of having an executive-level leader act as the "champion" or "sponsor" of a change initiative? One function of the sponsor is to demonstrate that senior leaders support this change and expect it to succeed, and thus the sponsorship communicates a veiled threat that resistance may provoke executive displeasure.

In many of the change initiatives that I see today, there will be an executive sponsor who wields organizational power to support the initiative. Some effort is made to identify and communicate the rationale behind the change. Usually there is some gathering of information from stakeholders that results in, first, a judgment about the current limitations or problems that need to be overcome, or the strengths and opportunities that could be developed, followed by a proposed solution for moving forward and a project plan for implementing the solution. At a minimum there is a communication strategy for communicating about the change with stakeholders, and sometimes this strategy presents stakeholders with opportunities to share their perspectives. Usually, however, stakeholder perspectives are flushed out, like a hunter flushing out his quarry so he can get a clear shot. Resistant stakeholders are identified, and actions are undertaken to diminish the resistance. Less frequently, people who are leading a change initiative invite stakeholders to contribute to a shared understanding of problems and solutions, and to help design and implement the solution.

This means that many change initiatives are based on a hybrid strategy that makes some use of power, reason, culture, and communication. Nonetheless, it is often possible to say that a given change initiative is essentially an exercise in doing things *to* or doing things *with* people.

Fallacies, Heuristics, and Situations

We are not quite finished with our consideration of the factors that give rise to human behavior. So far, we have examined explanations that human beings are rational agents whose behavior allows them to achieve their goals. Their goals might be to stay in the boss's good books, to receive a favorable performance review, to help bring a new innovation into use, to make a worthwhile contribution to the well-being of the community, to have some excitement, or to earn a year-end bonus. In all of these cases, there seems to be a clear and unproblematic relationship between the goal and the action. However, some recent science throws this into doubt.

For example, the fields of social and cognitive psychology, behavioral economics, and neuroscience have demonstrated the surprising fallibility of human decision processes.[12] The basic argument goes something like this. We humans think of ourselves as rational creatures. Oh, sure, we can be emotional, too, and we sometimes figure things out with a faculty that we refer to as our intuition. But for the most part we are rational. We notice problems. We gather information, we analyze, we run tests, and we arrive at conclusions. We can justify our decisions and our actions by calling upon our reason. However (the argument continues), we may not be as rational as we suppose. As long ago as 1739, the Scottish Enlightenment philosopher David Hume said that "reason is, and ought only to be the slave of the passions, and can never pretend to any other office than to serve and obey them."[13] Hume is claiming that we act on the basis of our passions, appetites, impulses, and intuitions, not on the basis of our reason, and only later do we bring our reason to bear in order to provide a nice-sounding explanation for our actions.

The problems go even deeper than Hume imagined. Not only do we not reason as frequently as we claim, but when we do reason, we often commit errors. These errors can include an inability to arrive at the facts that characterize a given situation – which most would agree is rather important for organizational leaders and change agents. We usually think that it is important to understand what is going on before we embark on a course of action. However, when we are trying to understand what is going on in a social environment, we necessarily make use of the human ability to draw inferences and make interpretations, and the result is that we often arrive at a description of a situation that is more our impressions and interpretations than a portrayal of the undeniable *brute facts*.[14]

One might also argue that the problems begin even before the act of perception occurs. We all have our favorite explanations and theories that allow us to see a coherent world. Some may believe that bosses are duplicitous, that unions are coercive, that middle managers are lazy, or that customer service representatives are uncaring; some believe that it is up to managers to make decisions, that staff should obey orders, and that workplace friendships get in the way of productivity. An organizational leader might believe that teamwork and collaboration will produce the best results, and a change agent might believe that a cultural transformation will work best when employees are given many opportunities to share and discuss their fears and aspirations. We all possess these theories that purport to explain the social world, and we often internalize these theories into mindsets or mental models that over time we believe correspond to the underlying structure or order of our social world.[15] These theories play an active role as we scan our surroundings and take in data. They lead us to filter out some disconfirming data and to pay particular attention to data that bolster and support our preferred way of seeing things.

There are two examples of how this tendency can interfere with our reasoning: the first is the phenomenon of confirmation bias, and the second is cognitive dissonance. Confirmation bias is the tendency to find and interpret evidence that tends to support our existing beliefs.[16] Too often, we find what we expect to find and miss contrary evidence that might lead us to alter our opinion. Scientific studies have indicated that people have a tendency to seek information that will support their existing beliefs, and they interpret information in ways that confirm what they believe they already know. At the same time, people tend to avoid seeking evidence that could weaken their current beliefs. Research has also uncovered an *anchoring effect* whereby we tend to overemphasize the importance of information gathered early in an inquiry or investigation and de-emphasize information that turned up later.[17]

Confirmation bias can clearly lead to problems in the reasoning of organizational leaders and change agents who are attempting to diagnose problems and propose solutions. Equally troubling is the likelihood that during a complex change process members of stakeholder groups who are appraising the merits of a proposed organizational change may themselves fall subject to confirmation bias and adamantly defend their preferred diagnoses and solutions while rejecting proposals based on new data.

The phenomenon of cognitive dissonance was brought to our attention through Festinger's research into the unexpected behavior that arose in an odd cult in the 1950s whose members thought that aliens from another planet were going to destroy the world on 21 December 1954.[18] When the date of the supposed apocalypse came and went without incident, instead of abandoning their preposterous beliefs, cult members concocted an explanation that allowed them to continue to believe in the existence of the unseen aliens. They explained that their own goodness had spread throughout the world, and this had persuaded the aliens to spare the planet and its inhabitants. These findings and subsequent research led Festinger to suggest that when people experience an uncomfortable disconfirmation of a deeply held belief, they will sometimes refuse to abandon their belief and instead will seek explanations that allow them to disconfirm the new evidence – in other words, they will take steps to reduce the anxiety caused by their cognitive dissonance. The theory suggests that human beings have a natural tendency to try to reduce the discomfort that is experienced when a strongly held belief is threatened by new information. We will sometimes ignore or try to avoid the new information, and at other times we may concoct laborious explanations that allow us to continue to hold onto our unlikely belief.

Once again, the problems that can arise as a result of this tendency are obvious. Since change efforts often begin with data gathering followed by a diagnosis of the existing situation and the positing of a solution, and since we know that in complex social systems it is often difficult to come up with an accurate diagnosis and an effective solution, there is a danger that our initial ideas will be proven wrong, and yet we will have invested so much in the early work that we will be reluctant to set aside our approach. Instead of being open to new disconfirming evidence, we may close our minds and cling to erroneous beliefs.

Scientists have also uncovered a number of heuristics that can produce undesirable results when humans try to solve a problem. In Kahneman's words, "The technical definition of *heuristic* is a simple procedure that helps find adequate, though often imperfect, answers to difficult questions."[19] We might think of a heuristic as a cognitive procedure that human beings use to find answers to questions or to solve problems. We are not conscious of our use of heuristics. We just use them, as a routine part of the way that we think through the problems and questions that arise in our everyday lives. Consider, for example, the representativeness heuristic. Suppose that you learn that Cyber Robotics Corporation has just opened a facility on the edge of your town and has hired 200 employees. Most of the employees are in sales or customer service, and there is also a small group of engineers and computer scientists. Then a friend introduces you to Bob, a new employee at Cyber Robotics. Your friend whispers to you that Bob is a real nerd, and asks you to guess which department Bob works in.

Make your own guess before reading the next paragraph.

According to research conducted by Daniel Kahneman and Amos Tversky, most people would answer the question by saying that Bob probably works with the engineers and computer scientists.[20] They make this guess because of a single piece of information, not necessarily reliable, indicating that Bob is a nerd, and they think that nerdiness correlates with – is representative of – the engineering and computer science professions. However, the statistical likelihood is that Bob is a member of one of the larger groups in the company, and works either in sales or customer service. The question can be approached as a matter of probability (using a basic understanding of statistics, which would lead us to notice that it is likely that Bob would be in one of the larger groups) or as a matter of representativeness (in which we make a link between engineering and computer science and Bob's supposed nerdiness). In other words, one might choose to answer the question by considering the base rates of employment at the new company (where most people are employed in two functional areas and only a few are in the third area), and by considering the quality of any countervailing evidence. Research has shown that most people rely more on the representativeness heuristic than on a consideration of statistical evidence when answering these sorts of questions.

If you are working with a client system and a few dissatisfied employees tell you that the boss is a bully, and if you notice the boss contradicting an employee during a meeting, are you likely to conclude on this evidence that the boss is indeed a bully? But perhaps the employee had been repeatedly raising irrelevant issues. Perhaps the boss has been told that unless the unit achieves its productivity target that month the boss will be reassigned and most employees will be laid off, and she is feeling a strong motivation to help these employees to keep their jobs. The representativeness heuristic gives us an easy way to link conclusions with scanty evidence, and too often we fall prey to it.

And then there is the availability heuristic. This heuristic suggests that individual human beings will all have their preferred theories and ideas about how the social world works, and when they encounter a novel situation that requires an explanation they will look first to these preferred theories. Frank Dumont tells us how this works in the context of clinical psychologists: "The character of the information that we find salient is strongly influenced by our training and our theoretical orientation. We perceive clinical details in the measure that they fit a template that gives them significance. We simply pick up more quickly on cues that we have been trained to find meaningful than on those that have a neutral import for us."[21] Paraphrasing Dumont, we might say that a leader's knowledge structures and character will significantly influence the leader's interpretation of new situations and may sometimes result in familiar but incorrect diagnoses of organizational dysfunction. The proclivity to confirmation bias and the innate desire to reduce cognitive dissonance could then result in the retention of the false diagnosis, perhaps to the detriment of the organization and its members.

As Nisbett and Ross have asserted, "The most general and encompassing ... theory of human behavior ... is the assumption that behavior is caused primarily by the enduring and consistent dispositions of the actor, as opposed to the particular characteristics of the situation to which the actor responds."[22] They call this the *fundamental attribution error*, and their insights on this cognitive trap are of great value to organizational leaders and change agents. They define the error as "the tendency to attribute behavior exclusively to the actor's dispositions and to ignore powerful situational determinants of the behavior."[23] This is the situation encountered by William Kahn when he consulted to the surgical department in a New England hospital that was encountering performance difficulties.[24] A few years before Kahn's arrival, an accident had occurred during a surgical procedure that resulted in the death of a patient. The doctors, nurses, and other health care personnel were never given a chance to talk about what had happened. To protect the hospital's reputation, personnel were muzzled and were told not to communicate with the press or the public. Over time, a dispiriting and draining pattern of interaction developed within the surgical unit, which included a particular set of behaviors on the part of the unit's nurse manager. She established procedures by which nurses would double-check the surgical procedures proposed by doctors, in effect protecting patients from potential surgical errors. This caused much resentment, and unpleasant exchanges within the unit became common. Kahn's analysis shows that the inability of the hospital to allow members of the surgical unit to make sense of the traumatic event resulted in the creation of a dysfunctional and unpleasant environment. The nurse manager played a particular role in this environment, but her behavior arose from the overall situation that had evolved in the workplace and not from an innate disposition to be a bully. Nonetheless, the hospital's senior leadership decided that the best way to improve the situation would be to fire the nurse manager, and that was the solution they opted for.

Other social psychologists have conducted research that confirms that much human behavior occurs in response to the situations in which people find themselves, rather than as a result of their individual personalities or traits. Solomon Asch convincingly demonstrated that peer pressure can often lead people to support judgments and opinions that they know to be false.[25] A few years later Stanley Milgram conducted experiments about our tendency to comply with instructions given by authority figures.[26] A voluntary research subject was told that he would be placed in the role of a teacher in an experiment intended to help us understand the importance of punishment in learning (this, of course, was a ruse – the person playing the role of the learner was a confederate of Milgram's, and the research subject was not told in advance about the true purpose of the experiment). The teacher would read out a series of word associations (for example, the teacher would say "blue" and then would say "sky"), and the learner was supposed to remember the associations. Then the teacher would repeat the sequence, this time offering three possible words to complete the pair (for example, the teacher would say "blue" and then would say "sky, lake, ink"). The learner (who in most experimental situations was in another room, speaking into a microphone) would then say the word that he thought was the correct completion of the word pair (in my example this would be "sky").

If the learner gave an incorrect answer, the teacher was to administer an electric shock by pressing a lever on an ominous-looking device. With each subsequent error, the shock became more intense. Following a pre-prepared script, the learner would intentionally provide incorrect answers, and more and more shocks were administered (of course, no actual shocks were administered, though the teacher did not know this). In some of the experimental conditions, after a while the learner would begin to scream in pain, complaining of a heart condition, and would insist that the experiment be stopped. Meanwhile, the scientist – an officious man in a white lab coat – would calmly tell the teacher to continue with the experiment.

Before conducting his experiment – which he repeated many times, with small changes to the experimental conditions – Milgram had asked groups of psychiatrists, middle-class Americans, faculty members, and college students to predict how many experimental subjects would be likely to continue to administer the shocks, regardless of their supposed intensity or the reaction of the learner. As Milgram writes, all groups predicted similar results: "They predict that virtually all subjects will refuse to obey the experimenter; only a pathological fringe, not exceeding one or two per cent, was expected to proceed to the end of the shockboard [and administer a severe shock]."[27]

They were mistaken. Milgram's findings show that many subjects were fully compliant with the scientist's instructions, regardless of how specific details of the situation were arranged. When the learner was placed in a separate room and could be heard but not seen, and protested by pounding on the wall, 65 per cent of test subjects were fully obedient. When the test was repeated, but this time the learner vocalized his demand that the experiment be stopped, 62.5 per cent of test subjects remained fully compliant. When the learner was seated in the same room as the subject, 40 per cent of test subjects continued to fully obey the scientist's instructions.

Though these results may make us uncomfortable, it seems likely that Milgram's experimental subjects were reasonably representative of American citizens in the 1960s. Milgram's experiments were replicated a number of times (sometimes outside the United States),[28] and in 2007 Jerry Burger conducted a clever repeat of the experiment at Santa Clara University that was necessarily adjusted to ensure that it met the standards of the university's research ethics board (these boards had not existed when Milgram carried out his experiments in the early 1960s).[29] These replication efforts have confirmed Milgram's original results, and also confirmed that the results are similar regardless of the gender of participants. Human behavior – even behavior that seems brutal or inhumane – can arise out of the situations in which people find themselves, regardless of their personality traits.

Summary

When we attempt to bring about social change, we do so on the basis of a theory of action. We theorize that action X will produce result Y. If I provide education about the health risks associated with obesity, more people will engage in exercise and will consume a healthy diet. If I explain how the company's new order entry system can increase our revenue and provide greater job security and better year-end bonuses, more employees will fill out the order entry screens correctly. If I create and implement a policy saying that all of the institute's research teams must include at least two people whose lives will be affected by the new knowledge generated by the research team, then research will be more likely to focus on issues that are important and relevant for stakeholders.

Our theories of action necessarily contain within them assumptions about the causes of human behavior. Some people believe that human behavior tends to be motivated by the ways in which people respond to the use of power, reason, and cultural norms. Others suggest that human social behavior is tightly linked to processes of sensemaking that invariably occur as organizational members interact with each other. Some claim that human beings possess personalities that are characterized by certain traits or dispositions and that these personality factors predispose people to behave in certain ways. Others suggest that human behavior arises out of the social situations that people encounter and that to alter behavior we need to understand and influence situational factors. Finally, some have pointed out that human beings make sense of situations through innate cognitive procedures and that these procedures sometimes lead people to arrive at erroneous conclusions that produce unfortunate courses of action.

All of these points apply equally to those who intend to bring about change and those who will experience the change – they apply to the change agents and to the stakeholders.

Social change is clearly going to be a complex and uncertain undertaking. If we are to navigate these stormy waters, we will need a method that allows us to move toward our desired goals while reacting appropriately to new and unexpected situations and information. This method should also encourage us to pause from time to time, and to reflect with others on the change process and consider whether we have been making reasonable decisions along the way.

So far, we have focused on the human experience of change. I suggested that we might consider change in terms of the relationship between those who promote social change and those who must bring it into being through their attitudes and actions. I also suggested that there are different theories about the causes of human behavior, and that these will have an important bearing on the strategies we devise to bring about change. I then pointed out that human cognition, for all its wondrous achievements, is fallible and can lead us astray through a variety of biases, heuristics, and errors, and that this should lead us to regard categorical ideas and approaches with caution.

Next, I would like to consider what it is that leads us to believe that change is needed.

CHAPTER THREE

Searching for Answers

We usually change things because something is wrong.

The climate is becoming warmer. Smoking causes cancer. We are losing revenue to new, more agile competitors. Our research innovations are not being applied by practitioners. Enrollment in our graduate programs is falling. Employee turnover in the Claims Management Department is causing instability. Cracks have appeared in the foundation of the public library building. Statistics show that suicide rates among war veterans are ten times higher than in the general population. And so on.

Something is wrong. And somebody decides that something should be done about it. We seek change because there is something wrong with the status quo. These things that are wrong we generally label problems.

I want to make two points about the way in which problems occur for us. First, problems do not usually appear before us *holus bolus*, fully formed and ready for remedial action. Indications that something is wrong are noticed at different times and by different people. These people interpret what they are noticing, and talk to others. Over time, an opinion takes shape – or a variety of opinions – and ideas about what should be done begin to be debated. Sometimes a group will move to action quickly, *jumping to solutions* as some people term it, before the problem is well understood. At other times a group might engage in a long process of collective rumination, in what some have called *paralysis by analysis*, before taking action.

We tend to engage in a process of problem framing as we try to understand the problematic aspects of a troubling or uncertain situation.[1] One might say that the problem initially presents itself to us (and hence I will refer to "the presenting problem" as the problem's appearance at the start of a change process) through a variety of indications or symptoms. Typically, we consider these symptoms and compare them to our past experiences, or to things that we have read or heard about, and we formulate working hypotheses about what might be going on. When possible, we test these hypotheses, sometimes by finding ways to confirm or disconfirm the hypotheses, and sometimes by gathering more information or engaging in discussions with others.

Our goal at this stage in the process is to frame the problem as a problem that can be solved. Some might object that this is not the case. Our goal is (or should be) to frame the problem as it is in and of itself, to frame it through an accurate description of the problem and its causes and effects as they exist in the objective world. This might sometimes be true. If we are concerned about the cracks that have appeared in the public library's foundation, we might be concerned solely with understanding the causes of these cracks and the consequences of taking no remedial actions. However, we might be concerned not just with the cracks themselves but also with the extent to which the public library continues to serve a useful function and to receive support from residents of the community. And we might be concerned with the priorities currently being faced by our city council and what sort of funding might be made available to repair the library's foundation or to construct a new library building. If we are thinking in terms of all of these concerns, having to do with engineering, demographics, social trends, and political realities, then we are thinking not merely about *what is*, but also about *what is possible* in a complex and changing social environment. In this case, being pragmatic human beings, our tendency is to look for ways of framing the problem that will allow us to devise and implement a favorable solution.

This brings me to the second point that I want to make about problems. Several authors have pointed out that problems tend to come in two distinct types.[2] There are problems that we already know how to solve, and there are problems for which we do not have a solution. Some have termed these technical as opposed to adaptive problems.

A technical problem is a problem with a known solution. Engineers know how to shore up the library's foundation, ensuring that the building remains stable and intact for another fifty years. The solution to the problem of the cracked foundation is known and available.

Adaptive problems are problems that do not have a known solution. Finding a solution will involve a search, a process of exploration and trial and error. We don't know how people are going to react to a new unexpected expense showing up on the city's budget. What other projects might have to be canceled or delayed? What trade-offs will be necessary? Who will support the library renewal project, and who will oppose it? What are the costs, what are the benefits, and what unanticipated surprises will occur once we start down this road?

The engineering and construction work needed to effect the repair to the foundation can be estimated and planned with some precision. The social mobilization needed to gain political and public support for the project is less certain. We might devise a three-part strategy: first, we lobby the city council; second, we feed information to the media; and third, we launch a new "Night Out at the Library" campaign with free movies in the auditorium and authors reading from books and professors and public figures offering lectures. But then we learn that the city's Municipal Recreation Center, with its public swimming pool and hockey arena and basketball court, is scheduled for a major engineering upgrade, and other infrastructure renewal projects have also been planned. We find out that the editor of the local newspaper thinks that "bricks and mortar" libraries are antiquated and can be replaced by providing more digital access to information, and we find out that owners of some local businesses – book stores and theaters – are complaining that our Night Out campaign is hurting their business. Clearly, we need to revise our strategy.

An adaptive problem usually cannot be met with a ready-made solution. Instead, it requires a change *process*. As we go about trying to understand and solve the adaptive problem, we will learn new things. We may discover who wants to help to solve the problem, who is indifferent to our efforts, and who opposes us. We could learn that the problem is causing difficulties for some people, and that it creates opportunities and provides benefits for others – in our library example, perhaps the crumbling building infrastructure has created some new jobs for the building maintenance crew, and these people could lose their jobs if a more permanent solution is implemented. We might discover that there are different opinions about the role of community libraries, and about the social benefits provided by libraries. We might also learn that the city's new development plan includes rezoning the area around the old library building for more industrial uses, making the location problematic. All of this learning could influence the way that we think about the problematic situation that is troubling us.

Here is one more wrinkle in the challenge of responding to adaptive problems. This sort of problem, which we do not know how to solve, may lie beyond the reach of our current thinking. We may lack the conceptual tools to analyze and understand the problem. We may lack the vocabulary to describe it. The solution lies in a cognitive area that has yet to be explored.[3] At the very least, this means that to solve an adaptive problem we will need to change both ourselves and some aspects of the social situation that gives rise to the problem. As Kegan and Lahey point out, "meeting adaptive challenges requires, first, an adaptive formulation of the problem (that is, we need to see exactly how the challenge comes up against the current limits of our own mental complexity), and, second, an adaptive solution (that is, we ourselves need to adapt in some way."[4]

Consider the following change process. A few years ago, almost all large organizations in North America and much of the rest of the developed world were organized as top-down hierarchies. An organization was divided into segments, with a manager assigned to each segment. Segments were organized in a pyramid shape, with lower levels reporting up to higher levels. Decision making paralleled this hierarchical structure. The manager made the final decisions on behalf of the segment that he managed (it was usually a "he" in those days), and decisions were ratified or overturned by the next level up the pyramid.

As the human world experienced the technological and social up-heavals at the end of the twentieth and beginning of the twenty-first centuries, this began to change – at least for some organizations. Many jobs became more technical, more knowledge-intensive. Organizations employed workers with highly specialized knowledge who became the experts in their job functions. Work became so complex that it was no longer possible for a manager to possess all of the knowledge needed to make good decisions on behalf of the work unit. One result of this emerging problematic situation was that faulty decisions became more common. Another result was that decision making slowed down in some organizations, and some managers became adept at playing political games that allowed them to evade responsibility for errors.[5]

Imagine an organization where this problematic situation is taking shape. Some organizational leaders can see that something is wrong and that change is needed. They live in a top-down, hierarchical world, and that world is no longer capable of producing desirable results. They realize that the organization of power, authority, and decision making needs to be revamped. There is no ready-made solution available that would allow them to fix the problem. What are they going to do?

Looking back with today's hindsight, we know that one solution to this problem would be to create new decision-making processes that would draw upon the intelligence and knowledge of the skilled workers, to empower workers with more responsibility, and to change the role of manager to put less emphasis on technical expertise and more emphasis on the skills needed to facilitate collaboration among diverse workers. You may recall the tremendous emphasis placed on the concept of emotional intelligence a few years ago, and on skills needed for effective teamwork. These ideas were bound up with the social forces that were unleashed by the enormous changes that began to occur in our organizations.

At the time, however, the leaders who wanted to find solutions to the problematic situations that were holding back their organizations did not have access to these ideas. They knew they needed to try something new but did not know precisely what to try. One thing is certain. The first step that these leaders took toward the new organizational forms that we have today was taken from the position of the old hierarchical forms that prevailed in the past. Think of it this way. The first step in the move from command-and-control hierarchies toward more collaborative workplaces took the form of thoughts, actions, and structures that were consistent with command-and-control thinking. This sort of thinking was all that was available to those leaders, and so their first step toward the new way of being was taken from a stance consistent with the old way of being. In effect, well-intentioned organizational leaders ordered their subordinates to become empowered, while simultaneously finding themselves unable to relinquish their right to have the final say.

In other words, the first step failed. It produced errors. And those leaders had to recognize that the first step produced errors. They had to analyze and try to understand those errors. And then they had to try something new. With each step, with each mistake, they generated new information that could lead to new ideas, new hypotheses, and new tests.

We may experience an urgent need to solve the problem quickly and completely. But like it or not, as we reach out for the new, we invariably find ourselves in a stance that is embedded in the old. Our first step to reach the new is taken on the old path, with the old techniques – and is therefore likely to fail. Solving adaptive problems will almost always involve mistakes and errors, especially at the beginning of the process.

This is very disturbing for many people.

If I really try to solve this adaptive problem, I will make mistakes. Who is going to be blamed for the mistakes? Who will be accountable? What is going to happen in my next performance appraisal? Maybe it would be better to just do things I know I can succeed at and try to keep below the radar. Let somebody else stick their neck out.

Alternatively, some people might try to simplify an adaptive problem by treating it as though it were a technical problem. We act as though we know the solution to the problem, and then we go about trying to implement our solution. Consider the following example. Suppose there is a municipality that wants to begin to use recycled water for limited purposes within the community. The recycled water will be used to water the lawns and gardens around municipal buildings and schools, and also for some industrial purposes. It will not be delivered to households, and it will not be combined with the municipality's supply of potable water. The water authority and city government decide to carry out a publicity campaign, informing the public of what they are doing, and explaining that this use of recycled water will help to keep municipal taxes low. Press releases are issued, and the water engineers and some city politicians are interviewed by newspapers and radio and television stations. However, it turns out that many people are alarmed at the prospect of the city beginning to use recycled water. Some people believe that this is a slippery slope and that before long the city is going to try to fob off recycled water onto city householders. "Does anybody really want to drink the city's sh**** water?" a popular newspaper columnist asks in an editorial comment? A deluge of complaints floods into city hall.

The response of the city government and water authority is to step up their communications campaign. After all, they have the solution. They are right, and everyone else is wrong. They just need to work harder at getting their message out. New press releases come out; more interviews take place. A full-page advertisement is taken out in the local newspapers, explaining once again the rationale for the use of recycled water and outlining the many benefits of the program. However, two days later another full-page advertisement appears in the newspaper, sponsored by the Citizens Committee for Clean Water, blasting the mayor and his government for its irresponsible and unsafe water policy. The protest gathers momentum. Demonstrations and marches take place. Rival politicians assure city residents that if they are elected in next year's municipal elections, they will scrap the program. A few weeks later the mayor's office announces that the recycled water program is being shelved for the time being. A potentially useful water policy joins the list of failed change initiatives.

The city engineers and politicians failed to recognize that they were dealing with an adaptive problem. They thought that the only salient issues were those relating to the ability of existing technology to recondition waste water and render it fit for certain uses, and the ability of existing water infrastructure to deliver this reconditioned water to locations where it could be used. The publicity campaign was conceived of as an add-on to the technical program that was ultimately going to save the city money by making it unnecessary to find new, additional sources of clean, potable water for the city's growing population.

They were mistaken. The prospect of introducing recycled waste water into the city's water system provoked strong reactions among city residents. People read articles and listened to newscasts about the issue, they talked to each other, and they formed opinions. The policy was presented to them as a *fait accompli*, as a packaged solution to a problem that most were only dimly aware of. To many people it felt as though a draconian policy cooked up by unfeeling engineers and scientists was being foisted upon them.

The problems faced by the city's water authority were adaptive. Certainly, there were some technical issues that needed to be considered and resolved, but that was the easy part. It was also necessary to discover the different attitudes that people might have about the use of recycled water, to show that a variety of alternatives were considered, and to see what solutions were agreeable to the majority of citizens. None of this was done.

In the 1990s I was invited to participate in a multi-year project being undertaken by the National Water Quality Institute. The institute had been commissioned by numerous water authorities across the United States to investigate the ways in which people perceived water re-use projects, and how they would like to be involved in those projects.[6] I was one of twenty-one participants on an advisory panel for the project, which included a literature review, three detailed case studies, the production of white papers, collaborative workshops allowing for discussion and debate, and large group deliberative methods such as the nominal group technique. Among the various outcomes from this work were the identification of five critical areas that need to be considered when developing a water re-use initiative: assure a flow of relevant information among all interested stakeholders; show individual and organizational commitment to the process; engage in comprehensive two-way and interactive communication; make decisions in a manner that is recognized as fair and effective; and focus throughout the process on creating and sustaining trusting relationships among all stakeholders.

In my example of the failed water re-use initiative, perhaps things would have gone better if the city government and water authority had approached their challenge as an adaptive problem, and if they had designed a change process (rather than a solution) that drew on some of these five areas.

None of this is intended to imply that using technical expertise to solve technical problems is easy or unimportant. Technical know-how will be vital in our efforts to reduce or eliminate the damage that human beings are inflicting upon the natural environment. Surgery and other therapies used to treat many chronic medical conditions call for the skilled application of technical knowledge. When an emergency situation arises – a tsunami crashes upon an ocean coastline, or a mine tunnel collapses and traps people beneath the earth – it is often technical expertise that is needed to save lives and repair damage.

I am merely saying that for some types of problems, the technical problem-solving approach will not work. When we are dealing with interventions into complex human systems to resolve problematic situations and to bring improvements to the social and task environments, we are almost always dealing with adaptive problems. To respond to an adaptive problem, the change agent needs to focus on creating and leading a change process rather than on selecting and implementing a solution.

To summarize – problems first appear to us in the form of indications or symptoms that arise out of a problematic situation. We know that something is not as it should be, but we are not sure how to frame this troubling situation. We create hypotheses, we seek information, we talk to people, we test our ideas, and finally we frame the problematic situation as a problem that can be solved. We say things like: the real problem is that the level of employee engagement in the Claims Department is low; or, what's wrong around here is that people still think of libraries as buildings full of books and not as public gathering places where all sorts of community events take place every day; or, the problem is that we have created a culture of maintenance when what we need is a culture of innovation. Once the problem is framed, we begin to think about actions that we could take to remedy the situation. If the problem is an adaptive problem for which no known solution exists and which requires that we bring groups of people together to search for ways of resolving the problematic situation, then our intention will be to create an adaptive process for our change initiative.

Searching for Solutions

But still, you might object, if we are going to create a process that will search for a change, where will that search take place? What are we looking for, and where are we looking for it?

Solving a technical problem generally does not involve a deep challenge to the schemata or mental models of people who are affected by the change process. Prevailing attitudes and assumptions remain unchallenged.

Solving an adaptive problem, however, usually requires that existing mental models are challenged and shifted. This means that the change agent will help organizational members to take a critical look at their existing attitudes and assumptions, their existing ways of thinking about their social world, and their behaviors and social structures.[7] This type of change initiative will almost always involve changing attitudes, behavior, and (often) existing social structures that help to hold attitudes and behaviors in place.[8] In the public library example, the change being promoted by those who want to see the library building restored could encompass the attitudes of politicians, administrators, and members of the public, as well as behaviors of these groups – politicians need to support a policy to restore the building, administrators need to take action to implement the policy, and the public need to demonstrate their intention to use the library in ways that justify the expense. The restoration of the library might also be evident at the level of social structures – the municipal legislation to undertake the construction project is a social structure, and it is possible that the library itself might adopt new institutional policies and procedures to assure its ongoing relevance in the community.

The same is true of the water re-use example that we considered. To bring about the desired change, which would see the adoption and use of recycled water for some purposes in the community, the advocates of change might need to help the public to overcome a "toilet to tap" attitude with a perspective on recycled water that emphasizes the effective use of scientific and engineering knowledge and the responsible stewardship of limited natural resources. Potential users of recycled water would need to be encouraged to take action, and social structures – consisting of municipal policies and operating procedures that, in part, ensure the safety of the new measures – would need to be created.

Since we are dealing with bringing about change in human systems, we also need to conceive of our efforts to change patterns of thought, action, and structuring as occurring at a variety of system levels. If we are hoping to improve the decision-making process used by a particular project team, we may need to focus our efforts on a few key individual team members, on the team as a whole, on the department that houses the team, and on the executive leadership of the organization that houses the department. Some large-scale change efforts – for example, introducing a new attitude and approach to care in a national health system – might also require a sector-wide or industry-wide focus.

To bring about change in a human system it is often necessary to intervene at more than one system level. The same intervention framework – thought, behavior, structure – can be used to organize one's thinking about the intervention at each level. The change agent would thus consider what is currently known about the presenting problem and what actions might elicit more information, or what actions might shift the system in the desired direction. Actions are designed that might provoke shifts in the patterns of thought, behavior, and structuring evident at the level of individuals, groups, organizations, subsystems, or full systems. Table 3.1 provides a framework that can be used to think through this planning process.

To illustrate how this looks in action, let's briefly consider a specific case: the way in which people with dementia are treated in Canada. As in many other countries, Canada's population is aging. The average age of Canadians in 2000 was 41.1 years, and by 2020 this had risen to 41.4 years.[9] Seniors are the fastest-growing demographic segment of Canada's population. In 2011 approximately 5 million Canadians were at least sixty-five years old, and this figure could reach 10 million by 2036 and 15 million by 2061.[10] Up to 25 per cent of Canada's population will be senior citizens by 2051.[11] With this growth in the number of seniors in Canada, we can expect new strains on the health care system. Elderly people tend to have more chronic medical conditions and require more health care. For example, the Alzheimer Society of Canada reports that

Table 3.1. Intervening at multiple levels in a system

	Thoughts	Actions	Structures
Individuals	Individual motives, aspirations, fears, goals, etc.	Individual patterns of behavior	Roles, jobs, and other structures that affect individuals
Small Groups	Team purpose, goals, rules, norms, culture	Collective patterns of interaction	Team mandates, regulations, occupational rules (scope of work), etc.
Large Groups	Divisional purpose, goals, rules, norms, culture	Higher-order and interconnected patterns of interaction and workflow	Divisional mandates, strategic plans, organizational arrangements, productivity targets, etc.
Subsystems	Subsystem purpose, goals, rules, norms, culture	Still higher-order and interconnected patterns	Subsystem mandates, plans, legal frameworks, organizational arrangements, etc.
Full System	Full system purpose, goals, rules, norms, culture	Even higher-order and interconnected patterns	Foundational laws, overarching organizational frameworks, system-wide performance targets, etc.

747,000 Canadians were living with dementia (including Alzheimer's disease) in 2011, and this is likely to increase to 1.4 million by 2031.[12]

People with dementia experience changes in their brains that affect their cognition, emotions, judgment, and behavior. Sometimes they are unable to communicate their needs and preferences by making verbal statements or requests. Instead, they may express themselves by grabbing someone or making loud noises. They might curse or complain or exhibit agitation or wander about. Dementia caregivers refer to these sorts of behaviors as *responsive* behaviors.

The behavior represents the way in which the person with dementia is responding to a situation and expresses important information about what the person thinks and how the person feels.

For many caregivers, however, these responsive behaviors seem violent and unnecessary. The caregiver may experience a temptation to walk away, or to respond angrily, or to take steps to compel the person with dementia to act in a more compliant and cooperative manner. In the early years of the twenty-first century, health leaders in Canada and elsewhere were trying to devise better ways of interacting with and providing care to people with dementia, and the issue of responsive behaviors caused a great deal of concern. How can caregivers be persuaded to consider the possibility that these seemingly aggressive behaviors can be looked upon as attempts to communicate? What can be done to help people living with dementia to lead more congenial lives? Here is a classic instance of an adaptive problem with implications at a variety of levels within the health system, from individual caregivers and people with dementia right up to the level of province-wide health policy.

A group of health leaders in Ontario took it upon themselves to search for solutions to this dilemma.[13] These leaders located and obtained funding from a variety of sources (enough to pay for some teleconferences and webinars, to reimburse some local travel expenses, and to pay part of the salary of a knowledge broker), and then designed and implemented a flexible strategy to look for ways of bringing about change. They identified local leaders from the different health regions across the province of Ontario (which is a vast territory of over 1 million square kilometers, larger than Spain and France combined), solicited assistance from a provincial health agency called Health Quality Ontario, and then began to hold numerous "local conversations" among small groups of health care providers across the province whose work brought them into frequent contact with people living with dementia. They discussed

attitudes toward people with dementia who exhibit responsive behaviors, and identified existing health and community resources that
were available as well as gaps in important services. The conversations yielded ideas for a new framework and supporting principles
that offered a productive way to think about providing care to this
patient population. The conversations and the reports that the core
team produced reached people living with dementia, caregivers, local programs and caregiving teams, regional institutions, and policy
makers who worked for the provincial health ministry. Ultimately,
policy makers decided that the groundswell of support for the initiative, along with the tangible benefits that could improve system
performance (for example, better care could reduce the number of
hospital days attributed to long-term care patients with dementia
who exhibit responsive behaviors and who cannot be transferred to
a more appropriate facility because of concerns about the behavioral
issues) justified additional investments, and a new province-wide
initiative was launched, with significant new funding that allowed
for the hiring of new health care professionals who would be dedicated to providing services for patients with responsive behaviors.

In this example, the intervention process was targeted at multiple
levels, and was intended to bring about a shift in the way people
thought about this patient population and the health services that
were intended to help them, along with shifts in related behaviors
(such as the behavior of individuals, groups, and organizations
when responsive behaviors arise in clinical situations, and the behavior of subsystem and system leaders as they set priorities and
monitor performance). The intervention was also intended to have
an impact on structuring by influencing provincial health policy,
and by creating new roles within institutions and programs and
new teams who would focus on delivery of educational and clinical
services. Table 3.2 shows how this intervention can be thought of in
terms of the framework for intervening at multiple system levels.

Table 3.2. The dementia case: Intervening at multiple levels in the health system

	Thoughts	Actions	Structures
Individuals	Local conversations explored a variety of ways of thinking.	Participants gathered information, analyzed processes, and devised possible improvements.	A framework was created that offered a new way to think about dementia care. A new provincial initiative offered a supportive social structure with new roles and teams.
Small Groups	Teams and programs considered their service offerings in relation to the framework.	Teams and programs experimented with ways of overcoming silos and aligning offerings.	Mandates were revised to allow for better alignment and links to new services offered through the provincial initiative.
Large Groups	Institutions (for example nursing homes) considered services in relation to the framework.	Health care providers began to interact with patients in new ways.	Mandates were revised to allow for better alignment and links to new services offered through the provincial initiative.
Subsystems	Health regions were informed of the initiative and invited to participate. The new provincial initiative offered access to new resources. New priorities were formed.	Health regions began to access and implement the new provincial resources.	Mandates were revised to allow for implementation of the recommendations and resources offered by the ministry.
Full System	Senior policy makers saw how supporting this dementia initiative aligned with their own strategic priorities.	Senior policy makers made new resources available and asked initiative leaders to report on impact related to provincial priorities.	New initiatives were created, staff hired, programs designed and implemented, and evaluation plans developed.

Thinking and Acting Together

Human beings are problem-solving animals.

Every day we encounter a host of problems that must be solved. How are we going to get our work done now that Ruth and Don have both phoned in sick? What is the best way to introduce an important new treatment innovation into a primary health care practice that is already struggling with its heavy workload? Where do we draw the line between vigorous debate and vicious hectoring?

To solve a problem, regardless of how serious and puzzling it is, we must first frame a situation as a problem that has a solution. Then we identify and appraise possible solutions. Then we make a choice. And then we act. When we are dealing with an adaptive problem, it will often be the case that our first choice and our first set of actions will not produce the results that we hoped for. We still do not fully understand the problem, and so we are acting on hunches and on behavioral options that we are fond of. It often turns out that we begin by making an error. We then hope to recognize the error, reflect on what the error means for our original diagnosis, and revise our thinking and try something new.

Gino and Staats, writing in the *Harvard Business Review*, point out that people in organizations have a tendency to move too rapidly into action.[14] They suggest that this is one of the tendencies that can limit an organization's ability to solve problems. This is consistent with Donald Schön's argument in *The Reflective Practitioner*, where he says that, when we encounter a problematic situation, we begin our problem-solving process by framing the problem as a problem that we can solve.[15] Schön is pointing out that we are creatures of action. We are constantly bringing our ideas into being by taking action, and when we encounter a problematic situation, we find it difficult to sit still and think about the situation. Instead, we want to do something.

When facing an adaptive problem many people want to take action quickly. We feel acutely uncomfortable with the uncertainty of the problematic situation, and we want to make it go away. One way of doing this is to ignore the uncertainty in the situation and to incorrectly posit the problem as a technical issue that can be resolved with a single-order solution. This helps to account for the popularity of methods and techniques that are often invoked to bring order and predictability to confusing social environments. Business process reengineering, highly structured change management methods, project management disciplines – all of these techniques are sometimes used to create a sense of order in situations that are emergent and unpredictable. Sometimes, however, it is necessary to tolerate the uncertainty in a situation, to experience the uncertainty in order to learn about the situations and interactions that are giving rise to it, to take small steps in order to provoke reactions, before assembling the symptoms into a fully framed problem that one can then put significant resources against.

Several years ago, I served on the board of directors of a business association whose purpose was to develop more capacity for improvement and innovation throughout a regional economy. Each year the board sponsored a dinner with business and community leaders to discuss emerging issues and trends and to talk about the sorts of services that the association could be providing. One year the dinner's attendees included the president of the biggest university in the region. When she was asked about the biggest trend that was affecting her institution, she thought for a moment and then said, "The biggest issue is that people no longer have time to think." The pace of change, the rapid generation and dissemination of astonishing quantities of new knowledge, and the connective technologies that create ever-increasing ways for us to communicate with (and interrupt) each other were creating new habits of mind, new ways of thinking and acting, that favored the soundbite over the essay. People react without thinking.

Gino and Staats were able to demonstrate the negative consequences that arise when people do not have time to reflect on their work. They write:

> We studied employees during their initial weeks of training. All went through the same technical training, with a key difference. On the sixth through the 16th days of the program, some workers spent the last 15 minutes of each day reflecting on and writing about the lessons they had learned that day. The others, the control group, just kept working for another 15 minutes. On the final training test at the end of one month, workers who had been given time to reflect performed more than 20% better, on average, than those in the control group. Several lab studies we conducted on college students and employed individuals in a variety of organizations produced similar results.[16]

This brings me to the final point that I want to make about how people think about change – sadly, we often *don't think* about change. Instead, we act.

Thinking is hard work. It is often easier to go with our hunches and intuitions rather than to identify all of the variables at play in a situation, consider how those variables are interacting with and influencing each other, and calculate the probabilities associated with alternative actions. Besides, most of us are not rewarded for spending time in our offices quietly thinking things through. Thinking by ourselves can be valuable, and thinking together with others can also be valuable.[17]

Thinking, Behaving, and Structuring

I have said that the target of an intervention into a human system will usually consist of the patterns of thought, action, and structuring that occur at various levels within the system.

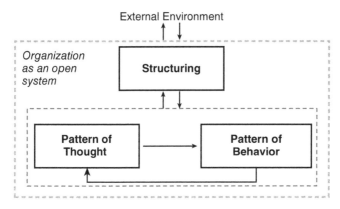

Figure 3.1. A human system as a pattern of thought, behavior, and structuring

Figure 3.1 shows the most useful and flexible model that I am aware of to depict the essential functioning of a human system.[18]

The model offers a way to understand the functioning of a system in context, and it can also be used to understand how an intervention might function across system levels (table 3.1 illustrates the use of the model across system levels). The model depicts a bounded human system that is open to influences from an external environment, and that in turn is able to exert some influence on that environment.

The model envisages a system consisting of an intertwined pattern of thought, pattern of behavior, and the structuring that arises from and supports these patterns. This offers the interventionist a flexible way of thinking about any human system that has asked for help in bringing about beneficial change. As the interventionist enters into the system and begins to interact with system members, she can observe the behaviors of system members. She can also see some of the structuring that occurs within the system, and she can inquire about the thinking – about the aspirations, goals, strategic objectives, and cultural norms – that is characteristic of the system.

As she encounters the full, rich dynamic that brings this model to life in a specific human system, she may begin to see the affordances and constraints that arise from the dynamic. A human system's patterns invariably display certain affordances. The system is able to understand and accomplish certain things – often things that this particular system regularly encounters. An emergency department in a hospital may be adept at responding to the unexpected arrival of a seriously injured patient. A team of accountants may display skill and creativity when looking for ways to handle a client's unusual tax situation. The administrators at a school may be recognized for their ability to respond appropriately to concerns raised by the parents of students. Similarly, the system's pattern invariably displays constraints and limitations. Some issues and problems – some situations – seem to confuse and defeat system members, seem to lie outside the system's current abilities. A team of scientists may become confused and uncertain when a colleague refuses to provide them with access to portions of their shared database. A skilled and dedicated operations group may be unable to integrate an innovative technology as they cope with a heavy workload. The managers and team leaders at a community library may struggle when they are tasked with designing and implementing a community outreach program.

The experienced interventionist will be able to see how the beliefs and assumptions that characterize the system give rise to actions that make up the system's behavioral routines, and how the results produced by these behaviors tend to reinforce and support the prevailing beliefs and assumptions. She will notice how certain structuring arises from these patterns, and in turn supports and holds the patterns in place. The pattern of thought defines what is considered possible and valuable within the system, and the structuring sustains the behavioral pathways that are consistent with the pattern of thought. The interventionist begins to consider the assumptions and beliefs that might need to be challenged, the behavioral routines that will need to be disrupted, and the structures that might have to be adjusted or abandoned.

The point of the model is to help the interventionist to organize the information about the client system that she gathers as she works with system members. It allows her to create a coherent picture of the unique reality of this client system – a picture she can then bring to the attention of system members so they can begin to understand how their own pattern of thought, pattern of behavior, and structuring interact and produce a shared social reality that is coherent, functional, and perhaps also dysfunctional.

The model includes a dotted-line box that encompasses the system's pattern of thought and pattern of behavior. The correlation of thought and behavior is critical for the work of the interventionist. I find it useful here to paraphrase the first law of performance proposed by Zaffron and Logan: how people act correlates with how the situation that they are acting in occurs to them.[19] Put simply, behavior correlates with thought. The pattern of thought includes how the situation occurs for the people in the system. This may include their goals and aspirations, their beliefs about the work that they do and about each other, and their expertise or tacit knowledge. I say this is a pattern of thought because for each individual system member their thinking tends to be organized by the mindsets – the mental models and heuristics – that characterize their cognitive experience; and for the collective as well, their thinking will tend to coalesce into a pattern. This does not mean that everyone is thinking the same thing.[20] It means that the thinking that occurs in the system will arrange itself into a coherent and more or less stable pattern.

The system's pattern of thought correlates with its pattern of behavior. The way that people act correlates with their cognitive experiences, some of which may be rational and deliberate while others may be rapid cognitive experiences governed by heuristics. System members take action, and their actions produce results. They notice and reflect on these results, and this in turn can influence their beliefs and assumptions. We are capable of changing our minds. New thinking can lead to new ways of acting, and new ways of acting can influence thought.

The model also recognizes that structuring is an integral part of any human system and that structuring arises naturally from the patterns that human beings inevitably create. Structuring arises from, and then in turn influences and supports, the patterns that we create. In some cases, working only on the pattern of thought and behavior may fail to produce sustainable change, because the compelling force of a system's structuring will push the behaviors back into the previous routines. Similarly, in some cases working only on a system's structuring may fail to produce sustainable change because the compelling force of a system's pattern causality will undermine and overturn efforts to create change through structure.[21]

So far, I have been applying the model to the human systems that an interventionist seeks to influence. It is also true to say that the intervention process itself will consist of a pattern of thought, action, and structuring. The intervention, designed and implemented by a group of interveners, is itself a human system. We, the interveners, have our ideas about the problematic situation that needs to be tackled. We have our theory of action about what actions are likely to produce positive effects that may either bring to light more information about the presenting problem or ameliorate the problem and its unpleasant outcomes. We take action. And we often create social structures to define and hold our intervener team in place – a project plan, roles and responsibilities, a schedule with milestones, an advisory committee, and so on.

To solve an adaptive problem, we need to put in place an adaptive change process. What's more, we must ensure that our adaptive change process allows time for reflection, so we can identify mistakes, reconsider our assumptions, and adapt our change strategy to the affordances and constraints evident in the situations we are operating within.

Summary

We seek change because there is something wrong with the status quo. These things that are wrong we label problems. We tend to frame problems in two ways. Technical problems are problems for which there are known solutions. Adaptive problems are problems for which there are no known solutions. When faced with an adaptive problem, the change agents must embark on a search for a solution. Unfortunately, some people respond to an adaptive problem by trying to impose a technical solution, and this will usually not work.

To solve an adaptive problem, we must have time to think and to act. We must try something, see how it goes, consider alternatives, and then try something new. We attempt to influence the existing patterns of thought, behavior, and structuring, and we often do so at different system levels in order to produce a sustainable solution. Change is a *process* rather than an object.

Change involves solving a problem. We start by framing the problem as something that can be solved, and we then design and implement an intervention that solves the problem. When we intervene, we, the interveners, think, act, and structure an intervention into the patterns of thought, action, and structuring characteristic of the human system that we are acting upon. We must often focus our actions at multiple levels, including individuals, small groups, larger social units, and subsystems and systems.

In part 2 we consider how to do all of this.

PART TWO

The Doing of Change

The next five chapters discuss how an interventionist facilitates change in human systems. We will focus on facilitating change in the patterns of thought and behavior produced by system members and in the structuring that arises from and supports these patterns.

Thought, behavior, and structure are the grist in the interventionist's mill. Many change theorists and practitioners have focused most of their attention on changing human systems by altering social structures. However, a focus on structure alone is often not sufficient to bring about sustainable change. When we propose a change to a human system, the change must invariably be reflected in the behavior of the people who are part of the system. The patterns of behavior must change. If you alter a social structure without engaging with people at the level of their cognition and behavior, the existing patterns of behavior will usually attempt to reassert themselves.

For example, let's say that we are looking at the claims processing department within a large insurance company. This group has learned that productivity is vital to its success. The importance of productivity is reflected in a supportive structure in the form of a monthly bonus plan for claims examiners who achieve certain *productivity targets*. Over time, however, the quality of the claims examiners' work suffers. An innovative manager decides to correct this by introducing a second bonus plan (a new structure) that rewards claims examiners who achieve monthly *quality targets* (measured by the ratio of claims processed without errors). To be rewarded with a full monthly bonus, claims examiners now need to meet both their productivity and quality targets.

The plan is introduced, but the habit of considering productivity as the most important aspect of department performance remains. Supervisors notice that as quality improves productivity declines. This results in backlogs and bottlenecks. The existing system of work is not designed to handle backlogs, and thus strains appear within the department. Managers complain about the bottlenecks and tell supervisors to fix the problem. Supervisors respond by encouraging claims examiners to meet their productivity targets and to merely do their best to meet quality targets. Over time, productivity once again becomes high, and quality falls to its previous level. Now, however, you have claims examiners who are confused and resentful. Their productivity bonuses are offset by their failure to achieve quality targets. Turnover begins to increase.

The problem illustrated in this example is that a change in structure often does not produce the desired change in the prevailing pattern of behavior. Instead, the change leader must intervene directly in the pattern itself, accessing the knowledge and experience of people who work on the front lines and engaging in inquiry, conversations, and specific actions to change the patterned routines of the workplace.

Of course, the opposite can also be the case. Let's revisit the example of the conflicted claims examiners, but tweak the situation slightly. Suppose the claims examiners become confused and resentful as they see their productivity bonuses vanish due to the imposition of penalties for failing to meet quality targets. The tensions result in the formation of two factions, one made up of a small group of people who are sometimes able to meet both the quality and productivity goals, and the other made up of a larger group who consistently fail to meet both goals. The struggling group asks for help from the more successful group. The more successful group correctly estimates that if they provide the help then they too will fail. Tension builds, arguments erupt at team meetings, and the atmosphere of the workplace becomes increasingly strained.

Let us also suppose that a manager notices these tensions and conflicts and concludes that the productivity of the workplace is being undermined by unresolved interpersonal conflicts. The manager persuades the vice-president to allow him to bring in a human relations intervention in the form of conflict resolution training. He surmises that if people are better able to understand and work through conflict, the tensions will be reduced, and work will be conducted in a more congenial and productive manner. An expert conflict resolution consultant is contracted to provide the training, and the claims examiners all participate in the workshops.

What happens? For a short period, things seem to improve. There is less tension on the floors, and people seem to be getting along better. However, after several weeks the arguments and bad feelings are once again evident. The conflict training increased the capacity of the workers to cope with conflict, but it did not remove the cause of the conflict – which is the maladapted structure that requires claims examiners to meet both productivity and quality targets that are simply out of the reach of most workers.

The interventionist must consider the three critical dimensions at work in the client system: the pattern of thought, the pattern of behavior, and the structuring that arises from and supports these patterns. The interventionist must work with client system members to create the conditions that allow them first to see the factors that are creating the problematic situation that is undermining their work, and then to consider new patterns and structures that could produce more desirable outcomes.

This brings us to the four critical balancing acts that I introduced in the preface. To create deep and enduring change, the interventionist must be persistent. He must maintain his balance as he engages with the complexity of a human system that contains both functional and dysfunctional elements. He must balance four critical priorities:

1. The interventionist must balance the need to create psychological safety for the client with the need to respect the client's determination to change and improve. Psychological safety creates the preconditions for risk taking and change. However, too much emphasis on the creation of a safe social container for the client will promote stasis rather than experimentation and change. I have seen several good graduate students become enamored with this single aspect of the interventionist's craft while neglecting the need to encourage and sometimes push the client toward success.

2. The interventionist will engage in work that could easily result in a close working relationship with the client. However, the interventionist must balance the need to promote closeness and safety and the need to become part of the client system with a countervailing need to remain separate and apart. A serious pitfall of this work is that the interventionist can be seduced into colluding with the client's prevailing patterns and tendencies, and when this happens the interventionist is no longer in the stance of a helper whose role is to facilitate improvement and change. Instead, the interventionist has been subsumed into the prevailing patterns of the client system. As the saying goes, he has become part of the problem.

3. Because the intervention process is intended to create client learning that can then become the basis for sustainable change, the interventionist must resist the urge to do things for the client.

He must balance the inclination to tell the client his opinion and his interpretations with the need to create the conditions in which members of the client system can discover the answers for themselves. At times it is appropriate for the interventionist to assert his views. However, assertions must always be tempered with inquiry.

4. The interventionist must also balance the planned with the emergent. This balancing act recognizes that the problematic situation that interventionist and client are working on is not just "out there" in the organization. It is always present when members of the organization, including those who are collaborating with the interventionist on the change initiative, gather together to talk and work. This means that the problematic situation will often appear in the room as interventionist and client are working together. The interventionist must balance the need to follow the plan, to keep working through the agenda, with the sudden and unexpected opportunity to confront the problematic situation that has just shown up in the room. These emergent interventions are critical if the client is to be able to transfer the learning about the problematic situation into a new capability to recognize and interrupt dysfunctional routines and replace them with something more productive.

One distinctive feature of the *balancing acts* approach to organizational change is the recognition that an interventionist must design and implement a formal, evidence-based plan for bringing about desired change while also noticing and acting in response to emergent phenomena that arise as the formal plan is implemented. In effect, the interventionist operates within two time scales. The formal plan is based on a big picture that sees the change being put in place over the longer term – a period of weeks, months, or even years. The emergent planning deals with aspects of the problematic situation as they show up in the here and now, as interventionist and client work to implement the formal plan.

Most books and articles about organizational change emphasize the former and neglect the latter. For example, John Kotter offers a way of thinking about organizational change that has proven immensely popular.[1] His view of the change process is panoramic and strategic.

Kotter's model has eight steps. Organizational leaders begin by instilling a sense of urgency around the change. They form a coalition of change leaders who create a vision of a transformed organization. The coalition then communicates the vision to the broader organization, using numerous communication vehicles including small meetings and one-on-one interactions. The change leaders empower stakeholders to become involved in and contribute to the change, in part by creating some "quick wins" that demonstrate that the change program will work. They then consolidate their progress and continue to implement changes, and finally take steps to anchor the change into the organization's culture – a process that can take up to ten years, Kotter suggests, when dealing with transformative change efforts in large organizations.

Kotter makes many useful points, including his emphasis on the importance of both leadership and management for the change process. He sees leadership as an inclination toward innovating and adapting, while management is an inclination toward stability and short-term results. With this conceptualization, management is needed to consolidate gains and operationalize the new organizational routines. His discussion of how to consolidate gains includes a simple but effective discussion of organizational complexity that emphasizes the interdependence of groups and activities within an organization.

However, Kotter's account of organizational change is of less value for people who must move away from a panoramic view of the formal change plan unfolding over several years, and who need to enter into the scrums, the project war rooms, the production lines, and the cubicle forests where the day-to-day work of the organization is accomplished. Kotter offers a popular way to think about change that many have admired (and in which others have found shortcomings),[2] but his work remains at a very high level. For an interventionist – a project manager, an OD practitioner, a task force member – Kotter is less helpful when we are sitting down with a group of organizational members who are trying to understand a dilemma that cannot be grasped by their current cognitive and behavioral routines.

Stouten and colleagues recently published a review that encompassed popular change management models (including Kotter's) advanced by expert practitioners or scholar-practitioners as well as the scientific literature on organizational change.[3] They found both scientific and practical support for the proposition that organizational change efforts should include six specific processes. Table P2 summarizes the six evidence-based processes and indicates how the *balancing acts* approach supports and enacts them.

The next five chapters deal with "the doing" of intervention. What does the intervention process look like? What tasks must be carried out? How is the relationship with the client developed? While intervening in the client system, the interventionist will be engaging in these balancing acts.

This is strenuous, demanding work. One bit of reassurance that I can provide is that if you lose your balance momentarily, you will not plunge from the high wire. You will be able to regain your balance and carry on. You will be asking yourself, "Is my client ready to try something new, or do I need to keep building trust for the time being?" "Should I stick to the plan or should I draw people's attention to what just happened?" "Am I starting to get too close to some members of the client system, or am I still maintaining the

Table P2. Acting on the evidence through the Balancing Acts approach

Evidence supports the importance of …	These important areas are handled by the Balancing Acts approach as you …
Diagnosing the problem	Explore, understand, and frame the problem through a collaborative process with significant stakeholder involvement.
Creating a plan	Create a formal project plan that becomes housed in a temporary, transitional project structure, *and* allow for an ongoing process of emergent planning through which you take action when the problem shows up in the room.
Involving and empowering stakeholders	Because it is the attitudes and behaviors of stakeholders that must develop and change in order for the project to succeed, invite the relevant stakeholders to play meaningful roles in the change process.
Developing and aligning knowledge, skills, and ability	Use the change project as a vehicle for allowing stakeholders to develop, apply, and practice new attitudes, insights, ideas, skills, and abilities.
Monitoring and evaluating progress and making adjustments	Monitor and evaluate progress throughout the implementation of the change, so you can test ideas in action, identify misconceptions and shortcomings, and revise plans when needed.
Institutionalizing change in structures and systems	Stay focused on the thought-behavior-structuring model to ensure that change outcomes become part of the prevailing mindsets and structures, and eventually (for transformative change) meld into the fabric of the organizational culture.

appropriate distance?" "Do I need to provide some hints to help the client to see what is going on, or are they moving in a useful direction?"

The first step in the practice of a skilled interventionist often involves forming a relationship with a new client. This is where we begin our examination of the doing of change.

CHAPTER FOUR

Creating a Contract with Your Client

In this chapter and in the three that follow I will discuss the phases of an intervention into a human system.

Some theorists and practitioners suggest that we think of change in relation to certain phases or steps. The sequential model of change was first proposed by Kurt Lewin in the inaugural issue of the journal *Human Relations*.[1] After discussing much of the research that he had conducted over the previous decades, he suggested that successful and sustainable change involved three stages: *unfreezing* the present situation, *moving* toward the new situation, and *refreezing* the new situation. Lewin conceptualized the social situation as being held in place by opposing forces, which produced an uneasy and impermanent (Lewin uses the term "quasi-stationary") equilibrium.

Suppose a new department manager wants her department to achieve a higher level of productivity. Workload is increasing, and the manager wants case managers to provide services to 10 per cent more clients and to handle the corresponding higher volume of weekly transactions. According to Lewin, this would involve recognizing both the forces that currently allow the case managers to be productive and the opposing forces that prevent the case managers from achieving greater productivity. The forces that promote productivity must be increased, and the opposing forces must be reduced. Lewin suggests that a sustainable change will often involve allowing the case managers to analyze the existing situation for themselves, which would include asking them to consider the benefits of and methods for increasing their productivity, and then allowing them to try out new approaches and to discuss results. Lewin recognized that this change process could be psychologically challenging for participants, and that to disrupt the satisfaction or complacency with the existing situation it might be necessary for the interventionist "to bring about deliberately an emotional stir-up."[2] For Lewin, then, unfreezing would include a process of identifying and discussing the problematic situation that is confronting the group. Moving includes the exploration of the forces that hold the current situation in place and experiments intended to shift the situation in the desired direction. Refreezing might include steps to ensure that the workforce has the needed competence and skill, along with the alteration of existing social structures and the creation of new social structures (such as incentive schemes, standardized work processes, and supportive equipment and technology) that will help to sustain the new situation.

Some have pointed out that Lewin's model seems to rest on the assumption that organizations are often in a state of frozen equilibrium, and this does not seem to fit well with our own lived experience of organizational life. I recall meeting with a client a few years ago to begin discussions about a proposed change initiative, when the vice-president of operations cautioned us to be wary of change fatigue. He proceeded to catalog four major change initiatives underway in the organization that were altering how they managed data, fulfilled work orders, developed leaders, and segmented business activities, while a fifth initiative was integrating the operations of a recent acquisition into their culture and operations. Organizations are fluid, not frozen, and a change process is less like melting a block of ice and more like arriving late to a meeting where people are engaged in a heated debate about a topic that you know nothing about.

Nonetheless, interventionists need a way to think about the change process that allows them to organize themselves and get their work done. We make sense of our past experiences and create plans for experiences that are about to unfold by developing narratives that typically take the form of beginnings, middles, and endings. In his popular work *Managing Transitions,* Bridges suggests that a change process begins with a phase in which people release their hold on the existing situation, then move through a "neutral zone" as they try to create a new situation, and finally arrive at the conclusion of the change process, which is described as "a new beginning."[3] Kotter's eight-step change process includes energizing titles such as "create a sense of urgency" and "build the guiding coalition."[4] Block offers a more concrete model that focuses on the pragmatic aspects of the relationship between interventionist (he prefers the term consultant) and client, and suggests that this relationship moves through phases of contracting, discovery, analysis and decision making, implementation, and termination.[5] Block, however, emphasizes that his model is more iterative than sequential, and focuses as much on the dynamics of the relationship between interventionist and client as on the activities that characterize the different phases.

It is clear that change, like all human processes, unfolds through time. Human beings have developed ways of thinking about human experiences that create orderly sequences. We think of human life in terms of a lifespan that can be divided into developmental phases. We see experience in human groups as falling within phases, each with its own challenges and opportunities. For some, history itself unfolds in a dialectical manner, with a certain *Weltanschauung* giving rise to opposing inclinations and forces that ultimately produce a new synthesis that starts the process anew.

Earlier in the book we considered the extent to which initiatives to bring about planned change often end in failure. The discipline of project management arose in part out of a desire to increase the success rates of organizational transformation and technology implementation. If we break the change process down into steps; and if we define these steps in terms of activities, milestones, and deliverables; and if we follow the plan with discipline and rigor, then surely we will improve our ability to implement desirable social changes.

This emphasis on sequence and progress faces challenges when we are dealing with adaptive change. In such cases, we are not implementing a prefabricated solution. Instead, we are embarking on a process of discovery, and through the process itself (rather than merely through the creation of deliverables) the new way of being, with its new patterns of thought, action, and structuring, comes into existence.

Our desire for project discipline must be balanced with the need for exploration and discovery. Each phase in the change process should move the human system closer to an awareness, understanding, and resolution of its problematic situation, and should do so through processes of discovery, problem framing, interaction, and commitment and action. Discovery does not come to an artificial end at the close of the project's initial phase; commitment and action are not saved for the grand finale.

I agree with Peter Block that an intervention usually begins with the negotiation of a contract between the interventionist and the client system, and that is what I will discuss in this chapter. Once the contract is established, the intervention usually moves into a phase of exploration and discovery, where the interventionist and client gather valid and relevant information that is needed to promote a useful and shared understanding of the problematic situation. Once the data have been gathered, the intervention moves into a third phase of collective sensemaking and action planning. At this point the interventionist and client system make sense of the data, reach agreement on the salient features of the problematic situation, and identify the new attitudes, actions, and structures that are needed to

Intervention Phases

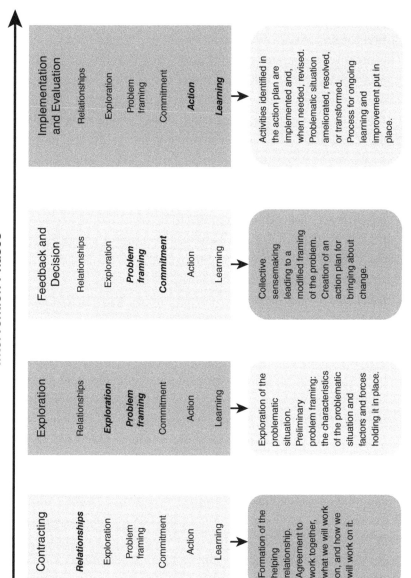

Figure 4.1. The phases of an intervention into a complex human system

bring about sustainable change. In the fourth phase the client, with assistance from the interventionist, implements the action plan and evaluates the results of the intervention and the lessons that can be learned for future endeavors to bring about planned change.

Figure 4.1 summarizes these phases.

Although this looks like a tidy, linear process, the lived experience of an intervention is often contentious and surprising. The intervention moves in unexpected directions and produces unintended results. Contracts often need to be renegotiated as the real nature of the problematic situation becomes apparent. When hypotheses are disconfirmed, it can be necessary to gather new data even though the exploration and discovery phase was seemingly complete. The formal intervention plan often needs to be revised or abandoned.

You will notice that figure 4.1 shows the same six activities occurring in each of the four phases: each phase will see some work on relationships, some exploration, some problem framing, some commitment and action, and some learning. In each phase it is usually the case that one or two of these activities is pre-eminent. Nonetheless, the interventionist is always working on relationships, exploring the client world, seeking a better understanding of the client problems, committing to interpretations, carrying out interventions, and learning from the results produced by the interventions.

You might therefore consider an intervention as a problem-solving process that emphasizes the need for interventionists to reflect on their plans, actions, and results as the intervention moves forward. Each phase of the intervention will contain some of the elements of an experiential learning cycle, which is usually thought of as including action, reflection upon the action, analysis and planning based on the reflection, followed by further action.[6] Then again, you could think of the phases of an intervention as taking the form of a process of continuous quality improvement such as the Plan-Do-Study-Act (PDSA) cycle, where change moves forward through small, incremental steps that include planning followed by action (or implementation of the plan), which in turn is followed by reflection and analysis of the impact of the actions, which then can result in revisions to the plan and a new PDSA cycle.[7]

When dealing with adaptive problems, an intervention does not move forward through the formulation and rigid implementation of a plan. Instead, the implementation moves forward through a process of learning. Information is gathered; tests are conducted; new ideas, behaviors, and structures are experimented with; and, when needed, plans are revised.

Throughout these four phases, the interventionist engages in the four balancing acts that are critical to the stance of a compassionate and rational helper. During the contracting phase, the critical balancing act has to do with the creation of the helping relationship discussed in the previous chapter: being accepting of and compassionate toward the client, while also encouraging the client to abandon the status quo and move into new and uncertain territory.

The Critical Balancing Act of Contracting: Being Compassionate and Confrontational

During contracting it is especially important that the interventionist balance the need to challenge and at times push the client toward success with the need to create safety and to show compassion for the client. The interventionist is confrontational *and* compassionate.

One must balance the need to create the conditions for psychological safety with the need to create the conditions for successful change. One must be authentic, empathetic, and accepting, and one must be prepared to join with the client in facing uncomfortable facts. The consultant will often find it necessary to show the client situations and processes that the client has been studiously avoiding, and the consultant must then be prepared to remain calm, authentic, and reflective when the client's defensive routines are provoked.

Through my own experience gained from numerous consulting engagements I have learned in a visceral and immediate way that my effectiveness depends significantly on my ability to co-create a generative helping relationship with my client.[8] After about fifteen years of working as a consultant, I began to encounter the literature that I have used to construct this chapter. Reading this literature was, for me, a process of validation rather than a process of discovery. It was validating to learn that other consultants and scholars had come to conclusions similar to mine.

However, this may create a dilemma for someone who as yet has little or no experience of forming a helping relationship with a client. As Combs and Gonzalez write, "there is a vast difference between knowing and behaving. Effective learning comes about as a consequence of discovery of personal meaning. It is not enough simply to know; helpers must understand so deeply and personally that knowledge will affect behavior."[9] In other words, it is all very well to learn about something while sitting in the stands. Eventually, however, an intervener into human systems must go down onto the court and play the game. This is where interveners discover for themselves what works and what doesn't work when forming relationships with clients. I know from my work with students who have no practical experience of intervening in human systems that the thought of moving onto the court can be daunting.

Here is some advice.

First, remember that virtually everyone who comments on the need for a secure and trusting consultant-client relationship says that the consultant must be congruent or authentic when interacting with the client. In other words, you must be yourself. Don't worry about impressing anybody, or about appearing smart or important or powerful. Just be yourself.

Second, we all occasionally have the need to form a helping relationship with others. Chances are you have provided help to family members. If you have ever acted as a teacher, or as a coach, then you have formed helping relationships. Our friends sometimes come to us for help, and we do our best to support them. It is likely that you have learned the importance of listening carefully to people who have come to you for help, to give them a chance to fully express their anxieties and concerns, and that you have had some practice in helping people to create new ways of thinking and to develop new action plans about the things that trouble them. All of these experiences are already part of your behavioral repertoire and are available for you to draw on when you begin to work with clients.

Third, many people find it useful to identify a person outside of the situation where they are going to intervene and ask this person for support during the process. Just as you are going to support your client, you may find it useful to find someone who can support you. Arrange to have regular conversations with this person while you are working as an interventionist. While respecting your client's privacy, tell your confidant(e) about the situations that you have encountered, how they have affected you, and what you have struggled with. This person does not need to solve problems for you, or to tell you what you did right and wrong. You are just looking for someone who will listen, and who will ask questions to help you with your own framing of the ongoing situations that you and your client are working on.

Fourth, if you are worried about causing harm to your client because you are unfamiliar with the art and science of social change, try to begin with something small. Stay away from vast corporate mergers, from communities recovering from violent trauma, and from comprehensive cultural transformations. Begin by helping with a relatively small change, such as the move to a new physical workspace, or the introduction of a new computer program, which will certainly affect people's experience of life and work in the social milieu but does not strike you as overwhelming and intimidating. Even in small change processes there is much to be learned.

Fifth, always begin with inquiry. Do not start by attempting to shuffle the chess pieces on the board. Instead, try to understand what is happening on the board, and do so by asking people questions. Pay attention to how you communicate with people. You should notice that most of the time when you are in a consulting stance, you are asking questions. Initially your questions will probably aim at putting together the facts that concern the client's problematic situation. What is going on, how do people feel about what is going on, and what ideas have they generated so far? In time, you will begin to form hunches and hypotheses, and your questions will take on a diagnostic flavor. You will ask questions that probe in particular directions. It is best to hold your hypotheses with a light grip, because it is often the case that your original hunches will be disconfirmed as you access more perspectives.

There Is No Recipe for the Client Relationship

I offer one caution about the relationship that you form with clients.

Be wary of categorical assertions when you are dealing with human beings. Assuming that a certain kind of relationship is *always* necessary to create a climate where change can occur may be incorrect. It may be that with some people and in some circumstances a warm and empathetic relationship is needed and with other people and in other circumstances this is not the case.

This is why Argyris states that when a client is in a state of crisis "the interventionist may ... have to focus more on helping the system to survive than on developing its problem-solving competence."[10] The interventionist may thus need to be directive with the client, rather than finding ways to create opportunities to learn and grow.

For example, one of my research teams was recently creating evidence-based deprescribing guidelines – guidelines to help physicians, nurse practitioners, and pharmacists when considering the pros and cons of stopping or reducing medications for elderly patients who are taking multiple medications. We piloted the guidelines in six frontline clinical sites. We did not have the time to create warm, empathetic, and authentic relationships with people in all of these sites. Instead, I think it fair to say that we conducted ourselves in a respectful manner, and for the most part we were business-like and efficient. We did not try to provide members of these client systems with a sense of validation or confirmation. We did not place considerable emphasis on ensuring that we listened carefully and at length to all of their concerns. Instead, we provided information and answered questions.

Nonetheless, the sites engaged meaningfully and with determination in attempting to adopt and use the guidelines and to bring about behavior change in their practices. In this case a good result did not depend so much on establishing warm or genuine relationships between change agents and frontline participants; instead, the important fact seemed to be the credibility of our change agent team (which included expert clinicians and scientists who used rigorous methods to develop the evidence-based guidelines). Participants saw that the change agents were credible, and concluded that the information being provided was also credible and that behavior change was therefore desirable.

Perhaps what is going on here is an interplay of four factors:

- The extent to which the proposed change makes sense to frontline participants
- The difficulty of implementing the change that is being proposed
- The credibility of the people proposing the change
- The quality of the relationship between change agents and frontline participants

Table 4.1. The coherence and difficulty of the proposed change

	Proposed change makes sense	Proposed change does not make sense
Easy to implement the proposed change	Case 1: High motivation to change	Case 2: Some motivation to change
Difficult to implement the proposed change	Case 3: Some motivation to change	Case 4: Low motivation to change

The coherence and difficulty of the change can be represented in a two-by-two table (table 4.1):

With case one, where the proposed change makes sense to front-line participants and where it will be relatively easy to implement this change in the social milieu, credible change agents may be sufficient to move the change forward. It is likely that this change is a technical problem rather than an adaptive problem. If you consider my deprescribing example, this situation might apply to a health care site in which health care providers are familiar with the problem of polypharmacy (the use of multiple medications) among the elderly but have not yet designed a deprescribing process, and where existing work processes include regular reviews of patient medications. It will be relatively easy to include deprescribing as part of these regular medication reviews, and health care providers will be willing to participate in this new activity.

With case 2, credible change agents and a warm relationship are necessary to move the change forward. Sticking with our deprescribing example, this situation may arise in a health care site in which existing work processes include regular reviews of patient medications but where health care providers are not familiar with the problem of polypharmacy or the extent to which this problem exists among their patients. The formation of a helping relationship may help members of the client system to face the fact that their existing practices could be causing harm to some patients, to accept their responsibility for this situation, and to institute the needed changes.

With case 3, credible change agents are necessary to move the change forward, and a warm relationship will also be helpful. This situation could arise in a health care site where health care providers realize that polypharmacy is a serious problem that affects some of their patients, but they have not developed work processes that allow for the regular review of patient medications, and they have no other work processes that could easily be used to facilitate deprescribing. Instead, they have other priorities that have been given to them by health system leaders, making it difficult to somehow fit in deprescribing among their numerous workplace activities. In this case, the formation of a helping relationship may allow members of the client system to recognize their own helplessness to improve their practice, and to devise strategies that will allow them to lobby and advocate among health system leaders to change their priorities so deprescribing can be made feasible.

With case 4, credible change agents and a warm relationship are necessary to move the change forward, and the process can be expected to take longer than in the other cases. In this case, health care providers are not aware of the problem of polypharmacy, and existing work processes cannot be adapted to include deprescribing activities. The creation of a helping relationship may first of all allow members of the client system to recognize the problem of polypharmacy, to see how it exists within their own patient population, and to accept that they share some responsibility for this situation. They may then be able to create a strategy that will allow them to lobby for changes to their priorities so that deprescribing can be included, and then to redesign their existing work processes to include deprescribing activities. Here we see a need to educate and to motivate, to lobby, and to redesign. The change process is likely to be time consuming and will probably encounter unforeseen difficulties along the way. We are now dealing with a problem that is more adaptive than technical.

The Tasks of Contracting

The primary purpose of contracting is to reach a general agreement on the nature of the problematic situation that is to be investigated and to surface the assumptions that the interventionist and client are making about the work that is to be done. The following story will illustrate why it is important (and sometimes difficult) to begin an intervention with some work on these two concerns.

Some years ago, I accepted a contract to work with a leadership team to help them prepare for their upcoming strategic planning process, and to help them develop more capacity to create and implement strategic plans.[11] The organization was a somewhat loosely knit entrepreneurial group with a large leadership team of about eighteen members.

At the conclusion of my first meeting with the full team, I contracted with two team members to work with me to design some activities that we would bring back to a larger group in four weeks. I had made similar contracts with other people on other projects in the past, and I anticipated that this contract would be straightforward and clear, and that we would complete our work without incident. This, it turned out, was an error.

Ours was a verbal contract with simple terms. I invited two members of the leadership team (I will call them Donna and Keith) to help me to prepare some materials that would assist the team in understanding the challenges and opportunities that the organization was facing as it prepared to launch a new round of strategic planning. That was the only contract that I offered, and that is all that I expected from them. We would work together, I would do my share of the work (or perhaps even the lion's share of the work, though I did not explicitly state this to Donna and Keith), and they would pitch in. To help us get started, a package of reading material had been put together by members of the leadership team. I negotiated with Donna and Keith a date and time when we would meet to discuss this reading material and to consider how to proceed. I suggested a date that would give them plenty of time to complete the reading, though I realized that they might not be able to read everything. I did not articulate any other expectations, and neither Donna nor Keith said anything to suggest that they believed that there were elements to our contract other than those I put on the table.

However, without saying anything to Donna or me, Keith had in his own mind added some elements to our contract. Keith had concerns about how the organization's leadership team functioned. He believed that some members of the team said one thing and did another. They were out of integrity. They talked about the importance of teamwork, but they often took action and made decisions without consulting colleagues. They talked about the collegial atmosphere within the leadership team, but they engaged in manipulative tactics to try to get their way when decisions were being made. Keith wanted to influence our work in ways that would result in a session plan that would highlight this lack of integrity and force certain leadership team members to explain themselves.

Similarly, Donna saw our contract in a way that differed from my view and from Keith's view. Donna thought that she and Keith would do most of the work to prepare the activities for the leadership team. She wanted to meet with Keith before the two of them met with me. She thought that she and Keith needed to read all of the materials in advance and then create a detailed plan for the way in which the group would work through its challenges and opportunities. Donna thought that my role would be simply to review their proposed plan and suggest ways of improving it.

I now realize that I, too, had included unstated elements in our contract that Donna and Keith were not aware of. I was helping this leadership team to work on their capacity to create and implement plans. We had agreed that we would do this work by creating and implementing a strategic planning process. It seemed to me that by *doing* planning, and then by reflecting on how the planning had gone and what it had accomplished, we would together create a naturally situated school of planning from which all participants would learn. For each step in our process, I wanted to involve some members of the leadership team who would act as planners and who then could share their insights and experiences with the rest of the team – who in turn could comment on what it was like to receive the sharp end of the planning stick.

I did not explain any of this to Donna and Keith. I just said that together we were going to plan some activities for the coming meeting.

The three of us were operating on the basis of different contracts that were composed of unstated assumptions. We all thought that we had a firm and clear grasp of what was to be done and how it was to be done. However, we were all mistaken. I thought that we would work together to create a plan for the session, and that perhaps I might end up having to do most of the work. My goal was to create an experience of planning that could form the basis for learning – I was looking to create what a teacher calls "a teachable moment." Keith saw our contract as a way to address some of his personal concerns about individual members of the leadership team and how they affected the work of the organization. Donna saw the contract as a task that she and Keith would collaborate on, with support from me, so the two of them could develop new skills in designing interactive planning sessions.

When we met again, I began by saying that the purpose of the meeting was for the three of us to discuss what sort of design might be appropriate for the next meeting of the full leadership team, and how we might incorporate the suggested reading materials. Donna started things off by handing us a piece of paper with a proposed design for the session. Donna's design included a brief presentation by one of us to summarize the key points from the reading material, followed by small group discussions about how these key points could inform a strategic planning process, and culminating with a full-team discussion to derive lessons and next steps from the group activities.

Keith then told us that he had been thinking along different lines. He did not have an alternative design or any fully worked out ideas about how the session would work. The one concrete suggestion that he described was to invite some suppliers and customers to the meeting to provide the leadership team with a variety of perspectives on what it is like to work with the organization.

After a lengthy discussion, we agreed that we would use Donna's activity, and I invited Keith to give his idea further thought. The next day Keith sent me a friendly email in which he said that Donna's activity sounded good, that he was not making headway with his own idea, and that he had lots of other work to do and was withdrawing from our planning team.

Assumptions were made by all parties. I assumed that my offer was understood and accepted by everyone, and that we would meet at the appointed time and work out what to do. Donna assumed (and I am inferring this from what she said at the time and what she told me afterward) that she and Keith should come to the conversation with a plan. Keith assumed, like me, that the planning would occur during the phone call, and that it was okay for him to add his own objectives to the process without first negotiating them with Donna and me.

When the full leadership team met, I explained that Donna had developed an interesting design for us to use, and invited her to explain it. She did so. We went through the planned activities, and everything seemed to go very well. Then at the end of the session we debriefed the session. I thanked Donna for her hard work, and I invited people to tell us how they had experienced the plan, and how they felt about the work they had done during the session. At this point Keith spoke up, saying that he had felt disrespected by me throughout the day. I had singled out Donna for praise and had ignored the very significant amount of effort that he had put into our planning process.

I was surprised by this statement, in part because things had seemingly gone so well and everybody else had seemed pleased, and in part because I had not been aware that he had put significant effort into our planning process. Before I could reply, Donna spoke up in an angry tone, essentially saying the very things that were going through my mind. There then ensued an angry exchange between Keith and Donna.

When emotions and frustrations become apparent in a client group, I often let them surface for a while rather than covering them up (I will explain why when I discuss the idea that "the problem is in the room" in chapter 5), and so I did not intervene right away. After a couple of minutes other members of the leadership team intervened and smoothed things over.

The basic problem that triggered this outburst – and that continued to plague the leadership team through several more meetings – originated in our contracting.

Assumptions had been made by all parties. I assumed that my offer was understood and accepted by Donna and Keith, and that we would meet at the appointed time and work out what to do. I also assumed that our planning exercise would create an opportunity for us to reflect together on the experience of planning in the context of this leadership team. Donna and Keith were not aware of my assumptions.

Donna assumed that she and Keith should come to our planning meeting with a plan, or at least some concrete ideas and suggestions that could become the basis for a plan. Neither Keith nor I were aware of Donna's assumption.

Keith assumed, like me, that the planning would occur during our meeting. However, he also added some personal objectives to our contract, and did not inform Donna or me that he had done so. Neither Donna nor I were aware of the changes that Keith had made to our contract.

The result was confusion during our planning meeting. Donna's assumptions did not collide with my own intentions, and so her behavior made sense to me. Keith's assumptions remained hidden, and he was not able to explain clearly the activity he was proposing or how it related to our purpose, and thus I was unsure of how to incorporate his ideas. This incorporation was supposed to take place afterward, but Keith withdrew from the process. My objectives had been met. I realized later, however, that Donna and Keith had experienced a great deal of emotion and frustration, and they both carried their frustrations into the leadership team meeting.

To fulfill the purpose of contracting, four tasks must be accomplished:

- Agreeing on the problematic situation that the work will inquire into
- Surfacing and sharing hidden assumptions, agendas, intentions
- Agreeing on a process for moving forward
- Signing the contract

Agreeing on the Problematic Situation

I have said that the main purpose of contracting is to reach agreement on the nature of the problematic situation that is to be investigated and to surface the assumptions that the interventionist and client are making about the work that is to be done. I acknowledge that this is a somewhat unorthodox stance. Most people assume that the purpose of a contract is to establish the terms of agreement around the exchange that is to take place. What is the offer, what is to be delivered, and what consideration will change hands when the contract is fulfilled? This implies that a contract is mostly about goals, activities, milestones, and deliverables.

These are important. However, if your contract is an agreement in which you are to act as an interventionist who is trying to help a client system to change itself so as to resolve an adaptive problem, then it is even more important to explicitly create the basis for *shared intentionality* with the client. By *shared intentionality*, I mean that it is important that you and members of your client system be honest and forthright and that you agree about the nature of the problematic situation that you are trying to resolve, that you are not operating on the basis of hidden assumptions or intentions that might later undermine your work, and that you agree on the process by which you will tackle the problem.

The contracting process begins when an interventionist is, in some fashion, presented with a problematic situation that is intolerable.

This can happen in a number of ways. Because I worked and continue to work as an external consultant, for me it usually happens when a client sends me an email asking if I am available to help with something. If you are an organizational leader, it might happen as you begin to notice a variety of puzzling situations in your workplace – an increase in turnover, a decrease in sales or in the quality of your team's work, the development of a conflict among members of your team or between your team and other organizational units, a growing tendency of your colleagues to grumble about disrespect or bullying or unreasonable time constraints, or an inability to move forward with an initiative. Perhaps your senior leadership team has presented you with new objectives that cannot be easily implemented within your existing work environment. Perhaps your organization's board of directors has issued a new mandate for the organization that is inconsistent with the way that work is currently organized.

In my own case, as I said, contracting usually begins with a brief inquiry about my availability, and it might include a query about whether I have expertise in a particular area. When I am asked about my expertise, I try to find out if the client wants to contract with somebody who has content expertise in a particular method or technology or if they are looking for help in creating and implementing a process to bring about beneficial change. If it is the latter that they need, then I usually continue the conversation.

Since I am an external consultant, sometimes the initial query is an invitation to participate in a Request for Proposal (RFP) process. This is a competitive process in which a number of consultants or vendors are invited to review a formal description of client needs and then to present a proposal outlining the consultant's qualifications, proposed approach, and suggested budget. I am usually quite happy to participate in these competitive processes, as long as the work looks interesting and as long as I believe that I am qualified to provide the help that is needed.

Regardless of how the contact is made, the most important first step for the interventionist to take is to try to understand as much as possible about the problematic situation that the client is facing. This includes trying to understand the problematic situation in itself, and also trying to grasp how this situation is occurring to the different people who make up the client system.

To do this, it is advisable to conduct a brief environmental scan.

An environmental scan takes the form of gathering data about the system and the problematic situation that it faces. You can often find useful data in sources such as annual reports, strategic plans, and websites. Sometimes it can be useful to also undertake a brief scan of the social science and management literature, to see if anything useful has been published about the issues that your client is facing. If you are responding to an RFP, the client will usually have included details about its current situation and requirements in the RFP document, and you will often have a chance to submit questions to clarify important details.

An environmental scan also involves engaging the client in conversation about their experience of the problematic situation. It is especially useful to hold several separate conversations with different people. This allows you to access a variety of perspectives on what is going on. If the client system organizes power in a hierarchical manner (as most organizations do), then it is always advisable to speak with the person or people in charge. In addition, the interventionist should try to speak with other people who represent at least two other perspectives within the system.

If I am intervening in a long-term care home about a problematic situation that is evident on the home's residential floors and involves frontline workers, I might try to speak with the person who contacted me (this would be someone like the general manager or the director of care), someone from the nursing staff, and someone from the basic care staff (these workers are often called personal support workers or health care aides). I would often ask myself what individuals or groups are probably going to need to participate in the change process. I want to speak with these individuals and with representatives of these groups.

If I am intervening in a call center that provides customer services for a technology company (a computer services outsourcer, for example, or even a cell phone or cable TV vendor) about a situation concerning the breakdown of existing problem-resolution processes and some internal conflicts that have recently developed, I might want to talk to the manager of the unit, to one or two supervisors, and to a few customer service representatives.

I want to gain access to several different perspectives because it is likely that different people are experiencing the situation in different ways. Several years ago, I was invited to work with a technology support unit that was part of a large government department. The unit's long-time director had recently retired, and a new director had been hired (he was the previous assistant director). He wanted me to help him to shift the focus of his unit from efficiently handling a high volume of work to focusing on understanding and meeting the needs of internal customers in the department's operational units. He said to me: "We are focused inwardly. I want us to focus on our customers." I carried out an environmental scan before finalizing the contract, and I discovered that others in the unit shared their new director's dissatisfaction with the status quo. However, they had different ideas about what was going on.

One group told me that there was a great deal of jealousy, frustration, and conflict within the unit, and that this was due to the previous director's insistence on always being positive and on never giving employees any constructive (or negative) feedback. "We are the top unit in the department," she liked to say at staff meetings, regardless of whether this claim bore any resemblance to reality. When some key long-time employees did not keep their skills up to date and were no longer able to perform their jobs, the previous director ignored that situation and hired new people to ensure that the work was accomplished. This meant that several long-time employees were no longer engaged in productive work and simply "coasted" through their days. It also meant that the new people began to notice that they were performing the work of these coasters, and that the coasters were paid more and were safely lodged in secure jobs, even though they contributed very little to the unit's performance. Resentment and frustration developed.

A second group told me that most managers were promoted because of their technical competence, not because of their leadership abilities. This created a situation where some of the unit's teams were led by technical all-stars who ended up doing all of the challenging work themselves while depriving their employees of challenges that would allow them to develop their skills. More resentment and frustration developed.

My environmental scan allowed me to access multiple perspectives that allowed us to create an appropriate scope for our inquiry. The new director was quite right in thinking that the unit had become inwardly focused in ways that made customer needs a secondary concern. This had come about because of certain management practices that had come to characterize the unit over the course of several years. These management practices had emphasized the importance of a congenial social environment at the expense of competence. As a result, the skills within the unit had languished, and resentment and frustration had grown. This, in turn, had created defensiveness within the unit. If the unit engaged openly and continuously with customers, its lack of competence might be revealed, and people would get in trouble. Better to remain behind the barricades, get work done in some fashion, and avoid trouble.

By starting the contracting process by talking to a number of different people you will produce another important benefit. This approach will accustom your primary client (the person who signs your contract and pays your bill, usually the manager of the people who make up the system) to an approach that endeavors to do things *with* rather than *to* people. You should tell your primary client that all conversations you have with system members will be confidential. This ensures that people feel safe when they are sharing their perspective with you (when problems arise in a human system, a natural response is to blame the problem on somebody, often the boss, and it is essential that your approach allows for some of this venting to occur), and in turn makes it more likely that system members will begin to trust you and will be willing to share their views and feelings about whatever is going on.

When carrying out an environmental scan, you generally want to ask open-ended exploratory questions. I like to begin by explaining why I am there, and then I give people lots of time to share their own perspectives. I do not assume that I might control or direct the conversation. If there is something important that the person needs to talk about, then that is precisely what I need to hear. I might say things like this:

I met with your new director, and he told me that he thinks this might be a good time for all of you to re-examine your current priorities. He wonders if it might be a good idea to focus more effort on the needs of customers, and on aligning your operations with customer needs. What do you think about this?

I would then be inclined to give the person ample opportunity to talk about whatever seems important in the workplace.

What are some of the challenges and opportunities that the unit is facing?

What problems need to be solved?

Which groups are most involved?

Can you give me a specific example of this?

How do you feel about the situation?

Are you satisfied with the situation here? Do you think others are satisfied?

Would you be willing to participate in a project that tries to understand and then improve the situation?

What would need to be in place or to happen to make an improvement project a success?

In carrying out the environment scan and in asking questions and interacting with members of the system, the interventionist is trying to meet two objectives. The interventionist wants to help the system, and the interventionist wants to gather useful and relevant information that can help all participants to reach a more complete understanding of the problematic situation and of ways that it might be ameliorated. While interacting with system members during the scan, the interventionist is attempting to form a partnership with people in the system.

The example that I have given is representative of my experience. It is often the case that by the time I have completed my environmental scan, it is clear that the problematic situation is being experienced differently by different people. This often means that my primary client (and other system members, too) is seeing only part of the problematic situation, and I need to negotiate an approach that can encompass the different perspectives that surfaced.

After completing the environmental scan in the consulting project that I have been describing, I once again met with the new director of the unit. Here is what I said:

> People seem to mostly agree with your assessment of the symptoms of the problem that needs to be fixed. The unit has become overly focused on internal needs, and customer needs are sometimes ignored. However, I noticed a variety of views about what is going on to produce those symptoms. If there are existing pressures that are producing this inward focus, you might need to identify and then do something about those pressures before designing a new customer-centered approach for the unit.

Originally, he had thought that we might begin by designing a project that would inquire into the ways in which the unit's organizational structure and work processes could be redesigned so they would align better with the needs of customers in other department units. After we discussed the results of the scan, he agreed that we should begin by inquiring into the causes of the current situation. This seemed important because, if we moved immediately to a new design, we might later find out that those hidden causes would act to disrupt and undermine the effort to realign the unit.

Surfacing the Hidden Assumptions

During contracting it is critical to surface the hidden assumptions that could, if they remain unacknowledged, undermine the work. This includes assumptions made by the interventionist.

Earlier in this chapter I gave an example of how unstated assumptions can lead to misunderstandings between interventionist and client, and how this can undermine the attempt to work collaboratively to bring about change. The effort to be clear about intentions and assumptions is an unending struggle, and all interventionists can expect to occasionally encounter this sort of problem.

Several years ago, I worked with a large public sector organization on an employee engagement project. My client had determined that their customer service levels were low, and they had a hunch that if they could improve the engagement of their employees, they could mitigate their problem. After meeting with them and conducting an environmental scan, I thought that their framing of the problem was plausible. Employees were organized within a traditional bureaucratic hierarchy. Managers set goals and made plans, and subordinates were expected to take action to implement plans and achieve goals. The workplace environment was characterized by a sense of drudgery and constraint. Allowing employees to engage more fully in the design and implementation of work, and in problem solving and improvement, stood a good chance of increasing the performance level of the various work units, and ultimately improving customer satisfaction.

I went to work with my client system to create a plan to encourage higher levels of employee engagement. When I met with line staff and supervisors our conversations were productive and stimulating. However, after meeting with the senior managers who had invited me into the system, I sometimes had an uneasy sense that something was wrong. Their facial expressions occasionally suggested that they were not sure what I was talking about. Now and then they made statements about what needed to be done that seemed unrelated to the project that we were designing. Perhaps they were extremely busy and were overwhelmed, and this made them distracted and occasionally unfocused?

After one of these meetings, it suddenly occurred to me that perhaps they were thinking of employee engagement in ways that differed from my own ideas about this concept. I did some searching in the literature on employee engagement, and sure enough I discovered that there were two separate views about this term.[12]

Some researchers, consultants, and organizational leaders saw employee engagement as having to do with the extent to which employees are able to bring all of themselves to their work by participating fully and meaningfully in work activities.[13] Engaged employees are able to contribute to the design of the workplace and work processes. They are organized in teams, they help to set their own goals, and they participate in problem solving to improve their own performance. Management provides a framework and principles to govern behavior. Within these broad parameters, employees are left with plenty of elbow room to be creative and innovative in their work. The term "engagement" is used to describe the many different actions and contributions that employees are encouraged to engage in. This was the notion of employee engagement that I was using.

However, other researchers, consultants, and organizational leaders saw things differently. For them, the term "employee engagement" denotes an attribute that characterizes employees and that exists in a form that can be measured or quantified. An employee is more or less engaged, just as employees are thought to be more or less satisfied, productive, competent, and so on. Engagement exists within employees as part of their current state of being. Just as we can use a thermometer to measure the body temperature of an employee, so too can we use an employee engagement question-naire to measure her current level of engagement. According to this view, when employee engagement is measured at a high level, a high level of that attribute exists in the workforce, and when a high level of engagement exists then this will cause customer satisfaction to be high.[14]

In other words, the senior managers in my client system did not want to encourage higher levels of employee participation in the design and conduct of their work. Instead, they wanted to measure the current level of engagement. If the measure revealed a low state of engagement, then they wanted to figure out why engagement was low, after which they would design interventions to prod the workforce toward a higher measure of engagement. Once they had correctly calibrated the level of engagement (like tuning the idle or timing speed on an older automobile), then the engagement at-tribute in the workforce would somehow cause another attribute, the "satisfaction" that exists as an attribute within customers, to increase.

It was not so much that they opposed the idea of encouraging more employee participation. Rather, they were indifferent to it. They wanted more employee engagement because they believed that would give them more customer satisfaction. When I talked about employee participation, they thought that I was musing about possible interventions that we might design in order to produce the attributes that they wanted.

After I noticed the different assumptions that we were operating under, I arranged to meet with my primary clients – the two senior managers who had signed my contract – and brought the situation to their attention. They confirmed that they conceived of employee engagement as a psychological state (or attribute) that could be measured with a questionnaire. They were surprised to hear that I conceived of employee engagement as a set of behaviors.

We then reviewed the contract that we had signed, and the description of the approach and the list of activities that fell within the contract, and negotiated a new, shared understanding of the problematic situation that we were working on, of the approach that we would take to ameliorate that problem, and of the specific activities that we would use to implement the approach.

One technique that I almost always use to mitigate the dangers that I am operating on different assumptions from my client, or that subgroups within the client system are operating on the basis of different assumptions, is the creation of a project charter. I learned the value of this when working on large change initiatives in the 1990s. Experienced project managers nearly always conducted a preliminary phase of work that focused on the creation of a charter for the project. This charter was more than just a plan denoting tasks, milestones, and deliverables – though most project charters do indeed include these items. The creation of the charter is also an occasion for project participants and stakeholders to meet and discuss the project's purpose, scope, benefits, challenges, and activities. It is a chance to consider the importance of involving stakeholders in the project and how these stakeholders might be included in the work. When creating the charter, participants can discuss the key ideas and technologies that will inform the work, and they can raise ethical issues and consider risks and how risks might be mitigated. The charter allows you to hold these conversations and to expose misunderstandings before the work begins in earnest.

I am an external consultant, and I generally follow the same sequence of activities. I begin with contracting, which includes an environmental scan and the formulation of a contract. Then I continue the contracting process by working with my client to develop a project charter. This charter is a much more detailed description of the project. It gives me the opportunity to continue forming positive relationships with members of the client system and to try to flush out the assumptions and potential misunderstandings that could hinder our work later on. Once the project charter document is complete and its content has been discussed and revisions agreed upon and made, my primary client and I both sign the charter.

Table 4.2 shows the sections that I usually include in a project charter, along with an explanation of what goes in them.

When I am in the stance of an interventionist preparing to work with a client, I invariably make a number of assumptions. Some are rather basic, and have to do with the amount of time that I need to contribute to the project, the amount of money that I will be paid, and whether I will personally have to handle administrative details such as scheduling meetings and preparing minutes (sometimes I handle these tasks, and sometimes my client takes care of them). Others are more significant, such as the assumptions I made in the case examples described earlier in this chapter.

Because different members of my client system may see things differently (and in fact it is usually the case that there are at least two different perspectives at work within the system, one held by managers or leaders and the other by employees or staff members), bringing these different perspectives to the surface, along with the assumptions and interpretations that they are based on, is an important part of the interventionist's job. When a problematic situation arises in a human system, it often shows itself in terms of the way tasks are organized and performed and the way social relations function. When trying to frame the problem, some people will focus largely on the task system. They will look for an explanation in terms of the skills and competencies of staff, staffing levels and role assignments, the appropriateness and functionality of equipment and technology, and the efficiency and effectiveness of work processes such as order entry systems, production lines, monitoring programs, and distribution processes. Other people will look

Table 4.2. The project charter

Project charter section	What to include here
Sign-off page	This page provides the names of the people who must sign off on the charter. Your name should be here, along with at least one name of a member of your client system.
Purpose of this charter	This is a very brief section that states what the charter is intended to achieve. You say here that the charter spells out the shared understanding of the project's purpose and how the purpose will be achieved.
Summary of the project	This is the charter's executive summary. It is a succinct and brief description (about two paragraphs) of the project's goals and of the activities that will be used and the deliverables that will be produced to meet these goals.
Background to the project	This is where you provide the information that is currently available about the problematic situation. Why did this client call you to work with them on this project? What is going on in the external environment and within the client system that is giving rise to the problematic situation that you are addressing? What are the known symptoms of the problem? Why did the client decide to take action?
Objectives of the project	This is where you provide the current framing of the problem and the approach to ameliorating the situation and bringing about some sort of change within the social situation. In a single sentence, state the objective of the project. Then, if needed, provide a list of more specific goals.
Approach to achieving the objectives	Here you provide a narrative description (that is, a description in paragraphs) of what you and the client intend to do. You might say something here about your method for gathering data, for organizing and analyzing data, for making sense of and drawing conclusions from the data, for developing a detailed action plan to bring about change, and for implementing and evaluating the action plan. For me, this section is providing context for the detailed chart that follows in the next section.
Schedule, milestones, and deliverables	This takes the form of a chart or table with four columns. The left column contains a range of dates. The second column names an activity. The third column is used to identify milestones (these are activities that represent decision points, where client approval is needed before the next steps can be taken). The right-most column identifies any deliverables that are produced by that activity.

(Continued)

Table 4.2. The project charter (*continued*)

Project charter section	What to include here
Scope of the project	This section describes what is included in the project, and what is beyond the scope of the project. This is very important for ensuring that your understanding of the work that must be done is the same as the client's understanding. How many interviews will you conduct? What data will be shared with the client? What languages will the work be conducted in? Who is responsible for scheduling meetings? What documents will be produced for the client?
Project organization	This section explains how decision rights are to be handled. You might think of it as an organization chart for the project. For larger projects, I usually describe the consultant (or consulting team) and explain their role and responsibilities, the client core team (usually from three to eight people) and their role and responsibilities, and a client or stakeholder advisory group and their role and responsibilities. I use the advisory group as a way to connect the work of the project with the larger organization that will be affected by the work.[15]
Details on specific project components	If needed, I include one or more sections that spell out the details on how a specific piece of work will be carried out. I do this to ensure that we all agree on how much effort, and what type of effort, will be expended on certain activities. Recently, for example, I worked on a project that included gathering data from various members of the client system, and that also included a benchmarking exercise that involved gathering information from people who worked for other organizations and who agreed to share their experience of certain organizational issues. Because I know that this sort of benchmarking exercise can have an almost limitless scope, and because I know that this can be used by client system members to deflect attention and effort away from painful internal problems, I created a specific section that explained in detail how the benchmarking exercise would be conducted.
Communication strategy	If needed, the charter can include a section about how information about the project will be shared with the rest of the organization or with external stakeholders.
Risk and risk mitigation	This section identifies any known risks and explains how any risks will be mitigated if they arise. It is another key section for identifying assumptions. For example, if the project will run over the December holiday season or over the summer holidays, do you anticipate that people may not be available to participate in the work? If that is the case, how will you handle this so that the project's timelines are not jeopardized?

(Continued)

Table 4.2. The project charter (*continued*)

Project charter section	What to include here
Change control and issue management	By including this section, your charter not only endeavors to flush out any hidden assumptions but also identifies a process to use if new assumptions come to light later. I usually say that any issues that suggest a significant misunderstanding exists among members of the project team must be brought to the attention of the charter signing authorities. These signing authorities then meet to confirm that a misunderstanding exists and how it can be resolved. The process will determine whether there is impact on the project's scope, budget, and timeline.
Attachments	These are created when needed. For example, you might decide that it would be handy to have an attachment that provides the name and contact information for all members of the consulting team, the client core team, and the client advisory group.

mostly at the psycho-social environment, and they will tend to point out the personality attributes of certain subgroups, the social conflict that exists between groups or individuals, or the presence of disruptive emotionality.

It is probable that a single problematic situation will give rise to symptoms in both the task and social environments. During the contracting phase, it is necessary only to get the symptoms onto the table so they can be examined, considered, and discussed. This must be done in a way that is civil and helpful. If the client system is divided into factions that are playing a blame game with each other, bringing these symptoms into focus will take skill. It is often useful to begin by simply agreeing on a set of facts and then acknowledging that different interpretations have been developed to account for these facts. The contract could then include an agreement that these different interpretations will be tested through the project's data-gathering and analytical activities.

Here is another way to look at this. We are here discussing the importance of surfacing the assumptions made by the interventionist and client during the contracting phase. My assumptions are my interpretations that I mistake for facts. For example, I might assert that my environmental scan has revealed that my client, a social services department, is unable to achieve one of its strategic objectives because the staff lack the needed competencies. I might claim that this assertion is a fact. However, facts – even facts concerning social reality – must have some ontological basis. That is to say, they must exist in the world, and they must exist in a way that allows them to be confirmed and agreed upon by human beings.

So, you might ask me, what is the ontological basis for your alleged fact that staff lack the competencies that they need? I might reply by saying that I base this on what I was told during conversations with six different members of the system. Five people told me that the department is unable to meet one of its strategic objectives, and two people told me that this failure is because staff do not possess the knowledge and skill needed to achieve that objective. You might then point out that this means that 40 per cent of the people interviewed during my environmental scan possess a belief that staff lack the needed competencies, and that this is the only fact that has been established. If I then admit to you that the other four people I talked to told me that they have no idea why the department is not achieving the objective, you might suggest that this might be an even more significant fact: that 60 per cent of the people interviewed are unable to form a hypothesis to account for the failure.

Being clear about assumptions is an important part of the process for framing problems. If we operate on the basis of unconfirmed assumptions that we mistake for facts, we may move too quickly to formulate solutions, and we may end up imposing an inappropriate and unsustainable solution onto the system.

Agreeing on a Process for Tackling the Problem

In addition to reaching a general agreement on the nature of the problematic situation that is to be investigated, and to surfacing the assumptions that the interventionist and client are making about the work that is to be done, determining a process for tackling the problem is a third important step that should be taken during contracting.

You will often benefit from considering two principles as you and your client start to discuss the process by which you will approach the problem. First, because you are searching for a greater understanding of the problematic situation and for solutions that might bring improvement, it is wise to create a process that is flexible. Do not immediately chain yourself to specific techniques and deliverables. Keep things as flexible as possible.

Second, members of your client system know the people, the workflows, the interconnections, and the patterns and situations that are characteristic of the system. Different people will have different perspectives, but together the people who inhabit this human system know the social reality of their workplace. What's more, just as the client system lives the problem (that is, they have created and are sustaining the problem as they experience it), the client must also live the solution (they must enact the solution in their patterns of thought, action, and structuring, and then sustain that solution over time). This means that you must work *with* the client. Because the leaders of your client system possess only one perspective (and an important perspective) about what is going on, you must work with them, and you must also work with their subordinates.[16]

Although it is impossible to make an organization's power hierarchies vanish during an intervention into a human system, those hierarchies will need to be mitigated during the intervention process. The less powerful people need to be assured that their participation in the process will not result in their being punished if their perspectives are unpopular among those with more power. To the extent that is possible, the project must incorporate structures (rules and policies) that will protect the less powerful from unfair retribution. However, at the same time it is best to be honest about the extent to which the existing power differentials will continue to be in operation during the intervention process. It is only fair to let less powerful participants know that they should continue to be careful about sharing perspectives that could invoke the displeasure of their bosses.

I like to distinguish between at least two types of client that I work with as an interventionist.[17] There is the client who has signing authority and decision rights over the project, given the way that power is regulated within this human system. Usually this is the person (sometimes it is two or three people) who has invited me to come into the system, who signs the project charter, and who has the authority to approve deliverables and invoice payments. I refer to this client as the *contract client*. The second client includes all of those people who have a stake in, or who are implicated in, the problematic situation that we are trying to resolve. I owe a duty to both of these clients. I will not function as a spy for the contract client, coaxing people into telling me their secrets and anxieties and then skulking back to the contract client to spill the beans.

I will discuss the ethics and ethical dilemmas of intervening in human systems later in the book. For now, I want to point out that as you are contracting with the client system, and especially when you are discussing how you will approach the work with your contract client, it is important to design a process that is free from deceit and manipulation. All who participate in the process should have the same understanding of the purpose of the work, the process that is being followed, and the way that information will be handled. This of course is desirable for ethical reasons, and it is also desirable for pragmatic reasons. To mobilize a process of change that includes all relevant system members, you must create relationships and a process characterized by a high degree of trust. If participants do not trust you, or if they have doubts about the ways in which their contributions will be used, they will not engage in the process in an open manner. Instead, defensiveness and impression-management will be triggered, and these will almost certainly limit the results that you are able to produce.

Your project charter should include a paragraph such as that which follows, and the contract client must sign the charter and thus pledge their word against these assurances.

All data gathered through interviews, focus groups, and discussions with project participants (including any notes or emails and other personal documents that are shared) by [your name, or the name of your team] will be treated as confidential. Participants will be advised of this at the start of all interactions intended to gather data. [Your name] will know the identity of the people who provided the data, but these identities will not be shared with anybody else. When data are organized and presented for discussion, care will be taken to ensure as much as possible that the wording used will not reveal the identity of the person who contributed the data.

When you are negotiating the process to use to carry out the intervention, the key point to remember is that the process should mirror the result that you hope to create. When this is done well, as the interventionist and client team work to design and implement an intervention, the process that they use to work together gradually starts to create the new way of being that is intended as the ultimate outcome of the project. For people unaccustomed to intervening in complex social systems, this can have a bewildering, almost magical feel to it. However, it is not magic.

I recently worked with a client organization that hoped to improve its capacity for sharing knowledge with stakeholders. To help this client, I created a process that was itself an example of how the exchange of knowledge could become integral to the organization's work. Working with the project's core team, we drew on the science of knowledge translation, the experience of organization members, and the perspectives of the organization's stakeholders. We created a project structure and approach that allowed for an open exchange of views, and for collaborative methods for working on deliverables. We also used techniques during the project that represented the different ways in which effective facilitation can be used to assist with the movement of new attitudes and practices across social boundaries. Our intent (which was stated in the project charter) was to create a process through which the project deliverables (which in this case included a written document that explained a knowledge-sharing model) were *about* knowledge exchange, while the project itself was an instance of knowledge exchange in action. This meant that by the end of the project the process of organizational transformation had begun.

The method for creating a project process that mirrors the desired result is surprisingly simple. As you carry out the environmental scan during the contracting phase, you listen for descriptions of the desired end state, the hoped-for way of being, that the client wants to create. You may hear different descriptions, sometimes even contradictory descriptions, during this process, and when this happens you have to resolve these discrepancies, or at least settle on a language that can encompass these different perspectives. If the goal is to create more collaboration, then the project process must be collaborative. If the goal is to create more effective communication, then the process must demonstrate effective communication. Table 4.3 offers some examples of how a project's process can mirror the project's desired results.

You will notice that in all of these approaches the interventionist works *with* the members of the client organization to bring new

Table 4.3. Matching the process to the project

When the project aims at creating …	The process should include …
More collaboration between organizational units.	Activities that invite members of the organizational units to work together on project tasks and deliverables.
More cooperation and mutual support among supervisors and frontline staff.	Activities that allow supervisors and frontline staff to share and explore perspectives, and then to cooperate and support each other as they contribute to creating the project deliverables.
More effective delegating of tasks by middle managers to staff.	Activities that allow middle managers to understand the problems that poor delegation creates, to create a framework for delegation (a new way of thinking about delegation), and to practice delegation using the framework.
A more thoughtful response by basic care attendants to the outbursts of patients who are confused by their Alzheimer's or dementia.	Activities that allow basic care attendants to frame the outbursts in a new way (not as "nasty aggression" but instead as "a confused attempt to communicate"), to reflect with others on alternative responses, to experiment with new responses, and to identify supports needed to sustain a more thoughtful approach to delivering care.
A new sharing of decision rights between managers and professional employees.	Activities that allow managers and professional employees to explore the limitations of the current approach, to recognize the needs that must be met through a new approach, to experiment with and reflect on alternatives, and to create the policies and procedures needed to sustain the agreed-upon new approach.

attitudes and perspectives, new activities and procedures, and new policies, frameworks, and other structures into being. Organizational members are included in the project process. The intervention is not something that is designed in a back room and then suddenly imposed upon the unsuspecting workforce. Organizational members are part of the process.

To make this work, you will sometimes need to translate an objectified goal into its behavioral correlates. For example, a client might tell you that they want you to help them to design and implement an intervention that results in higher levels of employee satisfaction on their annual employee satisfaction survey. It seems trite or even illogical to say that the project process must therefore include employee satisfaction. Instead, it will be necessary, as you carry out the environmental scan and the initial work to create the project charter, to help the client to understand what attitudes and behaviors correlate with employee satisfaction. It will also be necessary to work with employees to understand their perspective, and this could result in a very different framing of the project.

It is worth remembering that this book is about the design and implementation of interventions to solve adaptive problems in complex social systems. It is not about solving technical problems for which there are known solutions. It is about solving adaptive problems that require a search for a solution. If your project involves building a bridge across a river, you probably do not need to create a project process that looks like a bridge. But if your project is about creating inclusiveness, then your process should be inclusive. If the project is about sharing leadership, then the process should share leadership. If your project is about creating organizational learning, then the process should allow participants to experience the learning that occurs as people work together in groups.

Get the Contract Signed

I will make one final, pragmatic point. If you are an external consultant, chances are the quotidian pressures of making a living will require that you get the contract in place as quickly as possible, so you can start billing for your work. This is understandable. It might dismay you to think that you must carry out a cumbersome environmental scan and then create a project charter (which takes time and effort) before you start charging for your work. You might even worry that with the project charter in hand, your client could be tempted to cut you loose and then use your blueprint to do the work without your assistance.

My approach is to include the project charter as the first concrete deliverable in the project. I enter the client system, I conduct the environmental scan (usually by talking to at least three and sometimes as many as eight people), and then I sign the contract with the client. The contract sometimes takes the form of a standard contract that is used by that client organization, usually with a statement of work appended that I have prepared. At other times the contract is a memorandum of understanding that I have drafted and that the client signs. When the signed contract is in place, I begin work to create the full project charter.

Summary

Think of an intervention as a sequence of activities that unfold through time. At the beginning the activities involve gathering information, sharing perspectives, analyzing data, and framing the problematic situation. Later the activities involve doing things such as actively intervening to disrupt existing patterns, changing conversations, altering existing processes, and changing existing or creating new social structures. Because an intervention is a *search* for possible solutions, the intervention process is characterized by learning. At every step in the process, the interventionist encourages participants to consider what is happening, how they feel about things, what it all means, and what should be done next.

Most interventions have four phases. The intervention begins with a contracting phase, then moves into an exploratory phase, then focuses on collective sensemaking and action planning, then shifts into an implementation of the plan and an evaluation of the intervention's process and outcomes.

The interventionist will engage in the four balancing acts during the contracting phase. The critical balancing act of this phase is balancing the need to be understanding and compassionate toward the client with the need to be confrontational and challenging. The interventionist fosters psychological safety so members of the client system are more likely to experiment with new attitudes, behaviors, and structuring.

For an interventionist, contracting has three main purposes. Contracting allows the interventionist to reach agreement with members of the client system about the nature of the problematic situation that they want to resolve. Second, contracting ensures that the interventionist and client are not operating on the basis of hidden assumptions that might later undermine work. Third, contracting produces agreement on the process for tackling the problem.

Finally, an experienced interventionist will ensure that the process used to carry out the intervention mirrors the result that the client is hoping to achieve. If the goal is to create more collaboration, then the process must be collaborative. If the goal is to create effective communication, then the process must demonstrate effective communication. What's more, the process must be one in which the interventionist works *with* members of the client organization. Organizational members must be included in the process. The intervention is not something that is designed in a back room and then suddenly imposed upon the unsuspecting workforce. Organizational members participate.

CHAPTER FIVE

Exploring the Client System

With a contract in place, you are ready to begin your exploration of the client system.

Allow yourself to take in the connotations of the word *exploration*. You are venturing into unknown social territory. You are going to try to get to know the people, places, and activities that are characteristic of the territory. You will in effect be drawing a map of the territory, a map that brings to light the hitherto hidden nature of the problematic situation.

You are not the only one who is moving into unknown territory. Although members of your client system certainly know their own system, with its norms, culture, work processes, and competencies, it is also likely that none of these people can fully see the problematic situation that prevents them from being who they want to be and doing what they want to do. Something is blocking them. They may have tried to fix the situation, but so far nothing has worked. As you lead them toward the problematic situation, they too will be moving into uncertainty.

Most human beings experience some level of discomfort when they find themselves in uncertain situations.[1] They are unsure of the role that they are to play, they do not know how to act, they cannot predict how things might turn out, and they are unfamiliar with the patterns that are unfolding around them. This has been termed the "red zone" of transformational learning,[2] a zone in which people experience deep discomfort as they encounter threats to the coherence, identity, competence, and purpose that they associate with their workplaces and communities.[3] Your client will not enjoy these feelings and will want to find a solution, and fast. Part of your job is to make it bearable to live with the uncertainty for a period of time, so the data can be gathered that will allow people to begin to understand the problematic situation in all of its complexity.

Your primary focus during this phase will be on exploring the social and technical environment, gathering and organizing data, and beginning the process of framing the problematic situation in a way that may allow system members to ameliorate or resolve it. It is likely that you will also spend time developing relationships with the various people you work with. As you form hunches about what might be going on, you may encounter opportunities to intervene in ways that produce data that help you to create the map. You will almost certainly have a chance – during meetings with the core team, or with the advisory group, or with specific individuals – to discuss how the work is going and what new ideas are emerging based on what has happened so far.

The exploration phase can be a period of interesting discoveries and insights. Initially, a complex organization can appear as a confusing morass of people, relationships, processes, workflows, challenges, and opportunities. One often has the sense of encountering phenomena on the surface of organizational life and also of occasionally drawing the curtain and revealing secrets known to only a few. I recall a recent project during which I regularly received phone calls from two members of the client system who wanted to share with me their worries about the barriers that stood in the way of our shared intention to create new capacity for learning and innovation in the organization. They wanted to tell me about relationships between key organizational members, and about goals and challenges that were not generally discussed during meetings but that were important to some influential members of the system. It appeared that some things were happening out in the open, during meetings in the boardroom and teleconference discussions, and that there were also some "undiscussables" lurking in the shadows.[4]

The exploration is intended to create a map or a picture of the organization in relation to the problematic situation that you are investigating. It should reveal the affordances and constraints that characterize this human system – affordances that explain the ways in which the system acts on opportunities and creates value and benefits for organizational members and stakeholders, and constraints that limit the system's ability to adapt to new circumstances by acting in novel ways. In a sense, during the exploration phase you reveal that which has previously been unknown and invisible to most system members. Put another way, you make that which the system was constrained by and subject to into an object that system members can see, examine, understand, and act upon.[5]

We all make use of mindsets, mental models, ideologies, or assumptions to understand our reality and to produce actions that keep us safe and allow us to achieve at least some of our goals. These mindsets are often held below the level of consciousness, so we confuse our beliefs about reality with reality itself. Young people are entitled. Civil servants are lazy and overprotected. Entrepreneurs are selfish and greedy. Artists are fuzzy-headed dreamers. Movie stars are egotistical. Notice that all of these beliefs are stated in a categorical fashion. This group of people fits into this category. End of story.

But surely with a little thought and some open-minded observations we are likely to notice that young people cannot all be stuffed into a category labeled "entitled." Young people come in all shapes and sizes, with many different motivations, aspirations, and anxieties. It is absurd to think that you can usefully reduce this delightful variety into a single categorical clump.

Our mindsets have a hold of us. They offer us a quick way of understanding the world, so we can swiftly come to conclusions and take action. In a way, one might say that it is not me doing the thinking; rather, my mindset is using my mind as a vehicle. I do not have these ideas. They have me.

The exploration phase is an opportunity for us to discover the counterproductive patterns of behavior that hold the problematic situation in place, and to uncover the mindsets that give rise to these behaviors. These mindsets are probably below the consciousness of members of the client system, or they exist only as undiscussables – the colloquial "elephant in the room" that must never be openly broached. With the help of the interventionist, system members may finally be able to acknowledge that an elephant has been blithely crushing the system's desire to move forward with an important change.

During the exploration phase, the interventionist will engage in all of the balancing acts discussed in this book. I have often found that during exploration an interventionist forms rewarding new relationships with people and hears about some situations that she likes and others that cause her concern. This gives rise to emotional reactions, creating the need to remain somewhat distant from the client system to avoid being absorbed into the patterns of thought and action that she is trying to understand. The critical balancing act of exploration often involves both becoming part of and remaining apart from the client system.

The Critical Balancing Act of Exploration: Participating and Observing

An interventionist needs to be close enough to the human system she is intervening in to observe and understand the prevailing patterns of thought and action, to gauge the system's capacity for learning and change, and to take steps to disrupt the prevailing patterns in ways that could allow the system to develop more capacity to learn and solve problems. This means that the interventionist needs to be close to the client system.

At the same time, however, the interventionist needs to retain some distance from the client. The lure of collusion is an inevitable part of the work of an interventionist.[6] A human system attempts to sustain itself by pressuring newcomers to fit in. New actors will be assigned roles in the existing drama that is being acted out by the cast of this production. They will not be allowed to transform the performance so that it becomes an entirely different and new play.

This is one of the critical balancing acts that you must perform: you must balance the need to become part of the client system, so you can form relationships and gather information, with the need to remain distinct and apart, so you can avoid being absorbed into the client's characteristic ways of thinking and acting. You participate *and* you observe.

One way to understand these pressures is to consider the problems of induction and collusion. The word *induction* suggests that the interventionist may be inducted into the client system's patterns of thought, action, and structuring. The term *collusion* suggests that the interventionist may unwittingly aid and abet the client in maintaining their current, less than optimal patterns.[7]

In other words, the interventionist will understand the client system in terms of certain preconceived stereotypes, or stored understandings, that the interventionist has formed on the basis of past interactions with a variety of groups. Members of the client system will be doing the same as they start to get to know the interventionist. These stereotypes allow us to construct some quick, convenient understandings that allow us to begin our interactions with these new others. Over time, the interventionist's stereotypical understanding of the client system will be diminished as new information is taken in. For this to occur, however, the new information must penetrate the conscious understanding of the interventionist, without being filtered out by the biases, mental models, and assumptions to which the interventionist is subject.

Collusion can take a variety of forms.[8] Countertransference occurs when the interventionist finds that the client system is awakening some of his own unresolved needs. Usually, the interventionist is not aware that this is happening, and as the interventionist begins to act upon these needs the participant observer stance is destroyed. Projective identification occurs when members of the client system suppress their own strong feelings as an intervention takes shape, and the interventionist begins to feel the fears, helplessness, and anger that are bubbling below the client's placid surface. In effect, the client projects its emotions upon the interventionist, so the interventionist can deal with them on behalf of the client. If the interventionist begins to express these emotions and invent explanations for them, projective identification has taken hold. A third form of collusion, parallel process, occurs when salient features of the interventionist-client interactions reappear in other areas of the interventionist's life. For example, the patterns could appear in the interventionist's interactions with a boss or supervisor, or with a spouse or trusted advisor.

If several members of the client system see me as a benevolent father figure who is going to solve their problems for them and restore their sense of safety and security that has been disrupted by the problematic situation, I may, without initially realizing it, take on this role. However, I may have had a troubled relationship with my own father, and I may have a long-held and deeply suppressed desire to fix that relationship by becoming the good head of the family that my own father had failed to be. I now, without meaning to, unleash upon my client a deluge of paternal kindness and benevolent yet firm leadership. However, I am no longer an interventionist in the participant observer stance. I have been drawn into the drama that is being acted out in this system, and there is little likelihood that I will be able to disrupt existing patterns in ways that could produce new learning and change.[9]

This does not mean, however, that the interventionist should distance herself from the client system, or remain aloof and dispassionately objective at all times. To create psychological safety for the client, a degree of closeness is essential. To prompt the honest disclosures from system members that are needed to discover the different perspectives that exist on the presenting problem, a trusting relationship must be fostered. What is needed, then, is for the interventionist to develop the skill of recognizing the symptoms of collusion, and to take steps to arrest the process before she becomes submerged in the client reality.

Fortunately, there is also an upside to this. Becoming conscious of how one is fitting into the client's emotional field is itself a source of useful data. To manage this risk, the interventionist must become skilled in being consciously aware of all that is occurring for her as she interacts with the client. This includes awareness of what is being communicated by the client, and also awareness of her own reactions to the client. It is particularly useful to notice emotional states that appear unrelated to what is going on in the room. It can also be helpful to notice whether one is becoming attached to and sympathetic toward one subgroup within the client system, and critical toward another. I like to remind myself that there are no good guys and bad guys in my client system. Instead, there are roles that have been taken on and that are being acted out by different individuals. Setting aside the unlikely possibility that a member of the system is a dangerous sociopath or psychopath, it is probable that all members of your client system fall within a normal range of human values, preferences, and behaviors. If the boss is rather controlling and preemptive, if the administrative assistant is a grumpy gatekeeper, if the HR director is forever overwhelmed and distraught, your job is not to set things right. Your job is to help all of these individuals to create new roles for themselves, roles that allow for growth in the system's capacity to learn and solve problems.

For several years I have been teaching courses in human systems intervention to graduate students from around the world. For one assignment, the students are assembled into teams of three or four. They locate a real-world client who is contending with an adaptive problem of some sort, and they then contract with the client, and navigate through the various phases of the consulting process. In almost every instance that I have observed over the past twelve years (which involves approximately fifty consulting teams), the consulting teams have to some extent mirrored the patterns evident in their client system. As Deirdre Moyan has observed, in a rather mysterious way the client system's problematic situation is like a virus, and it is contagious.[10] The student consultants "catch" the virus, and part of their learning is to notice this, to take steps to eliminate the contagion, and to learn from the experience.

Earlier in the book I mentioned that a colleague and I recently consulted to a client system that is a top-down, command-and-control hierarchy that professes a desire to become more collaborative and to distribute power more evenly throughout the system. As we worked with this client, we took on some aspects of their own power dynamic. One of us became the Consultant in Chief, and called the shots as our work moved forward; the other became the good and compliant soldier, obeying orders and doing the grunt work. We noticed this parallel experience, and our discussions explicitly considered what this revealed about the affordances and constraints that characterized our client.

In another recent consulting engagement, the same colleague and I worked with a client system that wanted to engage differently with stakeholders across the country. They wanted to create a more open flow of useful information throughout the networks that they participated in. During facilitated discussions that involved members of our client system and stakeholders, conversations were guarded and somewhat tense. My colleague and I regarded this as important information about the current functioning of the system. Our client thought that the same situation must mean that my colleague and I were poor facilitators, and they began to issue very directive instructions to us. After receiving these instructions, I noticed that I was feeling defensive, and I wanted to write long, defensive emails in which I explained myself; my colleague noticed that she became angry about the impact of hierarchy on this group, and she wanted to conduct private conversations with the less powerful members of our client system. We were both being triggered into actions that would have led us to collude with the system. I like to work with a trusted colleague on interventions because we can intervene with each other, and help each other to extricate ourselves from the grip of collusive temptations.

In short, to be a participant observer means that you must allow yourself to participate in some activities with your client, but you must prevent yourself from taking sides. You should say to yourself that the client system will, undoubtedly, exert pressure on you to collude. Systems by definition attempt to rationalize foreign elements that enter into them. You are a foreign element that has invaded the body of your client system, and the client's systemic patterns will attempt to make sense of you.

To guard against this danger, you could keep a project journal, and after each client interaction you could shake off the contagion by writing as dispassionately as possible about the system that you are exploring, and also about the emotions that you are experiencing and the thoughts that are coming up for you. You could also ask a trusted advisor, preferably someone who shares your interest in intervening in human systems, to engage in a weekly debrief conversation with you. Or you could work as a team with a trusted colleague, and you could make a daily debrief part of your regular routine. Some questions to consider during your debrief conversations include the following: Am I remaining in the stance of the participant observer? Am I taking sides? Am I starting to play a role, other than the role of the dispassionate observer and helper?

Uncovering Perspectives and Mental Models

Before I describe the activities that are usually carried out during the exploration phase, I will illustrate the phenomenon of conflicting and hidden mindsets by describing one of my more memorable consulting engagements.

A few years ago, I did some work for a large financial services organization. This was a busy, successful organization that was constantly transforming itself as its external environment (the financial services industry and the changing competitive and regulatory environment that this industry existed within) was also transforming. As we carried out the exploration phase of the engagement, it became increasingly apparent that hidden assumptions were making it impossible for the organization to achieve its productivity and quality targets, and were also causing many newly hired young people to quit their jobs in frustration.

My client organization – I will call them by the fictitious name of FinCo – was a busy and hectic work environment, with numerous change projects underway, including a major merger and several enterprise-wide technology initiatives. FinCo was also somewhat staid and bureaucratic, as is often the case (at least in Canada) with large banking and insurance organizations.

The vice-president of Operations asked me to come by his office to discuss a situation that was troubling him and his senior team. I met with "Rob" (all names in this story are fictitious) in his large office that looked out on a busy confluence of city streets, and he asked three of his directors to join us. We sat at a round table in a corner of his office by the window, coffees and waters at hand, and he began to explain the situation that was puzzling him.

"Every quarter I ask my senior team to tell me about whatever it is that is causing them the most concern, and for the past year I keep hearing the same thing. We are wasting too much energy on recruiting new people to join our customer support teams, only to see many of them quit before their first-year anniversary. Something is wrong here. Our compensation and benefits plan is competitive with the industry. The work environment is pretty good. But something is causing these people to quit, and I want to get to the bottom of this and fix it."

I looked at the three men and one woman seated with me at the table and asked, "Do you have any ideas about what is going on?"

Tony, the director of Western Operations, nodded and replied: "I was in Calgary and Vancouver for most of last week, and I talked to the folks there, and then I checked with the people downstairs and called Cindy in Toronto. The two things that people mention most often is that there must be something wrong with our approach to hiring for these positions, and there must be a problem with how we train new hires."

It was not lost to me that I was talking to three directors who were responsible for Operations. They had noticed a symptom indicating that a problem existed in the organization, and they had talked to middle managers in the Operations units, and together they had concluded that the problem must originate somewhere upstream from the Operations units. We are experiencing a problem, and those guys over there are to blame.

However, I was intrigued. The fact that they knew that some sort of problematical situation existed, and that it was producing a consistent negative result – large numbers of new hires quitting within twelve months – suggested that an adaptive problem might lie beneath these symptoms.

I told Rob and his team that I was interested, but before settling on an approach to the work I wanted to talk to someone from the Human Resources group about the existing hiring process, and someone from the Training group about their training program. I pointed out that if their initial suspicions were correct, then the HR and Training groups would need to be involved in the work. We would stand a better chance of creating improvements to existing hiring and training processes if the relevant managers and staff were involved from the outset.

Rob and his colleagues readily agreed, and over the next few days I spoke at length to two HR managers and to the coordinator of the Training program at head office.

When I met again with Rob to discuss the scope of work and to finalize my contract, I suggested that my investigation should encompass the hiring process, the training process, the transition from training environment to the floor, and the day-to-day work routines on the floor. Rob agreed, and suggested that I also talk to some people in the Operations policy unit. These people created some of the work standards that new hires had to meet, and Rob wondered if these standards might be putting too much pressure on new hires. We then signed the contract, and I got to work.

During the exploration phase I gathered data by touring the relevant work areas, by interviewing (either individually or in small groups) managers and key staff members, and by holding focus groups with members of the customer service units. I gathered these data at head office and in three regional offices. As I sorted through the mass of data that I had gathered, I noticed that there were several different perspectives about the problematic situation. These perspectives are summarized in table 5.1.

My data revealed that management emphasizes teamwork, but people work alone. Staff are expected to be creative problem solvers, and yet they are closely monitored. Employees who encounter problems are expected to raise a red lever on the side of their cubicle, which is meant to be like raising a hand to ask a question. A supervisor will come to talk to the person within one business day. Supervisors routinely offer negative feedback on errors and shortcomings, ostensibly to help staff to improve. All supervisors used to be team members and were among those who were able to meet productivity and quality goals.

Figure 5.1 illustrates some of the different perspectives and assumptions that were revealed by the exploration.

It is useful to notice that nobody is entirely right and nobody is entirely wrong. Each group is having its own experience of the problematic situation, and each is making sense of the situation within the context of this experience.

The Operations directors, managers, and supervisors have noticed that an unacceptably high level of turnover is occurring in all of the units across the country, and they have identified this as a problem that must be solved. They have not noticed that employees believe that their bosses say one thing and do another: *the bosses say that we are innovative problem solvers, but in reality they treat us like unthinking drudges.* The leaders of the Operations units believe that the source of the problem must lie somewhere upstream, in training and perhaps also in the recruitment and hiring process.

Trainers are ready to accept the blame. Although they are expected to play the role of trainers, their own training has been inadequate. They have little confidence in their abilities, little confidence in their curriculum, and are insecure about their job security. They think that they are the cause of the turnover problem. The data, however,

Table 5.1. Differing perspectives, assumptions, and mindsets at FinCo

This group	Had this perspective
Operations directors, managers, and supervisors	They believe that they have designed and are managing an efficient and effective operational workplace. The teams they have built *ought* to be able to meet the quality and productivity targets, but often do not. They have created a congenial and pleasant work environment; they compensate people at levels that are at least equal to industry standards; and when appropriate they promote top performers to better jobs in the organization. They emphasize teamwork, and they offer tangible rewards in the form of quality and productivity bonuses. The workplace is a rational environment based on modern and enlightened ideas. People work in comfortable cubicles, and they are allowed to decorate their cubicle to make it their own personal space. They are given ample technological support, and the training program is extensive. There are also lots of fun activities – Halloween parties and contests, pizza days, birthday celebrations, employee of the month awards, and so on. As I visited the third work unit, it occurred to me that this workplace resembled a kindergarten classroom, with colorful posters, calendars, and photographs, and with people politely raising their hands to ask questions.
The trainers	Like the supervisors, the trainers have been promoted from the floor. They are good at achieving productivity and quality goals, and are known to be adept at solving the thorny technical problems that often arise. The trainers have no background in training or adult education. They "tweak" bits of their training, but they do not undertake a fundamental overhaul of the training. They do not meet with other trainers. The trainers feel isolated and blamed. They worry that the problems on the floor are their fault. They believe that they are inadequate as trainers, and that they have fallen out of the normal career path. While some supervisors and top-notch customer service people are occasionally promoted to better jobs in the organization, the trainers feel stuck, overlooked, and inadequate. They are ready to take the blame for the problems on the floor.
HR staff responsible for hiring	They work with all units in the organization, so have an expansive view of the entire organization. They report that Operations says it wants to hire creative problem solvers who are team players, and that is the kind of people that the HR group recruits for them. However, in reality Operations needs compliant people who can follow procedures and work alone. Operations pretends that they have created an innovative and modern work environment, but really it is a white-collar factory.

(Continued)

Table 5.1. Differing perspectives, assumptions, and mindsets at FinCo (*continued*)

This group	Had this perspective
The policy group	This group sets productivity and quality targets for the Operations teams, and establishes policies to govern how certain common customer service situations are to be handled. My discussion with them centered on the productivity and quality targets: how they are set, how often they are met, and how often bonuses are paid. These data revealed that only from one to three top performers in each customer service branch (about 10 per cent of existing staff) are able to routinely meet both productivity and quality goals. Another 80 per cent of employees are usually able to meet the productivity goals, but sometimes or often are not able to meet quality goals. The rest of the Operations staff rarely meet either of the goals.

The people doing the work on the Operations floors (there are three subgroups)

The "my job is my hobby" group	These are older people who have taken this job in order to make some money before their spouse retires. Most are women who stayed home with their small children. Now that their children are more independent, these women have decided to return to work. They prefer to work part time, they stay out of office politics, and they are not interested in a promotion. This part-time group makes up about 20 per cent of the workforce and is popular with supervisors, but is not interested in contributing beyond putting in their shift. These employees usually meet the productivity targets, and sometimes meet the quality targets. Few of them are part of the turnover problem.
The "biding time" group	This group consists of young people who have not yet figured out what to do with their lives. They needed a job, and they plan to stay with the company for only one or two years. Many of them dislike the work and are dismissive of those who are working hard and trying to get ahead. About half of this group usually meet the productivity targets, and about half only rarely meet productivity or quality targets. This group accounts for about one-third of the turnover problem.
The "career hunter" group	This group is made up of young people who are hoping to create a career in the financial services industry, and who entered the company through this department. Many have been told that this is a good way to get a job in the company. Most are trying to do a good job. Many have either a college or university degree. They expected to be working as part of a team and to be engaged in creative problem solving about customer issues, and many are disappointed to find that the work is routine and there are relatively few opportunities to advance. Many in this group began work in a positive state of mind and have become disillusioned after a few months of work. About two-thirds of the turnover problem comes from this group.

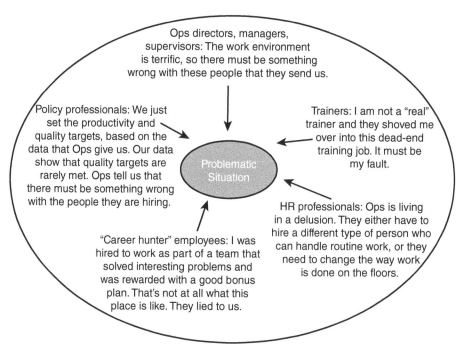

Figure 5.1. Differing perspectives about the same problematic situation

do not support this belief. The training could be structured and managed in a more professional and effective manner, but it is not fair to blame the turnover problem on the trainers.

The HR professionals responsible for hiring have noticed that there is a discrepancy between the work that is being done by these customer service representatives and the qualities that they are told to identify in new recruits. They are convinced that this must be the problem that needs to be resolved. The Operations group should change the qualities that they hire for, or they should change their internal management system. There is some truth in this, but the HR professionals are not seeing the entire picture. They are not seeing that there is room for improvement in the training program, that there may be problems with the existing productivity and quality goals, and that the leaders of the Operations units are attempting to cope with the inconsistencies between the company's old approach to customer service (which relied on standardized products and services) and the new demands of customers (for more tailored and customized products and services).

The policy professionals feel themselves to be somewhat removed from this fray. They notice that Operations has made up its mind about the nature of the problem. However, the policy group keeps looking at its metrics that show that productivity targets are often met and quality targets are rarely met. They believe that Operations might be more concerned with productivity than quality, or that the current targets are simply unrealistic.

Finally, the employee group that I have labeled the "career hunters," which is the biggest employee subgroup and the one that is most closely aligned with the hiring criteria established by Operations, is caught in two uncomfortable binds. First, they were recruited and hired on the basis of descriptions of teamwork and problem solving and innovation, but their actual experience of the workplace is one of routines and procedures and close supervision. Second, they are told that productivity and quality are both equally important, but they notice that their supervisors care more about productivity than quality and that they are encouraged to meet their unit's productivity goals at all costs.

Exploration involves forming and strengthening relationships with people, gathering the type of data illustrated in this case, and giving thought to the way in which the problematic situation might be framed with the client system. Your purpose here is not to unilaterally discover or create a solution to the client's problem. The client must be involved in framing the problem and in identifying solutions. Your purpose is to gather, assemble, and think about the data, and to mull over ways of presenting the data to the client that will be helpful.

The Tasks of Exploration

Every client, every contract, and every intervention is unique. Moreover, even when an interventionist develops a detailed contract with a client that includes a project plan listing numerous activities, milestones, and deliverables, once the work begins in the exploration phase it is likely that the lived experience of the intervention will be different from the expectations set forth in the plan. As a result, I cannot precisely anticipate what tasks I will need to undertake in my next intervention, which of course means that I also cannot anticipate what your tasks might be in your next intervention.

Nonetheless, my experience has led me to anticipate that certain tasks are often characteristic of the exploration phase. These tasks generally have to do with collecting, organizing, analyzing, and sharing data.

As you gather and work with client data, you also move through your client's social system. You accept the client as they are. You are honest about your own thoughts and feelings as you work with the client, and this includes acknowledging when you do not know the answer to a question that a participant has asked. You try to understand the perspectives and experiences of members of the client system as you interact with them, asking questions and making notes.

At the same time, you remind yourself that it is inappropriate to take sides. You are not going to advocate for the employee perspective or for the management perspective. You are there to help all members of the system to reach a better understanding of each other's perspectives, to see the problematic situation in new ways, to develop a new and greater capacity to solve pernicious problems, and to take actions that were previously not available. At times you might challenge and push members of the system, while always being understanding of the dilemmas and worries experienced by the people you are working with.

The exploration phase often includes the following tasks:

- gathering data, usually by using qualitative techniques and open-ended questions
- organizing the data that you have gathered in ways that make it easy for you and the client to work with and elicit meaning
- intervening when you notice that the problem is in the room
- responding to client resistance
- reflecting on what happens

Gathering and Organizing Data

When I have been asked to help a client system to resolve or mitigate an adaptive problem, I generally want to get started by learning as much as I can about the client system. I want to capture information confidentially, so I do not accidentally put people at risk because of power dynamics that I am not yet aware of. I want to meet with people individually and in groups, so I can get a sense of whether there are some things that people will not say in front of their colleagues.

I like to gather data using qualitative techniques. For me, this means primarily that I try to interview people, either individually or in groups of two or three. I also occasionally conduct focus groups that bring together approximately eight people at the same time, and I like to observe the behavior of people in their natural environment while engaged in their normal work routines.

I prefer to use these open-ended methods rather than surveys because I want to let people talk about the things that are important to them, using the words and phrases that are most meaningful to them. I want to give them a chance to tell me stories that they or others have created to make sense of important experiences. I want to probe and clarify. And I also want to observe their behavioral gambits, and to see for myself whether their behavior is consistent with their espoused intentions. My data should provide a picture of the thinking that goes on in the system – thinking about intentions, goals, aspirations, worries, challenges, frustrations – and the behavior that brings this thinking into action.

Surveys produce data that reduce the richness and variety of lived experience. As I explore the system, I am not interested in reducing things down to a few easy-to-manipulate variables. I want to open things up. I do not want to know what the strongest opinion about a subject is. I want to know about all of the opinions, where they came from, and what these opinions do for the people who hold them.

There are excellent books that describe how to use qualitative methods to find answers to questions.[11] Most of these books are written for graduate students and researchers who are attempting to find answers to puzzling research questions. If you have no experience in gathering data through qualitative methods then I suggest that you consult one of these standard texts. Here I will content myself with making four points about gathering data during the exploration phase.

Let people speak. Gathering data during the exploration phase usually involves talking to people. These conversations are often in the form of interviews, and you generally have a list of questions that you hope to ask in order to generate the data that you need.

I have learned that when a human system is confounded by a problematic situation, many people are experiencing distress. There is a pretty good chance that you will be the first person they have had a chance to talk to about what is going on. They may have a lot to say, and some of what they want – or need – to say may not fit neatly into your questions and categories. As you are interviewing a participant, they may seem to go off on a tangent, and you may want to intervene to bring them back to the topic. I have found that it is wise to resist this urge.

Let them speak. They have things to say, and sometimes this seeming tangent is actually taking you in the direction that you need to go. You undoubtedly did your best to come up with good questions that might bring to light important features of the problematic situation. But you were making informed guesses when you wrote those questions. Now, as you speak to the interviewee, you are in the process of exploration, and your interviewee may be showing you aspects of the territory that you – and your contract client – were not aware of. Be patient. Allow the person to say what they need to say. You can always bring them back to your question once they have gotten things off their chest.

Capture what is said in detailed transcripts. Make detailed notes as you are interviewing people. Try to make your notes directly on a computer, so at the end of the interview you have a rough draft of the transcript that just requires some polishing and editing. If you make notes on paper, you will need to type them up later, and this may not be the best use of your time. I have found it best to capture the interview directly on my laptop computer.

Some consultants and researchers I have spoken with have suggested to me that this might be distracting for the person being interviewed, and it might also affect my ability to pay attention to what is being said. I have not found using a computer during interviews to be a problem. I explain what I am going to do at the start of the interview, and people are sympathetic and understanding. Now and then I need to keep typing for a moment when a person stops talking, but I have found that people are patient. I also have not found that this approach unduly degrades my ability to pay attention. I am there with the interviewee, listening carefully to what the person says so I can capture their words in my notes. Now and then I ask a question to make sure I have understood them. I do not act merely as a transcriber. I make comments when appropriate, and express sympathy if the situation calls for it. I encourage you to create the rough draft of the transcript during the interview.

If you are gathering data through a focus group, I suggest that you do so with a partner. One person needs to ask the questions, to probe, to invite people to share their views. It is often useful for this person to capture key points on flip charts or a white board, because this can be helpful as participants are thinking of how they want to respond to your questions. Your flip chart points will not be sufficiently detailed to use as data, so it is essential that somebody be present who can make detailed notes.

I prefer not to use an audio recording device to create a digital recording of an interview or focus group. This is because I have become good at creating detailed interview notes directly on a laptop. I have colleagues who create an audio recording with their Smartphone, and who use a transcription app to create a transcript. I suggest that you experiment with these approaches and select the one that works best for you. If you do plan to record your interviews, let the participants know before you begin the interview.

Ask people to read and revise their transcripts. After you have interviewed a person, clean up and anonymize the transcript, and then show it to the person you interviewed. Invite them to make changes, including deleting passages if they wish. Ask them to make sure they are comfortable with how you have phrased things. Tell them who will see the data they have provided, so they can make an informed choice about how much they wish to share.

The information belongs to the person who provided it. This is their perspective, their experience, their ideas. If they are not comfortable making frank disclosures about workplace problems, you must respect this.

After the person has returned the transcript to you and indicated that they are satisfied, you can then begin to work with the information by copying and pasting it into your analytical working document.

If you have gathered data by holding focus groups, it may be difficult for participants to identify the portions of your focus group transcript that contain statements that they contributed to the discussion. Nonetheless, it can be beneficial to invite focus group participants to review and comment on the transcript. In this case, however, it is important to let people know that you will consider their suggestions but will not necessarily make the suggested changes. I sometimes indicate that if I disagree with a suggested change, I will leave the text as is but will add a footnote to show the change that was suggested by one of the focus group participants. Another technique that you can use with focus group data is to organize the focus group data for presentation back to your client system, and then show the presentation materials to focus group participants and ask them if this is a reasonable representation of the discussion.

Be creative. As you work with the data, do not become attached to a particular interpretation, conclusion, or solution. Look for imagery, phrases, or statements that are characteristic of the sensemaking patterns at work in this system.

One technique that I sometimes use is that I look for a particular phrase, metaphor, or story that recurs in the data, or that seems especially vivid and insightful. Perhaps people use words to indicate that they are always in a hurry in their workplace. They talk about not having time to think and being run off their feet. Maybe one person says the job is like running a marathon. Another person tells a story about how in the past it was possible to take the time to talk to customers and form relationships but now there is only time to complete the task at hand. This sounds like a pattern emerging from the data, and I would want to think about this and consider how it could be arising out of the problematic situation that we are investigating.

Or I might notice that that two people have used the metaphor of "a perfect storm" to refer to a significant event that occurred two years ago, and that both talk about how the people in the system are those who survived this deadly storm. They are survivors, they cope, they try to put things back together and keep moving forward. I would allow myself to play around with these images, and to consider how this language might help to provide a new framing of the problematic situation.

You must resist the urge to become the research scientist whose role is to find the answer to the research question or to conduct a definitive test of the hypothesis. You are creating the conditions in which the client can discover the way forward. It is best that members of the client system make the discovery for themselves, so they will create for themselves the ways of thinking, the mental models that arise from new neural pathways, that are needed to see past the constraints that are holding the problematic situation in place. Just as a hockey coach cannot score the winning goal for his team, you cannot act as a surrogate who experiences the needed insights on behalf of the client. An adaptive problem almost always requires that the people whose actions embody or enact the problem must experience a personal change, an internal change in the way they think and act, in order to resolve the problem. By definition, they must do this for themselves.

Intervening When You See the Problem Show Up in the Room

As you explore the client system, trying to understand more about the problematic situation that is limiting the capacity of the system to make progress toward important goals, it is useful to remember that the problem is in the room.

Suppose your client's problematic situation is experienced as a communication problem. Your environmental scan revealed that the client system is experiencing a limited flow of valid information between and within teams. People do not always share information that is needed to make good decisions. Members of the client system have said that they want to become more collaborative and cooperative. Your job is to help them with this transition.

Now that you have begun to explore the system, you notice that your interviews and observations have turned up lots of different ways in which people experience this problematic situation. Some say that new ideas are often shut down. Managers criticize more than they encourage. Not everybody is given a chance to speak. It is not safe to disagree with certain people. Team leaders are competing for resources and status.

As you work with this client, regardless of whether you are alone with the department manager in her office, or are in a scrum with one of the work teams, or are in a board room where three teams are gathered together – the problem is in the room.

This is often not apparent to clients. When you are meeting with people or observing people, they are gathered together to talk about something. For them, the topic of their conversation is almost always conceived of as "out there" in the organization. It is an object that is apart from them in the here and now of this moment. In fact, as you work with members of the system, they will have a tendency to fall prey to the fundamental attribution error that we discussed earlier. They will see the problematic situation as something that belongs to those other people, the ones who don't get it, the ones who get in our way, the bad guys. We are the good guys, gathered here in this room at this moment, to diagnose what is going on with those bad and ineffective others, and to come up with a solution.

However, if this human system is in its moment-by-moment lived experience giving rise to a phenomenon that we might term "a communication problem," then that problem of necessity is always in the room when members of this system are together. All system members are implicated in the problematic situation. The problem will always be part of this living moment, this unfolding experience, of the group that is creating the problem.

As you explore the system, you are (among other things) looking for the problem in the room. When you see it, you may want to interrupt the flow of conversation and test your hunch.

"You folks have said that one of the forms that this problem takes is that people shut down new ideas. A few minutes ago, I heard Rob suggest a survey, and his idea was criticized, and then you stopped discussing it. Just now Kelly suggested that you look at customer data, and once again the topic was dropped. Is this what you meant by shutting down new ideas?"

This sort of statement is an emergent intervention. It cannot be predicted and cannot be fully prepared for in advance. You notice the moment, you make a quick judgment, and you act.

The purpose of the intervention is threefold. First, the way the group responds will provide you with information about the patterns of behavior that are in place. Second, the intervention may introduce something new into the client conversation, and this could become part of the larger effort to bring about beneficial change. Third, by observing how the group responds to your intervention, you will gain a better understanding of the client system's current capacity to learn and adapt.

If your question poses a threat to the system's current way of functioning, it will be dismissed. In the example I just offered, you observed the "shutting down" phenomenon in the way people were working together in the room, and you intervened by drawing the pattern to the attention of the client. With your intervention, you have introduced something new into the conversation. Your prediction will be that it will be quickly dismissed. Because you are the external consultant (if that is your role in this case), the system may wish to dismiss you without offending you, to ensure that you do not try this objectionable behavior again. There may be some back-patting or reassuring along with the dismissal. If that is what occurs, then the pattern you observed is evidence that could help to confirm your hunch about the way the system is behaving.

However, it is possible that some members of the system who are participating in this discussion may indicate an openness to consider your observation. A few people might say, "You know what! It *is* an example of the problem that we are trying to solve. We are doing it right here in this room!" If that happens, you may notice a sense of helplessness in the group. Someone might say, "Wow. Just when we were getting a handle on this thing, it jumps up and bites us." People might seem discouraged or stuck. If something like this happens, you are seeing a willingness in the system to examine its own processes, and an inability to act on that willingness.

Regardless of the precise way in which the group responds to your intervention, you will get a better understanding of this client's current capacity to learn and adapt. In the former case, where the group rejects your observation and continues with the conversation, you are seeing that at this moment there is little capacity to learn and adapt. The client is either unable to see the problem in the room, or some members may be able to see it but they are not willing to do anything about it. Your initial focus may be on continuing to create the psychological safety needed for people to openly acknowledge and discuss the issues, and on helping them to see that the problematic situation is coming about because all system members are helping to create it.

In the latter case, where some members of the group acknowledge that you have pointed out the problem in the room but they do not know what to do about it, you have learned that there is some willingness to look at the problem but limited ability to take action. These people (or at least some of them) are able to acknowledge that all system members are complicit in the problematic situation. This means that they are close to recognizing that they hold the power to do something about the situation. In other words, if my current stance and behavior are helping to produce the problem, then I can help to change the situation and reduce the problem by changing my stance and behavior. I have personal agency and power here.

These emergent interventions during the exploration phase will help you to understand the problematic situation and also the client's capacity to change it. The information that they produce will be very helpful for you when you design the feedback session (which I discuss in the next chapter). Although these early, emergent interventions may seem to have little effect on the client, chances are there are people who are starting to form ideas and are starting to create a new way of thinking about what is going on. All of this will be very helpful as the client continues to work on bringing about change.

Exploratory emergent interventions can be very simple. You might stop the action during a meeting when you are puzzled by what you are seeing, and ask, "What is going on right now?" Almost certainly someone will respond, "What do you mean? Nothing is going on. Everything is fine." Depending on what prompted your intervention you could reply, "Thirty minutes ago there was all kinds of energy and excitement in the room. Now it feels like half of you are about to go to sleep. What happened?"

Remember that you are simply exploring. You are not going to solve the client's problem in one fell swoop, with a masterful intervention carried out during your first exploratory meeting with members of the client system. If the client tells you that you have solved their problem in one master stroke, you have almost certainly run up against the powerful seam of resistance that exists in your client's culture.

Responding to Client Resistance

The phenomenon that scholars and practitioners label "resistance to change" arises in almost all change processes. Instead of trying to find ways to batter resistance into submission, we might look at it as the system communicating its discomfort at the prospect of abandoning its current state of dynamic equilibrium and moving toward a new and uncertain state.

During the exploratory phase, your client system may exhibit its resistance by trying either to kick you out or pull you in. Both of these resistance strategies can be effective ways of preventing you from planning and implementing an intervention that could bring about beneficial growth and change. But do not be too quick to label client behavior as resistance. Sometimes the client system is engaged in important and difficult work, and it has managed to achieve a precarious pattern of thought, behavior, and structure that allows it to fend off threats and get its valuable work done. Your intervention may be seen as a threat to the system's ability to maintain this pattern and continue to provide value to stakeholders. The system is not trying to prevent useful change. It is trying to preserve important value.[12]

During the exploration phase the client may try to kick you out in a variety of ways. If you are dealing with an adaptive problem for which there is no known solution, in negotiating a contract with you the client system has to some extent acknowledged its own helplessness. This is an uncomfortable stance, especially for managers and leaders in fast-moving organizations. In our culture leaders are expected to know what to do. Your contract client may experience the contract with you as a sign of his failure to adequately perform his function. He may resent your presence at the same time that he is welcoming you into his system.

Your client system may try to kick you out by becoming truculent and uncooperative. They may look for reasons to question your competence. You may be creating a list of focus group questions and find yourself criticized for lacking the skill needed to create good questions. You may be told that your tone of voice is "wrong" (scolding, patronizing, or edgy). People might say, "We tried that already. That won't work here." Suddenly, brick walls are constructed all around you. The system is cornering you, fencing you in, keeping you neutralized and ineffective. Quite naturally, you might become confused and frustrated. All of a sudden there really is an edge in your tone of voice. The behavior of members of your client system pushes you toward uncertainty, defensiveness, and incompetence.

What can you do about this? First of all, don't panic. This is merely the natural tendency of a human system to neutralize or expel a threat. My basic rule for handling this form of resistance is to be firm, clear, and reflective. My client's behavior is telling me about the system's capacity to engage productively in an effort to solve problems and bring about change. We signed a contract. I have a job to do. Even though the client is now trying to push me out, the client also invited me in, and so I know that there is also some level of willingness to move forward. I am firm, and I try to control my frustration and to access my sense of compassion for the client. The client's behavior indicates that they are experiencing discomfort, that they are having a hard time. Let's keep moving. Eventually, more and more members of the client system will discover that the change process is not so awful, and they will begin to cooperate.

I also make sure that I explain and apply my confidentiality rule as I interact with people in the system. I say that I am not acting as a spy for the director or the managers. Everything you tell me will be kept confidential. If you tell me something and it then occurs to you that it is especially important that I keep this to myself, be sure to tell me. I will not directly quote you. I will not attribute statements to you. I am making the same promise to everyone, and I keep my promises.

And when I say that I keep my promises, I mean it. The secret fears and worries within the system probably do need to come out into the open, so system members can get a better idea of what is going on. But it is not my job to spill the beans or to point the finger of blame. I am there to see if we can co-create the capacity within the system to be more open and frank, and to find a way to ameliorate the problematic situation.

A second way in which client resistance can manifest itself during the exploration phase is by pulling you into the system. Think of it this way. It is as though the client system is putting on a performance. All system members have their roles in this unfolding drama. Every day they come onto the stage and act out their various roles. Now I have arrived, a newcomer. The system must quickly create a new role for me within the existing drama. It will attempt to put me in my place, assign me a role, and then carry on undisturbed.

However, I cannot let that happen. To do my job, I must disrupt the existing performance, not cooperate with it. Earlier in the chapter I discussed this when I introduced the third balancing act that the interventionist performs: balancing participation with observation. You must prevent yourself from being inducted into the client system's patterns, or from colluding with the system.

During the exploration phase, the temptation to collude often shows up as a covert invitation to take sides. At other times the temptation takes the form of an explicit challenge: "Perhaps this project isn't a good fit for you?" Almost always the system is characterized by subgroups that are engaged in disputes that often bubble away just below the surface. Employees have grievances against bosses. A leader is trying to implement an innovative and worthy strategy and finds herself blocked by uncooperative middle managers or employees. A functional group feels overworked and undervalued. Those of us who act as interventionists are often kind and compassionate people, and our sympathies can be evoked by what we experience as a good cause.

Be wary of this. You cannot help the system if you form an alliance with one subgroup. If you succumb to this temptation and become an ally to a single group, you are no longer helping the system as a whole to reach a new level of problem-solving capacity. Instead, you are helping this one group to beat down the others and secure a victory.

I also urge you, however, to be cautious of labeling behavior as resistance. It is often the case that a human system has created a pattern of thought, action, and structuring that allows them to carry out valuable work in the face of troubling adversity. The equilibrium that they have created is under threat, and system members are worried that if they cooperate with you then valuable activities will be destroyed and people will suffer.

Several years ago, I worked extensively with long-term care homes that provide services to the frail elderly. At that time, many of these homes were attempting to replace an old-fashioned medical model of care with a new and innovative social model of care. The medical model saw long-term care homes organized in ways that resembled factories or hospitals. Everything was set up for the convenience of the nursing and basic care staff. The elderly were cycled through a monotonous and uniform daily regimen that did not have room to take individual preferences into account. People living in these homes were often bored and unhappy, even though they were well fed and well cared for.

The new social model called for long-term care homes to be transformed into more congenial living environments. Residents would be able to get up when they wanted, eat when they wanted, and exercise autonomy over their daily routines. They could decorate their once-sterile rooms with personal items, including furniture. They could have plants and even pets. They might perform some of the jobs in the home, to give themselves a greater sense of purpose.

Many reform-minded leaders expected long-term care staff to embrace this new social model, because it would create such a pleasant environment for residents. Instead, many health workers were skeptical about the reforms, and were reluctant to cooperate with change initiatives. Leaders often concluded that these workers were stubborn and were strangely attached to their existing daily routines.

My own work suggests that these supposedly resistant staff actually had a reasonable explanation for their skepticism.[13] They had gradually seen more and more tasks added to their daily workload, to the point where it was common to see them literally run from job to job during the day. This meant that staff had fewer opportunities to simply spend time with residents, helping an elderly woman fix her hair or listening to an aging veteran talk about the last time he was able to attend a regimental reunion. Instead, it was all work, and they were not able to fulfill their duty to see to the psycho-social well-being of the residents they supported. A new change, even something congenial such as a social model of care, was seen as a threat to staff's ability to support their residents' quality of life. And hence they were skeptical.

When I encountered this phenomenon, it occurred to me that these workplaces could be thought of as environments in which an ongoing conversation was occurring. Each day the workers arrived and began their talk. They discussed the people they cared for, the work that had to be done, the situations that were arising (people who were ill, special activities taking place, a doctor visiting the unit, and so on), and they coordinated their efforts to ensure that basic care was provided and some level of informal social support was provided to residents. A change team that wanted to implement a new model of care was experienced as an effort to stop or disrupt this important ongoing conversation, and to replace it with something foreign and dangerous.

It occurred to me that instead of trying to impose a new conversation upon a workplace, perhaps an interventionist should seek ways to join the existing conversation.

Reflecting on What Happens

In my experience, one of the most significant contributions that an interventionist can make to a client system is to demonstrate the power and usefulness of reflective processes. Many of the clients I have worked with have created busy and competitive workplaces. People have a lot of work to get through each day, and they operate in an environment where winners are rewarded and failure and errors are punished. There is little time in which people can step aside from the pressures of the day and talk about how things are going. There is also little inclination to be open about problems, concerns, and mistakes when bosses and rivals are listening and may use your disclosures against you when promotions are being considered and performance is being evaluated.

However, when dealing with adaptive problems it is essential that people be willing and able to speak openly about what they have discovered, what seems to be working, and what is not working. When we try to understand and solve a problem for which there is no known solution, we are bound to make some mistakes. There is (or should be) no shame in this. Einstein made mistakes.[14] So did Hillary Clinton, Winston Churchill, Mahatma Gandhi, and Dr. Martin Luther King.[15] As we try to solve the turnover problem at a financial institution, or tackle the problem of polypharmacy among the elderly, or resolve a long-standing conflict between doctors and nurses in a surgical unit, or determine whether the use of fracking to access untapped reserves of natural gas is an appropriate stop-gap measure as we decrease our reliance on coal and look for new sources of clean energy – as we work on these adaptive challenges, we are bound to make mistakes. Being open and frank about errors is part of the process of finding a solution. It means that we are making progress.

When I use the term "reflective process," I am referring to a process by which a group of people can look at how they have been working together, what issues and constraints they have experienced, what opportunities may be taking shape, what they have learned, and what changes they would like to make in how they are working.

Every project meeting should include a period of reflection on how different people are experiencing the work, and what changes should be made to the group's process. Among other things, a reflective process allows people to acknowledge that their intuitive and emotional responses to each other and to situations cannot be fully controlled and thus often influence how the ongoing flow of work occurs for us.

There are many formal techniques that have been devised to structure a reflective process for a group. Kolb's experiential learning cycle could be used to create a healthy cycle of reflection, analysis, planning, and action in a group's way of working.[16] The PDSA quality assurance technique, the Shewart cycle, or the Deming cycle are other ways that reflection can be embedded in a group's regular work routines.[17] Developmental evaluation, with its approach to regularly gathering data about the work being performed by a group and then discussing the data at team meetings so the team can adapt its processes in ways that will make them more effective, is yet another way to create a reflective process in a group.[18]

Summary

The exploration phase is about discovery. You gather data and engage in interactions that could reveal the counterproductive patterns of behavior that hold the problematic situation in place, and the mindsets that give rise to these behaviors. You may bump into the "elephant in the room" that must never be openly discussed. With your help, members of your client system may finally acknowledge that their ability to share perspectives and information is blocked by a number of undiscussables.

During the exploration phase you form and strengthen relationships with members of the client system, you gather data, and you think about alternative ways of framing the problematic situation. Your purpose is to gather and assemble the data, to think about the information, and to mull over ways of presenting the data to the client that will be helpful.

As you gather data and interact with members of the client system, give people plenty of time to tell you what is on their minds. Sometimes they will want to talk about things that are not related to the questions you are asking. That is okay. The system may be revealing some of its important secrets during these conversations. As you accumulate data, do not become attached to a particular interpretation, conclusion, or solution.

During the exploration phase you are also balancing the need to provide psychological safety for your client with the need to support your client's success as people try out new ways of thinking and acting. You accept the client as they are. When appropriate, you honestly disclose your thoughts and feelings, and you acknowledge when you are confused or uncertain. Throughout the exploration phase you remain in the stance of the participant observer, balancing the need to get close to the client system with the need to remain apart from the system. You watch for indications that the problem is in the room with you as you interact with the client, and you may begin to make exploratory interventions that try to bring patterns of behavior to the attention of your client. You can also anticipate that you will encounter client resistance in a variety of forms, including efforts to pull you into the existing patterns of thought and action, and efforts to expel you.

At the conclusion of the exploration phase, you will have a significant amount of information about the functioning of your client system. You will also have a relationship with the client that establishes a paradoxical possibility: members of the client system now feel safe enough to experiment with new attitudes and actions. The next step is to work with the client to co-create a situation where these experiments will take place.

CHAPTER SIX

Making Sense of Things

When exploration comes to an end, it is time to create a map of the territory that has been explored. This is the primary purpose of the feedback and decision phase.

During the feedback and decision phase you bring members of the client system together at the same time and in the same place. Together you review the information that has been gathered. You consider what this information means, and you try out alternative framings of the problematic situation. If all goes well, you agree on a framing of the problem, and you agree on the actions that are needed to ameliorate or resolve the problem. At the end of the phase, members of the client system make personal commitments to a change process that begins as soon as the sensemaking session comes to an end.

In other words, members of the client system come to a new understanding of what is happening, and they begin to take new actions to bring about change. The feedback and decision phase functions as an intervention into the existing ways of thinking and acting that characterize this system.

The Critical Balancing Act of the Feedback and Decision Phase: Asserting and Inquiring

Throughout the feedback and decision phase, the interventionist continues to engage in the four critical balancing acts. For example, during the sensemaking session you will balance the creation of the psychological safety needed to allow for a frank exchange of perspectives with challenging and encouraging your client toward new ways of thinking and acting. By now you have formed relationships with members of the system, and you have seen things that you like and things that cause you concern. This means that as you continue to participate in the actions of the change process, you must also ensure that you remain distinct and apart so you avoid being absorbed into the client's patterns of thought and action. What's more, you will balance the need to be intentional and planful with the need to be flexible and emergent. For example, you will create a plan and agenda for the sensemaking session. However, as people come together and interact, it may be necessary to set aside the carefully wrought plan and deal with what is happening in the room.

During this phase of the intervention process, the critical balancing act is often a balancing of assertion and inquiry. You will need to balance your desire to tell the client your own opinions and interpretations about the client's situation with the need to allow people to make their own sense of the data and arrive at their own interpretations and conclusions. This balancing act now comes to the fore because members of the client system are trying to understand the information that has been gathered. They are faced with the facts of their situation, often presented in a fashion and with a directness that is new to them. Depending on what is revealed in the data, some may experience strong emotions as they encounter the data. At the same time, they will need to master their emotions and engage in a hermeneutic process of interpretation and sensemaking. They will frame the problematic situation in a way that allows system members to take action to mitigate or eliminate the problems. They will develop action plans, assign responsibilities, and create a method for monitoring progress.

While all of this is going on, the problem is in the room. The first steps toward a new and better way of being and working are taken from the present location and circumstances of the client system. They are taken from within the status quo, the current pattern of thought, action, and structuring that is producing the problematic situation. System theorists will know that the system is likely to attempt to thwart the change process before it can gain momentum, and thus it is almost inevitable that client resistance will show up during the feedback session. Members of the client system may disparage the data. They may argue that the interventionist's process is weak or biased, or they may attack the interventionist's credentials, demeanor, or tone of voice. They may notice that one or two people figure prominently in the data, and may try to mobilize opinion so that the full blame for the system's problems is dumped on these people.

This presents the interventionist with a subtle challenge. She must do her best to distinguish between reasonable and unreasonable criticism of the data, the interpretations that are developed, and the processes that are being used. If a criticism or suggestion seems reasonable, then it should be incorporated into the process. If some participants say that a theme in the data applies only to one specific subgroup in the organization, and if nobody disagrees, then it may make sense to revise the data to reflect this suggestion. If some participants say that they feel rushed and they need another twenty minutes to complete their discussion on an important topic, it may make sense to adjust the agenda so this discussion can continue.

However, if some participants make angry or frustrated statements that cannot be verified by examining evidence, the interventionist may wish to remain firm. Suppose that someone says, "That is utter nonsense! Nobody here believes that our product designs are too expensive!" The interventionist may reply, "The data are absolutely clear on this point. More than six interviewees made statements that align with this." The interventionist must ensure that she is not merely being defensive. She must remain grounded in the data that the system contributed to the change process. It is her job to represent the data accurately, and to be firm and resolute as she presents the data and perspectives that were offered during the exploration phase.

If some participants question the data or the interventionist's process or credentials, the interventionist must try to remain detached and calm. These may appear as personal attacks, but it is best to receive them as instances of the system protecting the status quo. While making these defensive moves, the client system also demonstrates its capacity to engage in a process of inquiry and change. All human systems possess both affordances and constraints. The interventionist will hold several questions in the back of her mind. Does this client system have the capability to engage in a respectful and open inquiry? Can the system find new ways of framing the problematic situation, which in turn could overturn old assumptions or beliefs and release a new pattern of thought and behavior? Can the system examine and alter the social structures that are holding the current patterns in place? Or, alternatively, are the defensive routines in this system so entrenched and pervasive that there is insufficient capacity to engage fruitfully in this change process? (I discuss how an interventionist assesses client capacity later in the chapter.)

The key to this balancing act is to give the client the opportunity to see the problem for themselves, to make their own discovery so their confidence is bolstered and they have a clear sense of ownership of the diagnosis and proposed way of moving forward.[1] The interventionist can help to point the way toward a diagnosis, but she probably lacks the tacit knowledge of the system's functioning that is needed to find the source of the trouble. The interventionist can help the client to remain in a productive and generative stance, to eschew an attitude of blame or a thoughtless leap toward a quick fix. It is usually necessary for the members of the client system to make their own discoveries.

Nonetheless, the interventionist at times may find it necessary to make direct assertions. Although much of the time the interventionist is posing questions and providing support, it is also the case that the client system is almost certainly stuck. They are caught in an ineffective pattern that is producing a problematic situation that they want to change, and they are unable to see the source of the trouble. Argyris sees this as a simple incongruence between a client system's espoused theory of action and the theory of action that can be inferred from the observable behaviors produced by system members.[2] They say one thing and do another, and somehow this incongruence must be put in front of the client for inspection. Kegan and Lahey see this as an exhausting tension produced when members of a human system are strongly committed to two mutually exclusive and contradictory goals.[3] The architecture of this unhealthy tension often takes the form of a commitment to an open and recognized strategic objective and a competing and hidden commitment to avoid the risks and threats that bold action (such as the actions needed to achieve the strategic objective) may entail. The point is that the client system is unable to see the problem. Their current mindsets do not allow them to see what is going on. They are aware of symptoms and of specific areas of discomfort, but they cannot see the systemic and enduring nature of the beliefs, interactions, and structuring that produce the problematic situation.

The interventionist's contract is to help the client system to see that which cannot yet be seen. If during the feedback session the client struggles to make sense of the data and to uncover the hidden source of its challenges, the interventionist will need to make a decision. Should she show them her map of the concealed social territory that is causing their distress? Her answer to this question will depend on the strength of her relationship with the client system, and on her diagnosis of the capacity of the client system to work effectively when faced with uncertainty and emotionality, to take risks while engaged in reflective conversation, and to recognize that all individuals and groups in this human system are in some fashion implicated in the existing patterns.

Before we review the major tasks of the feedback and decision phase, I want to delve further into the way in which an interventionist can create a map of the client's social reality.

When Exploration Ends, the Explorers Draw a Map

Chapter 3 introduced a simple framework for thinking about intervening in human systems. A human system creates and maintains a more-or-less state of equilibrium through its patterns of thought, behavior, and structuring. This means that a human system can be represented as shown in figure 6.1.

People who gather together in a bounded human system that is focused on a primary task (and perhaps some secondary tasks) will share certain mental models and assumptions about their joint enterprise. These mental models and assumptions form the pattern of thinking that characterizes the system and that gives rise to a repertoire of behavior that system members use to get their work done and to maintain the cohesion of the group. The behaviors and their effects will be noticed by system members, and learning will occur. In other words, system members notice whether the behaviors produce the desired results; they discuss these results, and these discussions inform the current pattern of thinking in the system – either by reinforcing existing views or by producing new explanations or new attitudes and ideas.

The pattern of thought and pattern of behavior thus exist in relationship with each other, and they in turn give rise to a pattern

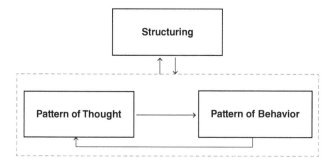

Figure 6.1. A human system as a persistent pattern of thought, behavior, and structuring

of structuring. The system creates structures that help to influence and enable the desirable attitudes and behaviors. These structures can take the form of policies, procedures, work processes, strategic plans, equipment and tools, quality assurance dashboards, and so on. The structures arise from the pattern of thought and behavior, and they in turn constrain and influence the pattern of thought and behavior. Once again, the three defining components of the system – thought, behavior, and structuring – exist in relationship to each other, enabling and creating each other while also constraining and shaping each other.

As a human group works together over time, its patterns of thought, behavior, and structuring encourage group members to view their shared world in a certain way. As beliefs are repeatedly confirmed, beliefs become assumptions. As behaviors continuously produce the expected results, behaviors become reflected in implicit norms about what works and doesn't work, about "how things are done around here." A culture is formed, and this culture acts as a taken-for-granted template for a functional social world. The culture permeates the mindsets of group members and establishes the basic rules for this human collective.

The simple framework depicted in figure 6.1 offers an insight that is of fundamental importance for interventionists. To help a human system to design and implement a beneficial change, it is almost always necessary to help the system to see its current way of functioning, and then to help the system to design and implement interventions that will affect the thinking, the behaving, and the structuring that produce the characteristic patterns of this system. A new procedure is usually not enough to bring about sustainable change. A training program is usually insufficient. A new policy can be overturned or ignored by the existing pattern of thought and behavior. Instead, it is usually necessary to consider what basic beliefs and assumptions need to be uncovered and challenged, what behavioral routines must be disrupted, and what supporting structures need to be altered or replaced.

I like this thought-behavior-structuring framework because during the feedback and decision phase it is often useful for the interventionist and client system to map the territory that has been explored. The word "map" denotes a depiction of the more-or-less equilibrium state of the client system as it produces the problematic situation. If it is possible to create such a map, then it will be possible to see the problematic situation, and it may be possible to notice potential intervention points that could be used to bring about change.

Consider a system consisting of three subgroups – a group of managers and supervisors, a group of professionals (they could be designers, technologists, engineers, clinicians, etc.), and a group of production workers. Each group will create its characteristic pattern of thought and action, and each of these three patterns will fit together to create a larger system pattern. The pattern, if described in narrative or in an illustration such as a map, will possess the characteristic of coherence. All of the parts of the pattern will cohere together in a way that creates a sensible, functional whole.

Let's suppose that the designers in this hypothetical system are highly motivated by a stringent set of professional standards that call for excellence in design. They want to create elegant, robust designs that are made manifest in functional, durable products. Let's say that they participate in regular quarterly meetings with members of the marketing and sales team, where they learn about what is working and not working in the marketplace. These meetings are an incubator for new ideas and innovations that are fed into the product development cycle. Given that the meetings produce new and better design ideas, they are consistent with the factors that motivate the designers to strive for excellence.

Now let's suppose that the production staff are motivated by management directives that call for stringent cost containment measures. They are charged with ensuring that products can be made with the cheapest possible materials and in the most efficient possible manner. Production staff are encouraged to make do with what they have, to get things done quickly, and to look for manufacturing shortcuts. They work in an area separate from the designers, and they do not participate in any regular meetings with designers or with the marketing and sales team.

The management team believes that it is their job to do the impossible. Somehow, they have to oversee a design, manufacturing, and sales organization that produces the high-quality products demanded by customers, at a price that can compete with offshore rivals who are able to bring cheap products into the country through international trade deals. So far, the management team has managed to keep the company afloat by adopting a "good enough" attitude. They have to persuade the frustrated marketing and sales team, the diligent design group, and the complaining production group to keep working and cooperating so product can be shipped and the organization can avoid the rumored closure or offshoring that emanates from the CEOs headquarters on the east coast.

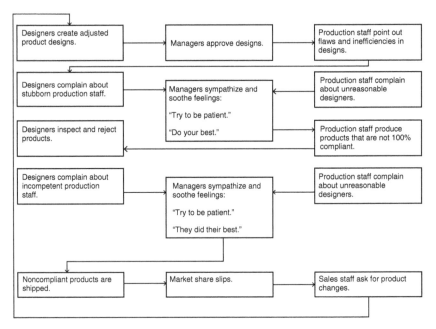

Figure 6.2. A coherent but dysfunctional system

Figure 6.2 illustrates a possible map of this system, in which different beliefs and assumptions on the part of managers, designers, and production staff create a coherent but highly stressed system. This illustration depicts the way in which work is done by the system. Given the frustrations that can be inferred from the illustration, it is likely that the social system is also fractured and troublesome.

Figure 6.3 shows another illustration of the system, this time highlighting the patterns of thought and behavior as a self-sealing web that leaves system members feeling caught and helpless. This sort of map can be constructed by organizing the data gathered through interviews, focus groups, and observations into the dominant themes that appear to exist in the system. I like to distill the data down into the main things that people say when they talk about their core

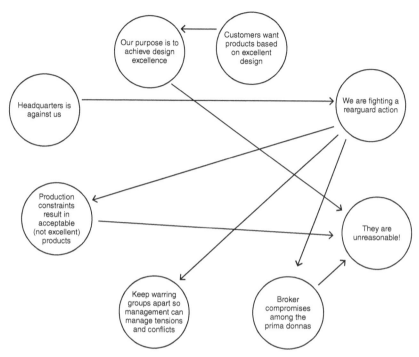

Figure 6.3. Interaction map showing the problematic situation as a web of assumptions and behaviors

feelings and beliefs about working in the system, and the critical behaviors that seem related to the predicament that they have asked me to help them investigate. I use arrows to show how one theme helps to create and sustain another theme. In this example we see that the system has worked itself into a permanent state of mediation. It is as though the management group are United Nations peacekeepers, and the design group and the production group are warring factions in a tribal dispute. What is notably absent from the map is any attempt at negotiating a permanent peace settlement. Instead, system members have accepted an assumption that the condition is permanent, and that the distant headquarters group will close the operation if they don't maintain a good enough quality at a cheap enough price.

It is worth remembering, though, that a human system is open to influences originating in its external environment. If the patterns characteristic of this design and manufacturing firm were entirely generated by the internal system members, then a well-designed and implemented intervention focusing solely on those internal patterns could bring about useful and sustainable change. However, if (as is more likely) the system is also open to its environment and is responding to both internal and external pressures, then an interventionist is wise to consider these external influences and to bring them to the attention of system members during the feedback and decision phase. This is the situation depicted in figure 6.4.

Here it is easier to see that the fate of the client system does not lie entirely in its own hands, and thus it would be misleading (and unethical) for an interventionist to suggest that the system can alter its internal patterns and thereby produce an entirely new, beneficial, and sustainable pattern. If the client system acts as though it is free from external constraints, it may institute actions that could lead to its swift failure in the marketplace. Nonetheless, bringing these patterns to the attention of members of the client system might yield some useful results. For example, it is possible that the interventionist and system members will agree that an intervention to ameliorate this system's problematic situation could consist of three parts:

1. Allow for more direct communication between the production group and design group. This could at least help members of the two groups to understand the motivations and pressures that are at work. It could also relieve the management group of having to focus considerable energy on mediation and dispute resolution. This could free up time for management to pursue a more sustainable long-term solution.

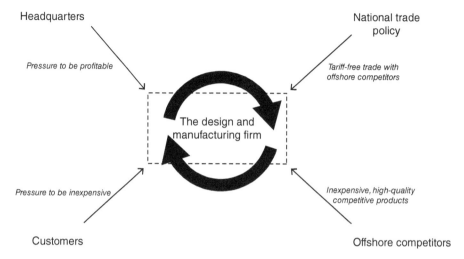

Figure 6.4. A human system that is open to influences from the external environment

2. Include members of the production group in the quarterly meetings with the marketing and sales staff. If the production perspective was directly represented in these creative brainstorming sessions, it might be possible to create innovative designs that take into consideration production constraints.
3. The management group could approach headquarters to inquire about the long-term plans for the design and manufacturing facility. Perhaps decisions have already been made, and thus local change initiatives could be off track or uncalled for.

The feedback and discovery phase is intended to create a map of the territory – the human system's existing task and social environment that is giving rise to the problematic situation – that system members can agree is an accurate and reasonable depiction of their current dilemma. This map is then used as the basis for formulating an intervention plan that calls for actions to alter the existing patterns of thought, behavior, and structuring.

Like the exploration phase, the feedback and discovery phase tends to be associated with certain tasks and activities.

The Tasks of the Feedback and Decision Phase

It is often the case that I contract to conduct a certain number of data-gathering activities (for example, my client and I might agree that I will conduct two focus groups and twelve interviews, and I will attend and observe three meetings). When these activities are complete, it may be possible to say exploration has come to an end, and the time has arrived to begin the feedback and decision phase.

Sometimes, however, the contract does not precisely specify the activities that make up the exploration phase, and thus the transition from exploration to feedback and decision is more fluid. If I am meeting with a core team at the end of each week, it is possible that after about half of the data gathering is complete our discussions at these meetings will begin to touch on the possible meaning of the data that have been assembled. This is a natural occurrence among people who want to create a coherent understanding of their social environment, and I do nothing to stop these speculative conversations. However, I do encourage my clients to avoid "jumping to solutions" at this point. We might be missing important information that will come to light in an interview that is scheduled for next week. We do not want to create an attitude or assumption in our minds that would cause us to inadvertently filter out this important information because we had already made up our minds about the situation that we are investigating.[4]

While you carry out the tasks associated with this phase, you strive to create the psychological safety needed for a frank and thorough discussion of your findings, and you attempt to create the conditions needed for the client to experience the success associated with a new framing of the problematic situation and the commitment to take new (and possibly uncomfortable) actions to bring about change. You model the behaviors needed to create a container for a productive discussion by being honest about your own feelings and fallibilities. When someone asks you a question and you do not know the answer, you acknowledge your ignorance.

During the feedback session some members of the client system may experience strong emotions, or conflict may surface between individuals or groups. You will try to help participants to remain grounded in the data, and to acknowledge that it is reasonable for different people to arrive at different interpretations of and responses to the data. You are professional in your demeanor. You are empathetic and compassionate, but you also strive to maintain some professional distance between yourself and the client.

Whether there is a clear demarcation point between the exploration phase and the feedback and decision phase, or a more fluid transition from one phase into the other, the following tasks are usually performed during the feedback and decision phase:

- The information that was gathered during the exploration phase must now be organized and prepared for use in a sensemaking session.
- A plan for the sensemaking session must be prepared.
- When designing the session, the interventionist must consider the client system's existing capacity.
- You may check in with certain people who could feel threatened by the data that you have gathered.
- The sensemaking session must be held, with the interventionist acting as session facilitator.
- You continue to create the conditions for safety and success.

- In the last part of the sensemaking session, and sometimes in the days following the session, the interventionist and client system must finalize their understanding of the problematic situation and move into action to bring about improvement and change.
- You reflect on what happens.

Preparing Materials

It is almost always the job of the interventionist to prepare the materials for the feedback session. This means that the interventionist organizes the information that has been gathered through interviews, focus groups, observations, and so on, and then prepares representations of this information that members of the client system can look at.

The goal is almost always to hold up a mirror for members of the client system. When they look at these materials, they should see themselves, their colleagues, and their work units. They should see how they, through their attitudes, actions, and structures, create and sustain the problematic situation that concerns them. Often, they will also see how external pressures contribute to the creation of the problematic situation.

Some people do not like to acknowledge that they themselves are implicated in the problems that concern them. They prefer to claim that other people – the imperious bosses, the tiresome employees, the demanding customers, the manipulative suppliers – are to blame. However, when we are dealing with a problem that is produced in a complex and dynamic human system, all system members are implicated in some way. Far from being a bad thing to be covered up and denied, this is a good thing to be searched for and acknowledged – good, that is, if system members want to change the situation and solve the problem. It is good because, if you are implicated in the problem, then you potentially have some influence over it. If you change your own behavior, you may alter the dynamic that produces the problem. You have personal power to do something about the problematic situation.

The interventionist's job in preparing materials for the feedback session is to show system members how they themselves are implicated in the problematic situation, and therefore to open up new ways of thinking that might allow feasible and sustainable solutions to be proposed.

When possible, I invite members of the client system to help prepare the materials for the feedback session. Often, however, I cannot invite them to work with me on the raw data because of confidentiality assurances that I have provided to the people who provided the data. Instead, I check in with the core team, and sometimes with other system members, to ask their opinions about the sort of materials that would be most useful. Then I take it from there.

I generally organize the data in terms of the questions that have been asked during the data-gathering process. If I have asked eight distinct questions during interviews and focus groups, then I try to find the patterns that emerged in the way that people answered these questions. I also try to retain some variety and diversity that is apparent in the responses. If my contract stipulates that system members are curious about the perspectives of subgroups, then I retain this detail as I organize the data.

Recall the example from earlier in the chapter. There the interventionist might have asked several questions while gathering data from designers, production staff, and managers. One question might have been, *What is currently making it difficult for you to perform your role, and for your team to perform its role?* If system members wanted to see the perspectives of the different groups, I might organize the data as indicated in figure 6.5.

It is possible that I would present these data on a sheet of paper, or I might display them on a slide or handout. In the example in figure 6.5, we are dealing with a system that is fractured into

Question 3: What is currently making it difficult for you to perform your role and for your team to perform its role?

Answers characteristic of all system members:

- Other groups in the organization are too focused on their own goals and needs.
- People don't see beyond their own functional silos. It is all "me" and not enough "we."
- Customer expectations create pressures that are difficult to manage.
- We get no direction or support from headquarters.

Answers characteristic of designers:

- Pressures from foreign competitors are heating up the marketplace and creating insane customer expectations.
- We create competitive designs, but the production department scales them back so that our products are not competitive.
- Other answers: inadequate professional development oppurtunities; not enough direct exposure to customer feedback; the organization has no long-term strategic plan.

Answers characteristic of production staff:

- Customers demand lower prices, and we struggle to find ways to meet this demand.
- Design department produces premium designs that we cannot afford to build.
- We do not receive a clear direction from management.
- Other answers: the scheduled retooling was cancelled; the salary freeze is in its second year; we aren't allowed to talk to the sales team.

Answers characteristic of managers:

- Everyone is stuck in their own little world, and the disciplines are not acting like we are all part of the same team.
- Headquarters is not providing us with the vision or support that we ask for.
- Other answers: not enough out-of-the-box thinking; we have a culture of "let's not rock the boat"; middle manager turnover is becoming an issue.

Figure 6.5. Organizing the data for the feedback session

subgroups, and that is dealing with a difficult problematic situation that will require a united response from the entire system. To help them explore the extent to which they can still act as a single, united group, I highlight the answers that seem characteristic of the entire system, as well as showing the distinct answers characteristic of each subgroup. This might help them to consider the possibility that they can set aside their differences and work together to produce more competitive products.

As I prepare these materials, I remain close to the data. I pull together my notes, I read and reread the answers provided by informants, I underline or highlight key words and phrases, I search for metaphors and figurative language, and I note down stories that informants use to make sense of their puzzling social reality. I do this because I want to guard against the danger of imposing my own interpretation onto this reality. The meaning of the information must emerge from the information itself. I am just organizing things to make it easier for members of the system to work with it. My beliefs and interpretations are not important. What is important is the way that members of the client system frame the problem. My role is to try to help them break free from the mindsets and assumptions that are currently limiting them and to help them see the problematic situation in a new way. But that new way of seeing must come from them, not from me.

In addition to showing how system members answered the data-gathering questions, I sometimes create slides that show themes that emerge from the data, and statements that exemplify the themes. A theme is a statement that describes a dominant pattern at work in the system and gives system members a chance to consider the main factors that are influencing behavior. If I am creating a theme, I make sure that the theme is well grounded in the data that I have gathered. I usually try to find at least three clear statements by three

Theme 4: They are unreasonable

- Designers create unrealistic designs.
- Production takes actions to undermine excellent designs.
- Management won't support the excellent designs that they ask us to create.
- Management won't support the cost containment measures that they impose on us.
- The design and production groups don't realize that we have no choice but to compromise.

Figure 6.6. A slide displaying a theme from the data

different people that support the theme. Figure 6.6 is an example of what this sort of slide might look like.

If I use a slide like the one illustrated in figure 6.6, I make sure that I give people a chance to dispute it. Perhaps I have misunderstood things that I have heard, or perhaps I became carried away in trying to construct an elegant depiction of the functioning of the client system. It is always possible that I have missed something, and it is very important that system members reach agreement about the meaning of the data that we generated.

I also try to present the client system with at least one map of their current way of being. Figures 6.2, 6.3, and 6.4 from earlier in this chapter are examples of maps showing the current functioning of and challenges facing our hypothetical client system of designers, production staff, and managers.

The materials you prepare should help members of the client system to see themselves and their current patterns of thought, behavior, and structuring. They should allow system members to see how the problematic situation arises out of these patterns and is, in effect, inevitable for as long as these patterns remain unchecked. The materials should be presented not as an *answer* that the interventionist is providing but rather as a comprehensive picture of the existing situation that the members of the client system and the interventionist have created together. The feedback session is an opportunity to look at these materials and to consider whether they are accurate or whether they need to be adjusted in some way. The materials are intended to help members of the client system to see something new, and then to shift their current way of thinking about the problematic situation that is affecting their workplace or community.

As the interventionist prepares these materials, there is a need to balance the desire to tell the client the answer with the need to create the conditions in which members of the client system can discover the answers for themselves. The interventionist will assert certain ideas through these materials, and will design a process for the session that allows participants to inquire into the factors that continuously produce the problematic situation that they want to resolve.

Designing the Session

While the interventionist prepares the materials needed for the feedback session, she must also design how the session will work. It is important that this design ensures that members of the client system play an active role in the conduct of the session, so that by the end of their discussions they agree on the framing of the problem, they are able to acknowledge that they are implicated in creating the problem, and they have begun to identify some actions that could bring about change and improvement.

To bring system members together to make sense of the data that I have gathered about the problematic situation, I schedule a meeting. Because I am usually working with a group of people, I have to make sure that the meeting takes place in a space adequate to comfortably accommodate the group, and at a time when all group members are able to attend. Usually, these meetings take place in a meeting room or board room in the client's workplace. Sometimes the client wants to take the group off-site, away from the routine interruptions that occur in the workplace, and prefers to hold the meeting in a hotel. On occasion, when I am working with a large group of people or with a community group, the meeting occurs in a large space such as a school gym, a church basement, or – on one memorable occasion – in the lounge overlooking a large curling rink. Wherever the meeting occurs, it should be in a space that can comfortably accommodate the participants and allow for the kinds of activities that are included in your design.

During the meeting I feed back the information that I have gathered over the preceding weeks. The form in which I share this information depends on a number of factors:

- In what form are members of this client system accustomed to receiving this sort of information? Do they usually receive information in the form of PowerPoint slide shows, or written reports, or oral presentations? Are they accustomed to sitting quietly and receiving information, or are they accustomed to playing an active part in the information dissemination process (for example, by engaging in small group discussions)?
- Given the nature of my contract, does it make sense to use the methods that the group is most accustomed to, or does it make sense to disrupt their existing way of doing things? For example, if the problematic situation has to do with the way in which information is shared and communication occurs within the workplace, it might be useful to use an unfamiliar information-sharing approach, to help participants see beyond their existing routines.
- Do the confidentiality requirements of the contract mean that I can provide written handouts, or is it important to ensure that no copies of the data leave the room?

The session usually begins with a discussion intended to create the conditions under which the meeting will be held. The next part of the session usually involves feeding back information to the group, and inviting people to react, to dispute points, and to reach agreement. The third part of the session usually includes activities that allow the group to consider various courses of action. The final part allows participants to reflect together on the process. Table 6.1 provides an example of how this might work.

Respecting the Client System's Existing Capacity

The session design will be informed by the interventionist's impression of the client's current capacity to solve problems and learn, and by the nature of the problematic situation that we are dealing with.

Every client system that I have worked with has been characterized by affordances and constraints. The system possesses affordances that allow it to get things done. Affordances have to do with the system's ability to accomplish and create. The system is also held in check by certain constraints. Its abilities and potentialities are limited.

I do not believe that this is a radical view, or that it represents an insult to the intelligence and capability of our species. A group of firefighters are likely to possess affordances that allow them to be good at fighting fires. They accept risks, they understand the need to work together and to help each other, and they move quickly to action. However, these very affordances also create constraints that may make it difficult for them to engage in slow and deliberative activities, to consider numerous alternatives before moving to action, or to spend time working in isolation on individual assignments.

It is likely that the problematic situation that you are helping the client to investigate is bringing to light the constraints that limit this human system, and it is possible that circumstances now require

Table 6.1. Sample of an agenda for a feedback session

Part 1: Creating the container

1. Create the psychological safety needed for success.	Allow the group to discuss the rules that need to be agreed to in order for them to have a productive session.
	Ensure that everybody agrees before continuing.
	If needed, add some rules of your own.
	Ensure that any confidentiality agreements are restated, and that people agree that participants can decide for themselves how much or how little they want to say.
	Be sure to acknowledge that you are going to show them how you have organized the data, and say that they will have a chance to dispute and clarify the data as you go through your findings.

Part 2: Feeding back the data and holding up the map

2. Show how people answered the questions.	Show representations of the data that summarize how each question was answered. Keep the identity of respondents confidential.
	After each question is considered, invite people to react to what they are seeing. Does this seem correct? What surprises (or excites, or worries, etc.) them? What does this mean for them?
3. Show the themes that emerged from the data.	This step is optional. I use it when the information strongly suggests to me that a small number of dominant patterns are of significance to this system.
	Show each theme (usually consisting of a theme name and then a short definition), and a few data elements that support each theme.
	Invite people to react. Ask questions such as: Does this seem accurate? Have you seen this? How would you describe this?
4. Show the map.	This step is optional. I use it when my assessment of client capacity indicates that people are willing to examine the root cause of the problematic situation but are unsure of how to do so. (I have more to say about client capacity in the next section of this chapter.)
	Show the map. Ask people to examine it silently for a minute.
	Invite people to react. Ask questions such as: Does this seem accurate? Do we need to make any changes? What does it feel like for you, to see this? Does this shed light on the problems that we have been working on?
	Stay with this until you have co-created a version of the map that everyone can support. If some people are reluctant, ask yourself if the problem is in the room. If one or two people are reluctant to endorse the map, consider whether they are in some way being "blamed" by the map.

(Continued)

Table 6.1. Sample of an agenda for a feedback session (*continued*)

Part 3: Moving to action

5. How do you react to this?	Depending on the number of participants and the nature of your contract, consider breaking the participants into small groups. Give everyone a chance to speak and to share their reactions.
6. What does this mean for you?	Bring them back into a large group to share highlights from the small-group discussions. Ask if the map suggests that system members may be acting on the basis of some assumptions that have never been tested. List the assumptions and ask participants if some of these assumptions may not always be correct.[5]
7. What can and should be done?	Ask participants to brainstorm actions that can be taken to bring about change.
	Ask participants to identify those actions that will have the greatest impact. Invite them to describe the causal reasoning that they are using to confirm that these actions will bring about the intended effects.
	Ask participants to sign up for actions. If appropriate, help them to arrange themselves into teams. Help them to commit to specific actions, deliverables, and deadlines.

Part 4: Reflecting on the process

8. How are you experiencing this project, and how did you experience today's session?	Invite participants to reflect together on how the project has gone so far, and on how they experienced the sensemaking session.
	Consider using an ORID design, which focuses first on the objective data (things that were seen or heard) about the session, second on how they felt about the project and the session, third on what the project and session mean to them and to the team or organization, and fourth on what is the first new action that they will take as a result of the session.*

* See Stanfield (2000) for a review of the ORID.

that the system overcome these constraints and transform itself so that it becomes capable of accomplishing new things. So far, however, it has not been able to bring about this transformation. That is why you are there. As you design the sensemaking session, you must ask yourself, first, what the current capacity of the system is, and second, what incremental steps system members might be capable of taking, so they can create new capacity and eventually become able to move past the current constraints.

The client system's capacity to change can be assessed on three key dimensions.[6] *First,* does the system have the capacity to work effectively when faced with uncertainty and anxiety? Is emotionality handled appropriately? Do people acknowledge the uncomfortable emotions that they experience without being disarmed or overrun by these emotions? Do some people seem curious and stimulated by the intellectual and operational challenges associated with new and uncertain situations? *Second,* is the system characterized by a reasonable level of respect and trust? Do people disparage or ridicule others? Have you seen examples of participants allowing themselves to be vulnerable, acknowledging that they do not have the answers, and sharing their own perspectives and views? *Third,* is the client system able to engage in self-reflection and to communicate openly? Are people willing to acknowledge that they all play a role in creating the current situation, and that they all will have a role in bringing about positive change? Can they "think together" by discussing their existing assumptions, behaviors, and outcomes?[7] Do you see many instances of passive-aggressive behavior, or do people communicate openly and share ideas that can be tested against evidence?

For example, consider a service delivery department that is composed of five interdependent teams. Each team contributes something to the service that the department provides to customers. Recently senior organizational leaders have noticed that the department's productivity and quality have been decreasing. Internal efforts to diagnose and correct the problem have failed. An interventionist is brought in by the department manager to help. The interventionist goes through an exploration phase and then begins to consider the data. The data indicate that people on each team are able to see that there is a problem that is affecting their performance. They can describe symptoms of the problem, and they evince a desire to fix the problem and improve performance. However, each team firmly believes that the cause of the problem lies outside of their team. Members of each team believe that one or two of the other teams are to blame for what is happening.

A session design for this hypothetical situation should take into consideration that system members are able to see and describe the problem, that the descriptions are unique to each team, and that system members are not yet able to see that they are all personally implicated in the problematic situation. Their problem-framing abilities are currently stuck in a stance of blame (consistent with the fundamental attribution error). At the same time, their behavior suggests that they are emotionally mature, and they demonstrate some capacity for self-reflection. A session design might allow each team to present their own experience of the problem. To do this, the interventionist might show how Team A answered the questions asked during the exploratory phase, and then invite the team to provide additional comments. Other teams would then be allowed to ask clarifying questions (but only clarifying questions). If another team tried to move into a blaming stance, or to make passive-aggressive comments, the interventionist would intervene to stop this behavior. The interventionist might say, "There will be a chance for more in-depth discussion later. For now, we are just getting the different perspectives on the table." The goal of this is to demonstrate that everybody recognizes that a problem exists, and that there are five distinct perspectives on the problem. This exercise is likely to allow some system members to begin to see things through the eyes of others and to realize that a bigger and better framing of the problem might be available.

The session design might also highlight the fact that all of the teams are committed to finding a solution. If there are different experiences of the problem, and if everyone wants a solution, then it should become apparent that the only way to solve the problem is to pool perspectives and ideas and to work together. If these activities went reasonably well, another component of the session design might be to form small groups made up of people from different teams. These groups could brainstorm possible framings of the problem or possible actions to take to resolve the problem. This is another way of allowing people to access the perspectives of the other teams, and also to provide them with practice in working together.

Another activity might be to ask small groups to create a diagram of how the current pattern of interactions is exacerbating the problem (that is, rather than the interventionist showing a map of the system, the system members are invited to create a map). If there are five small groups, this activity could produce five maps, which the full group might then use to create one master map that draws on the most persuasive features of the five maps. This could produce a useful deliverable, and also allow participants to gain some practice in working together in a new way.

A *poor* design for this situation would be one that allowed the warring teams to publicly castigate and blame each other. This would simply mirror the current system dynamic and might cause relationships to become further frayed.

If the client system is currently divided into silos, and the problematic situation has to do with the difficulty in sharing information and ideas across the silos, then your design should allow them to begin to form relationships and share information across the silos. If the client system is a hierarchy with decision rights concentrated at the top, and the problematic situation has to do with decision bottlenecks that ultimately will need to be relieved by sharing decision rights more widely, then your design might allow them to consider the issues associated with being responsible for making and acting on decisions, and to make a shared decision about the best way to move forward. If the client system operates on the basis of a norm that it is important to "be nice" to each other, and the problematic situation has to do with problems that arise when people are not willing to openly criticize or disagree with each other's ideas during project meetings, then your design might include an opportunity for people to evaluate alternative interpretations or proposals, with you actively facilitating the interactions to make up for their lack of skill in engaging in constructive conflict.

The main point here is to recognize the limitations that are currently holding the system back and to design activities that allow system members to begin to develop new capacity.

Checking In with Key Individuals

When human beings try to explain the events that occur in a human system, we have what appears to be a natural tendency to say that one person or a small number of people are responsible for these events.[8] For example, when a business enterprise performs better than expected by industry watchers, we usually give most of the credit for the superlative performance to the person who happens to be the CEO at that particular time. We do this despite the fact that many management scientists and social scientists have persuasively argued that it is often incorrect to attribute organizational performance (regardless of whether the performance is seen as excellent or poor) to the one person who happens to be sitting in the corner office at the time.[9]

When things go wrong, we also tend to assign blame for the problems by singling out one person or a small group of people.[10] Often referred to as scapegoating, this stratagem allows a group to cleanse itself by putting all of its problems (or sins) on one person, and then punishing that person, often by expulsion from the group.

Scapegoating sometimes rears its ugly head during the feedback and decision phase. If this happens, the data gathered during exploration will often show that certain individuals or groups are being singled out. An experienced interventionist will look for signs of this phenomenon in the data and will take steps to interrupt this dysfunctional pattern before the feedback session occurs.

For example, members of a client system sometimes believe that leaders are performing poorly and that this poor performance is largely responsible for the problems faced by the system. In other cases, a person with an important position in the milieu – perhaps a senior engineer, or a chief nurse, or a senior accountant – is blamed for the problems. The person being scapegoated is often a reasonably powerful and well-regarded member of the system.[11]

When your data indicate that scapegoating may be occurring, you have two challenges. You must find a way to present the data that is accurate and that diminishes the blaming. Second, you must determine whether to meet first with the person being scapegoated to help them to frame what is going to happen during the sense-making session.

One way of presenting information accurately so that it minimizes the tendency to inappropriately blame certain individuals for the system's problems is to focus on functions and roles rather than personalities or individuals. If the data include many statements in which people criticize the boss, then it might be possible to frame this as a concern about the way in which leadership is organized and delivered in this system. If the data suggest that a particular individual is to blame for the problematic situation, it might make sense to frame this by saying that system pressures are making it difficult to effectively perform certain roles. If the data point the finger at a particular subgroup, it might be possible to talk about issues concerning the integration of groups into a seamless and functional whole.

None of this is intended to whitewash or sidestep important concerns or issues within the system. Rather, the point is to frame the situation in a way that helps participants to see things in new ways, to consider new interpretations, and perhaps to begin to see a way out of their constraining dilemma. By using new words and by presenting the data in ways that differ from the current pattern of blaming and scapegoating, it is possible to help members of the client system to see the problematic situation in a way that produces a new conversation along with new ideas about how to bring about improvement.

The second challenge the interventionist may face is to consider whether it is wise to provide some advance warning to the people who have been singled out in the data. In making this decision, I like to consider this dilemma in the context of the client system's existing patterns. For example, do the data suggest that this client system is characterized by phenomena such as blaming, shaming, marginalizing, ganging up, or "blindsiding"? If some of these phenomena are evident in the data, then I would wonder whether the client system is pulling my information gathering and sensemaking activities into its existing patterns of behavior. If I just go ahead with a simple sensemaking session, it is quite possible that during the session some or many participants will feel blamed, shamed, marginalized, ganged up on, or blindsided. If this happens, there is a danger that the sensemaking session will simply reinforce the existing patterns and teach system members that it is too dangerous to inquire into these phenomena.

The interventionist's role is to design a sensemaking session that might interrupt these patterns. One way of doing this is to approach the people who have been singled out and see if it is possible to frame the data in a way that could produce a new and more productive reaction that would disrupt the existing pattern.

I will often prepare the ground for this sort of intervention during contracting or at the beginning of the exploration phase. When meeting privately with the manager or team leader I may say something like this:

When there are strains in a human system, one natural tendency of people is to put some of the blame on the person with the most power or authority. This means that it is possible that the data that I gather will include some dissatisfaction that is directed at you. If that happens, will that be uncomfortable for you?

I listen to what the person says, and I may add a few more points:

Dissatisfaction is often a powerful motivator to participate in change, so if we find dissatisfaction, that is not necessarily a bad thing. The very fact that you want to work on these issues suggests to me that you are also dissatisfied. If it turns out that most of your people are dissatisfied with a number of things going on in this system, including the current leadership, it might be possible to say that since the current leadership has not been able as of yet to resolve these issues then it is only natural that people are dissatisfied with the leadership. You might even say that you yourself are not satisfied with the current way of doing things, and that is why you have initiated this process to try something different.

You might be able to use the dissatisfaction of employees as a way of encouraging people to take responsibility for the ways in which their own attitudes and behaviors are helping to produce the issues that are holding you back. You could say, I want to learn about how I could handle things differently, so I can contribute to a solution. I also think that it would be helpful if everybody on the team does the same.

If I have had this prior conversation with the manager or team leader, then it is relatively easy to introduce the singling out phenomenon before the sensemaking session. I can let her know that we were correct to anticipate that some team members are dissatisfied with the current leadership, and then I encourage her to talk about how she might handle this during the sensemaking session.

If need be, I provide some coaching. It is sometimes helpful for the manager to release some of her own frustrations, including anger or disappointment directed at some specific team members. I let her put these frustrations on the table, and then I encourage her to consider how their behavior and her own behavior might be arising from the same problematic situation. I ask her how she might handle the interactions that could occur during the session. I encourage her to take responsibility for those things that she is really responsible for, and to let others take responsibility for their own attitudes, choices, and actions. By the end of this conversation, the manager has generally worked out a plan for how to handle the interactions that may occur during the session.

If the person being singled out is not the manager or leader, I often handle the singling out phenomenon by making some comments during the opening portion of the sensemaking session. I may say something like this:

> As we go through the data together, I want you to imagine that we are all movie reviewers. I want you to imagine that the data we are examining are in fact a new movie that we are trying to understand so we can all write our movie reviews for the newspaper. The people in this movie are playing roles. In our movie, these roles are imposed on people by the situations that characterize the workplace. Betty is assertive because the situation pushes her to be assertive. John is angry, Sophie is withdrawn, Lucas is gossipy, and Maya is mean, all because of how they are responding to the situation. When the data show that specific people are playing certain roles or are acting in certain ways, ask what it is about the situation that is pushing them in that direction? Be curious. Let us assume that nobody is acting out of an ill intent. Everyone is doing their best, and is coping with the same difficult set of circumstances. Let's dig beneath the roles, beneath the behaviors, so we can understand what is creating the problems here.

I might also offer some brief comments about the fundamental attribution error.

One of the most enduring and significant findings from social science research is something called the fundamental attribution error. This is an error that all people make from time to time. The error is this: we attribute a person's behavior to their dispositions or their personality, when in fact their behavior is being caused by the situation that they find themselves in. Our main question today must be: what situations are giving rise to the behaviors that we want to change? Because if we change the situation, then a lot of the unwanted behaviors will go away.

By introducing this idea, I will then be able to intervene in the discussion whenever scapegoating puts in an appearance. I can say, "Hang on a second. We are starting to talk about personalities. Let's get back on track. What is it about the situation that is producing this?"

I anticipate that some readers may be disappointed that I am not explaining how to deal with the troublemaker or the incompetent colleague who, they believe, *is in fact* responsible for the dilemmas faced by a human system. I do not wish to deny that there can be individuals who are unable to fit into a particular work culture and environment. In an environment that is nurturing and kind, a bellicose individualist might rub people the wrong way. In a workplace where people communicate in a direct and frank manner, a gentle and sensitive person may not fit in. Some people are promoted to roles for which they are unsuited or unprepared. Numerous articles and books have been published that explain how this sort of behavior comes about, and provide advice on steps that leaders and interveners can take to improve these difficult situations.[12]

And, of course, mental health professionals might remind us that some people suffer from antisocial personality disorder (studies estimate that the prevalence of the condition in the United States runs at around 3.5 per cent of the adult population)[13] and that such people tend to overlook the needs, rights, and comfort of other people. People who suffer from this disorder often break the law; they tell lies and steal and are cavalier about the safety of others; and they tend to feel and show no remorse when they harm others. A system-level intervention is unlikely to alter behaviors that arise from this mental health disorder. This subject lies beyond the scope of this book.

Often, however, the behavior engaged in by people in the context of a human system arises from the situations that are characteristic of that system. Nisbett and Ross have presented a compelling case suggesting that the same person can behave quite differently in different social contexts.[14] It is most often the situation, not the dispositions of individual actors, that accounts for the behavior that we witness in a workplace. For this reason, I urge readers to be cautious about joining in the chorus of blaming. If the behavior is arising from the situation, then to produce lasting change you must get at the factors that produce the situation.

Facilitating the Feedback Session

Another task that is characteristic of the feedback and decision phase is facilitating and managing the session itself. The interventionist is likely to act as the host or moderator of the session, though it is often wise to involve members of the client system in some facilitation activities. A poor outcome from the session would be for system members to feel dependent on the interventionist. The overall goal of the consulting engagement is to help the client system to develop new problem-solving capacity, so members become more independent and adaptive. For this to happen, people need to participate actively in the session.

Some interventionists like to meticulously plan all of the details of the session in advance and in effect create a "script" that provides a detailed roadmap of everything that is expected to happen. Others prefer to work with a loose plan, confident that they will know what to say and do as the situation unfolds. Personally, I do not think it matters whether you create a detailed or a high-level plan. The important thing is that you should have a clear intention for the session, that you should design a series of actions that move you and the client toward the realization of that intention, and that you accept the possibility that things may happen during the session that will lead you to abandon your design and take a more emergent approach.

For the most part, the appropriate facilitation style for a feedback session is rather hands-off. In other words, the interventionist speaks as little as possible and encourages participants to engage in discussion together. When I am feeding data back to the participants, usually by displaying a series of PowerPoint slides, I often will show the slide, perhaps read or paraphrase the title, and then allow people to quietly read the content for themselves. Then I invite people to make comments or ask questions. When a comment is made, I might ask if anybody in the group would like to respond. I function as a moderator, or as a sort of traffic cop, and I try to encourage session participants to engage with each other and to make their own sense of the data they are encountering.

Now and then I may offer a more assertive comment. For example, if one or two participants are trying to minimize or reject a portion of the data (perhaps by rejecting the way a subgroup answered one of the questions, or disagreeing with a theme that emerged from the analysis), and if I am confident that these data accurately reflect part of their social reality, I might intervene and say, "I heard this come up several times. It seemed definite and important to me. Have any of you heard these sorts of comments? What might be going on?" Notice, however, that my assertion is accompanied by a question. This social system is their reality, and it is up to them to agree on the meanings that will form the basis of action. I might also say, "A few people are skeptical about this. What do others think? Do some of you think that this is real and important?"

Of course, it is always possible that conflict may arise during a feedback session, and some interventionists (like many people in general) become uncomfortable when conflict occurs. However, the skilled interventionist must develop some capacity to remain effective and active when conflict occurs between individuals or groups. One strategy is to help people to remain focused on the agreed-upon facts. For example, one group participating in a feedback session may believe that the challenges facing the client system are upsetting and discouraging, while another group may find the same challenges exciting and inspiring. This could lead the two groups to disparage each other: "I wish you guys wouldn't always trivialize everything"; or, "I am sick and tired of being held back by the whiners and the quitters!" But these statements are reflective of the ways in which the two groups are interpreting the facts. It can be useful to help the groups to recognize that they are working from the same set of facts (declining sales, increased competition, resource shortages, etc.), and that their roles and responsibilities are leading them to interpret these facts in different ways. If they try to understand one another's perspective, it is often possible to change the conversation so that it becomes more productive.

Creating the Conditions for Safety and for Success

Another balancing act performed by the interventionist during the feedback and decision phase, especially during the sensemaking session, is to foster the conditions needed for psychological safety while also encouraging and supporting system members to take interpersonal risks that can lead to success.

To be open and honest with colleagues, we have to know that we can talk about things that worry or frustrate or frighten or anger us without triggering scorn or ridicule or punishment. Some research suggests that psychological safety can be created by asking questions whose purpose is only to inquire into the topic at hand (and not to trick or manipulate people), acknowledging one's own uncertainty and fallibility about the focus of the discussion (and thus allowing oneself to be vulnerable in front of others), and listening carefully to what others say.[15] In a psychologically safe environment, people are not punished for admitting that they do not know what to do, or that they have made a mistake.[16] For psychological safety to develop in a group, it is often necessary for the people with power and status to model the behavior. And this is a role that the interventionist can play.

To create psychological safety during the sensemaking session, the interventionist can do three things. First, she can include a preliminary item on the agenda for setting the ground rules for the session, and ensure that there are some items indicating that all participants should be free to say what they need to say without facing retribution. Table 6.1 earlier in this chapter showed how this might fit into the session design. Second, she can model the behavior herself during the session. It is likely that participants will ask her questions during the session, and it is likely that she will not know the answer to some questions. To model the behavior needed to create psychological safety, she merely needs to be honest. She can say, "I don't know." She can allow herself to be vulnerable – to step out from the facade that we normally use to protect our reputations and our status within groups. Third, she can support others who also model the behavior. She can acknowledge that some statements must have been difficult to make. She can thank people. She can point out that a new level of honesty is taking shape in the group, and that this candor is needed if the group is to gain access to the new perspectives and information that are needed to move beyond the problematic situation.

Moving to Commitment and Action

Another task that is characteristic of the feedback and decision state is to manage the shift from seeking to explore and understand the problematic situation to taking action to solve the problem. When the interventionist first arrived in the client system the people were stuck. They did not know how to think about the problematic situation, how to frame it as a problem that could be solved, and how to act in ways that might solve the problem. The interventionist's role is to help participants to move from thinking about the problem to doing something about it.

This is easier said than done. In a variety of fields, including secondary education and health care, many argue that it is relatively easy for frontline professionals to discover better ways of providing efficient and effective services, but it can be enormously difficult to translate these better ideas into concrete action in frontline workplaces.[17] For the past fifteen years, academic journals have been jammed with articles that attempt to provide advice on how changes are to be implemented in practice. Some argue that care must be taken to ensure that the change is implemented with fidelity.[18] Others emphasize the need for multifaceted intervention strategies that cater to a variety of learning needs present in frontline practitioners.[19] Some suggest that the involvement of knowledge users in the implementation process is a key to success,[20] and others wonder if the existing metaphors for organizational and practice change are limiting the way that people conceive of effective change processes.[21]

The approach taken in this book suggests that people may be unable to solve the compelling problems that are encountered in workplaces because they are unable to think effectively about these problems and to form clear and effective intentions based on a useful framing of the problem, and that these inabilities are the primary impediment to action. If your sensemaking session allows participants to think about their situations in new ways, and to devise some strategies for bringing about change, it is likely that this will help them to create the will and enthusiasm to move to action.

The interventionist should ensure that there is enough time at the end of the sensemaking session to engage in action planning. If the action planning is rushed or incomplete, then a follow-up session should be scheduled so this important work can be completed.

I encourage session participants to conceive of the changes they wish to make as a set of interrelated projects, and I invite people to identify the project that they are personally prepared to work on. Participants then form small groups and formulate their plans. I ask them to set a target or goal for their work, including the date when the goal might realistically be achieved, and then to identify the activities and milestones needed to achieve their goal. The groups then share their plans with each other and consider any overlaps or inconsistencies that need to be sorted out.

It is important to ensure that members of the client system become personally engaged in the process. People need to make commitments. The change process cannot be foisted on absent others. It is often wise for the core team to continue to meet, and to receive weekly progress reports from the people who are responsible for leading the actions.

I need to add one qualifier to this discussion.

A human system is best thought of as a complex adaptive system. A human system can be any human collective in which individual people interact and communicate and, often, work, and in which they create shared intentionality and patterns of behavior that give rise to social structures that in turn influence the thinking and behaving that goes on within the collective. On this definition, a human system is *not* a simple, linear environment where causes produce effects in an orderly movement into the future. Instead, a human system is a web of interdependence and influence. Outcomes emerge from multiple influences arising from players and processes within the web that are connected to each other in ways too complex to map.

This means that the interaction map that I present to client system members during the feedback session can only ever be a partial rendering of the forces and patterns at work in that human system. The map will depict the thinking, behavior, and structuring that occur in the vicinity of the problematic situation that we are exploring and that we have been asking about. It will undoubtedly miss other factors that are at work in the client system as a whole.

This also means that when the client creates an action plan to produce a desired change, the plan should be regarded as a hypothesis. This is what *might* happen if we have correctly identified some of the main causal factors, and if there are not other influences at work within the system that could reduce or deflect or transform the impact of the interventions.

And this in turn means that it is wise to create a process that allows the interventionist and members of the client system to observe what happens, and to learn.

As the interventions move forward and results are produced, the people involved must meet and discuss what is happening. It is wise to talk about the objective data – what actually happened; who did what, when, and where; and what concrete results can be identified. Did the results of employee satisfaction or customer satisfaction surveys change? Were revenue streams impacted? What happened to productivity and quality? Did unexpected events occur that impacted, positively or negatively, the promised results of the interventions?

Because this move into uncertainty can be troubling for people, it also makes sense to allow people to talk about how they feel about what is happening.[22] Are they becoming worried? Are they afraid that they might be blamed for the intervention's failure? Is their level of commitment to the change process changing? Are some people feeling intellectually stimulated by the unexpected results that are being produced, and are they engaging in new and unexpected research and analysis? Are some people excited by the challenges?

And then of course it is also important to encourage people to discuss what the progress of the intervention means, how it can be interpreted, and what activities need to be revised or dropped or created in order to keep the system moving toward its desired goal. Just as your feedback session might need to change based on what happens as people interact, the action plan that is produced at the end of the feedback session must itself be open to revision and improvement.

Reflecting on What Happens

The entire sensemaking session described in this chapter could be construed as a meeting that allows system members to look at new data showing how the system is functioning, and to reflect together on what the data mean and what actions should be taken to bring about improvement.

Even though reflection is integral to the sensemaking that occurs during the feedback and decision phase, I recommend that your sensemaking session include an explicit agenda item calling on participants to reflect together on the project and on the sensemaking session (see the sample of a feedback session in table 6.1 earlier in this chapter, and especially part 4 of the agenda, which invites participants to reflect together on the process).

I often use an ORID design for the reflective work that takes place at the conclusion of the session.[23] ORID stands for objective, reflective, interpretive, and decisional. By inviting people to talk about their experiences using this structure, you allow them to move up the ladder of inference from their initial encounter with phenomena in the shared world of objects and interactions, through their immediate emotional and intuitive responses to phenomena, then through their more reasoned interpretations about their experiences, and finally to their need to make decisions and take action.[24] The point of this reflective process is to look frankly at how the work is proceeding and to determine if any changes are needed to the intervention process. The interventionist might introduce this final part of the sensemaking session by saying something like this:

> We have been working together for about eight weeks now, and we have just spent the last four hours working through the data, figuring out what the data are telling you, and then deciding on some actions that you can take to improve your team's performance. Throughout our process we have occasionally paused and have looked at how we have been working together. This has allowed us to strengthen our own process, and also to validate that we are looking at the right things and that we are asking the right questions. I propose that we conclude our session today by once again reflecting together on our own process.

The interventionist can then facilitate this reflection by asking questions aligned with the ORID structure. Table 6.2 provides some sample questions.

By encouraging the client system to engage in reflective processes, the interventionist is helping to create new and important capacity. As you will see in the next chapter, an implementation process that attempts to resolve an adaptive problem is rarely straightforward. It is almost always necessary to carefully observe what actually happens, to be frank and honest about what is working and what is not working, and to make the necessary mid-course corrections. You might think of the implementation process as a series of experiments whose purpose is to discover and implement a sustainable solution to a troubling problem. Some experiments will succeed, and others will fail. The client system needs to develop the capacity to learn

Table 6.2. ORID questions participants can use to reflect on their process

The ORID structure	Sample questions
Objective	• What have we done so far during this project? • What did you see and hear today that stands out for you? • What are the highlights for you from today? • What for you was the most important conversation today? • What phrases or statements from today are you likely to remember? • What did we accomplish today?
Reflective	• When you think of the work that we have done so far, what excites you the most? • What worries or concerns did you experience today? • Did anything surprise you today? • What was difficult today? Where did we struggle the most? • What emotion are you experiencing as we wrap things up?
Interpretive	• What did you learn today, and what do you think this team learned? • What is different for the team now, after going through and discussing the data? • What are your top insights from the work we have done so far? • Did you have any "aha" moments today? Can you share them?
Decisional	• What is the most important action for the team to take? • If you were making a documentary film about this work that we are doing together, what might you call the film? • What factors must be in place for the team to succeed? • What do you personally need to do to help improve things? • What three things are most important for you to build on what we accomplished today?

from errors and to make corrections and move forward. This is the capacity offered by the interventionist's reflective process.

At this point in the intervention process, the client system is beginning to shift, and it also remains fragile. Old patterns continue to seem familiar and perhaps even attractive. The client will need support as they begin to implement the changes that have been agreed upon during the sensemaking session. By inviting people to reflect openly on how things are going, on how they feel about the process, and on whether the work seems sensible and likely to succeed, the interventionist reveals some clues about the system's current state and capacity, and also creates a precedent for the trial-and-error approach that will determine the success of the implementation phase.

Summary

After exploring a new territory, the explorers create a map. This is the main purpose of the feedback and decision phase.

The precise make-up of the feedback and decision phase varies with the circumstances of the client system. Nevertheless, this phase usually includes several important tasks. For example, the interventionist must organize and prepare the data gathered during the exploration phase for use in a sensemaking session, and must design how the sensemaking session will work.

The session design should be informed by the client's current capacity to solve problems and learn, and by the nature of the problematic situation that is the focus of the intervention. As the interventionist designs the sensemaking session she must ask herself, what is the capacity of this system? What limitations are currently holding the system back, and what activities might help system members to develop new capacity?

Sometimes specific individuals in the client system are singled out in the data as being to blame for creating the problematic situation. When this happens, the interventionist must present the data in a way that is accurate and that diminishes the blaming, and must also determine whether to meet first with the person being scapegoated to help them prepare for the sensemaking session.

It is important for the session facilitator to have a clear intention for the session, to design activities that move toward the realization of that intention, and to accept the possibility that it may become important to abandon the session design and take a more emergent approach. The interventionist must create psychological safety while also encouraging participants to try out new attitudes and behaviors.

Sometimes the interventionist must set aside the plan and deal with what is happening in the room. The problematic situation that the client system is working on is present whenever system members are interacting together, and this means that it will be present in the room during the sensemaking session. When the interventionist notices that the problem is in the room – perhaps affecting the flow of information or impacting the decision-making process – she can either follow the session plan or set aside the plan and draw attention to the problem as it presents itself in the interactions occurring at that moment.

A final task that is characteristic of the feedback and decision phase is helping the client to shift from exploration and analysis to action. Action plans should explicitly show how the planned interventions will produce intended results. That way, the participants will be able to monitor the success of their interventions and determine if plans need to be revised.

As is the case in all phases of an intervention, during the feedback and decision phase it is important for participants to reflect together on how things are going. This can be done in the final twenty minutes of the sensemaking session, when people discuss how the project has gone so far, how they experienced the sensemaking session, and whether they should make any changes in the way they are working as they move into the next phase of the intervention process.

CHAPTER SEVEN

Implementing and Evaluating the Intervention

The purpose of the implementation and evaluation phase is to alter the current pattern of thinking, acting, and structuring in ways that improve or resolve the problematic situation. This generally involves building upon the learning that has occurred among the core group of participants with whom the interventionist has been working and transferring the learning to the larger human system that is being constrained by the problematic situation.

This phase of the intervention process can yield enormous rewards and satisfaction for the intervener. When things go well, you see people come out of their shells. They show courage, intelligence, and resilience. They form new relationships and alter existing ones, they experiment with new ways of thinking and acting, and they push aside the barriers that have been limiting their success.

However, this phase can also bring disappointment. Sometimes it turns out that the system's current capacity for learning and change is less than it initially appeared. The system's patterns of thought and behavior may be more entrenched than anticipated, and old patterns may overrun the efforts to bring about change. When this happens, the interventionist may take heart from the fact that although the system as a whole did not shift toward a more productive and congenial way of being, it is likely that individual system members benefited from the learning available through the change process. New conversations may be occurring within the system, and new ideas may have infiltrated the mindsets of some people. The interventionist and others may be more aware of the current willingness and ability of system members to participate in a change process. Although change itself did not occur, the readiness for change may now be enhanced.

Sometimes the intervention process may be undermined when something unexpected happens in the internal or external environment. I have been involved in some large change processes that were derailed when the organization's board of directors unexpectedly terminated the contract of the CEO. When this happens, strategic initiatives often come to a halt until a new CEO is found and hired – a process that can take many months. The new CEO may believe that past initiatives are part of the problem for which her predecessor was fired, and may find it prudent to cancel or delay these projects until a new strategic plan has been devised – another process that can take many months.

I mention this not to discourage those who are interested in helping organizations and communities to design and implement improvements. My intention is to influence your expectations. The success of an intervention is not to be considered solely in relation to short-term deliverables and targets. It should also be considered in relation to the long-term effort to create and sustain an enhanced capacity to learn and adapt. Even when the immediate goals of an intervention prove elusive, it is possible that you have planted the seeds for creating new capacity within your client system. Your efforts may have fertilized the soil. You may have created the preconditions necessary for important change endeavors that will occur two or three years after you have exited from the system.

During the implementation and evaluation phase, members of the client system take steps to resolve the problematic situation. Although the work needs to focus on the patterns evident in the thinking, acting, and structuring that characterize this human system, many people find it easiest to work on a thing-like entity rather than on their own cognitive processes or behavioral repertoire. They prefer to change the external world rather than change themselves. This is often perfectly fine. While working to alter existing social structures – which can take the form of computer programs, reporting schemes, reward programs, or almost any other social arrangement – they will be engaging in discussions and taking actions. This means that the prevailing patterns of thought and action will be active and evident during the change process. The interventionist can thus ensure that some attention focuses on each of the three vital intervention targets: thought, action, and structure. Some members of the client system are likely to experience this as the interventionist's way of ensuring that the change process remains effective, and this is indeed what the interventionist is doing. The interventionist focuses on *how* the changes are implemented more than on *what* is being implemented.

Implementation is difficult and complex. It is a social process that requires a coordinated effort on the part of many people. For implementation to work, people must conduct themselves with integrity. They must say what they are going to do, and then they must follow through with congruent actions. It requires authenticity, integrity, and determination, and the interventionist must model these qualities. When implementing solutions to complex problems, people are bound to make mistakes. The implementation process must allow these mistakes to come to light so they can become the basis not for the dispiriting "blame games" that vex so many change initiatives but rather for new learning and improved plans.

The Critical Balancing Act of Implementation and Evaluation: Staying the Course and Changing Course

As this final phase in the intervention process unfolds, the interventionist continues to engage in the balancing acts that distinguish the stance and efforts of an effective change agent. He continues to foster relationships and interactions that promote psychological safety, while also encouraging people to experiment with the new way of thinking and acting. He will continue to enter into client interactions, while maintaining sufficient distance to avoid the never-ending pull of collusion. The interventionist will also balance his inclination to share his interpretations with members of the client system with the need to allow people to make their own discoveries and reach their own conclusions.

The critical balancing act of this phase involves the need for coherence and predictability and the need for openness and adaptability. The interventionist works with system members to implement plans and follow agendas, while also remaining open to emergent situations and opportunities.

During implementation the interventionist and client are following the map that was produced in the previous phase. They have agreed on shared intentions and have set a course to bring about positive change. This phase is about action. Some may see a moral imperative attached to the action: we said we would do this, and now we must show our integrity by following through on our intentions. To hesitate is to show that we are timid, that we do not have confidence in our own plans.

Moreover, the intentions and plans that were created at the conclusion of the exploration phase often create a reassuring structure that provides support as system members move into the uncertainty of change. Some have shown that humans have a tendency to form attachments to familiar objects and ideas, and these attachments provide scaffolding or support as we experiment with new ideas and behaviors.[1] The formal, agreed-to plan is an example of this scaffolding. We went to the trouble of investigating the problem, debating alternatives, and then agreeing on this course of action. We should stick to it and see it through. The plan keeps us safe.

But as with any journey into unknown territory, it is impossible to predict everything that might happen. What's more, the formal intervention plan is devised with the information that was available at the time about the patterns that characterize a complex human system. It is likely that some important information was missed (or was withheld) during exploration, and that this information may come to light as the interventionist and client move forward with implementation.

Consider the following situation. In the 1990s my consultancy was part of a consortium that was invited to submit a bid to outsource the desktop technology environment of a large financial services company. My company's role was to assist with the transition from the in-house delivery of services to the outsourcer arrangement, and to help design and write the policies needed to support a congenial and effective relationship between the customer and the information technology vendor that I had partnered with.

Our first step was to design the service offering and present it to the customer in the form of a detailed service proposal. The customer would review our proposal and the proposals submitted by two other bidders, and would then announce the winner of this competitive process.

Our team was led by a sales executive whom I will call Robert. He was a tall, lanky man whose ideas often occurred faster than he could express them, which sometimes produced a seemingly jumbled and iterative conversational style. But Robert was no dummy. He was committed and energetic, and he was determined that our team would submit the winning proposal. I supported him fully, and worked closely with him throughout the sales process.

The proposal was due on a Friday at five p.m., and as that final week began, we were in good shape. The proposal documents were clear and well-organized. Our technical information and our financial plan were laid out in clear provisions, backed up by tables showing support levels and pricing and service comparisons. Everything was looking good.

I will never forget the Thursday afternoon when Robert came into our project war room, shoulders slumped, with a grim expression on his face. He was wearing his inevitable gray suit pants, no jacket in sight, with the shirt tails hanging out, and he was carrying his well-thumbed copy of the customer Request for Proposal (RFP) document. "We're screwed," he said to me.

I told him he was crazy. "This is the best, most well-thought-out proposal that I have ever been involved in. I am doing the final proofread right now, and we can be printing by four p.m. The technical solution is solid, and the pricing is competitive, and our timelines are aggressive and realistic. We have the people right here on the ground. We beat the competition at every step."

"Except one," he said. He showed me a footnote from one of the technical appendices in the RFP. It was a section that I had only glanced at, because it did not concern my company's contribution and had been assigned to one of the technical teams. The footnote said that the customer expected to minimize costs and maximize service speed through the use of remote desktop support. "We missed it. The guys didn't include it. At least one of our competitors is going to go to town on this one feature. When I noticed this about an hour ago, I called Frank [this was the customer bid manager who was our contact during the competitive bid process], and he said that this one is a showstopper. Their vice-president of information technology is drooling over remote access. He expects it to be at the heart of the proposed solutions."

I sat in silence for a few seconds, trying to digest this bad news. Robert spoke first.

"We have to rewrite the proposal."

"You're crazy," I said. "We don't have time."

"We have ..." Robert looked at his watch. "We have almost twenty-seven hours. I am going to give you the service brochures on our remote offering. It is brand new, and the material is crappy, but it is something. And I am going to give you the number for the guy who heads up this area for us. He knows you're going to call him, and if he doesn't answer you are to page him. I will show you the sections where you need to weave this in. I'll work on the technical sections. I'll order a pizza, and then when the place is quiet you and I will rewrite the executive summary. We will need to reread the whole thing tonight, to make sure we have caught everything and that our remote support stands out as the real center of the whole thing. We can start printing and assembly at noon tomorrow."

I argued with Robert. Everything was in such good shape. I was looking forward to getting home at a decent time and finishing the project in a calm and orderly manner. Robert was turning my world upside down and creating a situation in which it became more likely that we would make mistakes and introduce errors into the proposal documents.

Robert heard me out, and then he asked, "Well, you tell me. Should we turn in a gorgeous document that tells the wrong story, or should we turn in an adequate document that tells the right story?"

I had no reply to this. I took out my notepad and listened as Robert repeated his instructions. I called my team together and, after giving them time to complain and remonstrate, I told them that I knew they were up to the challenge and that we could pull this off. Robert and I worked right through the night. I still remember the two of us, in our rumpled clothing that we had been wearing for two days, literally running up to the customer's receiving desk with our two big boxes of proposal documents at 4:55 p.m. on the Friday afternoon.

Our original plan had been rock-solid. It was implemented with passion and determination. We were hours away from delivering an excellent product. But new information came to light that showed our excellent product was the wrong product. Despite the frustration and pain, we had to change course.

This is the critical balancing act of implementation and evaluation. The interventionist must help the implementation team to press ahead with the action plan, and must also be open to revisiting and revising plans when new situations arise or new information comes to light. He must stay the course and change course.

The Process Is the Interventionist's Deliverable

Human beings are capable of moving mountains, and they are also capable of inertia, avoidance, and errors. We are prey to the heuristics discussed in chapter 2, which frequently lead individuals and groups to make poor decisions, or to concoct fatally flawed plans, or to privilege the management of our reputations over honest conversations about setbacks and problems. Argyris reminds us that people in organizational milieus are held tight by the defensive routines that limit learning and organizational performance, and that it takes effort and determination to loosen the hold of these limiting ways of being.[2] Kegan and Lahey have pointed out that people often form strong attachments to competing goals, a tendency that results in self-defeating behaviors that undermine valued improvement objectives.[3] To change an organization, it is often necessary for organizational members to also change themselves. Kahneman, Lovallo, and Sibony have shown that robust analytic and technical procedures are often unable to produce good decisions and results unless they are contained within a process that allows for the detection and management of cognitive biases.[4]

During the implementation and evaluation phase, the change *process* is the interventionist's primary concern.

Some of my colleagues and many of my students like to distinguish between the "what" and the "how" of work carried out to implement an intervention. The word "what" points us to what is to be done: the goals or strategic objectives that are to be achieved. We will implement an employee engagement plan that increases levels of engagement and ultimately improves customer satisfaction ratings. We will implement a new mentoring program that drastically reduces training timelines and costs and improves the satisfaction levels of new hires three months after joining their production team. We will introduce an evidence-based deprescribing guideline into rural primary care practices that results in increased deprescribing conversations with elderly patients on five or more medications during their annual checkup. This is the "what" of implementation.

The word "how" points us to the ways in which system members will act and interact, and the activities that will be carried out to produce the intended result. Rapid action teams will be formed to carry out each element of the action plan; the teams will consult with impacted stakeholders to explain the rationale for the project, finalize plans, and implement agreed-to changes; and the team leaders will meet together once a week to assure overall coordination. This is the "how" of implementation, and it is here where the interventionist's expertise is most needed.

The interventionist's concern is with the change process. You may find it useful to think of the process as a container for the various activities that system members are carrying out to bring about beneficial change. The process contains these activities, along with the emotions that people experience as they encounter new and uncertain situations. The interventionist will work with the client to create a process that offers psychological safety and support while also encouraging system members to experiment with new ideas and behavior. The process will often include actions needed to help system members to set aside old ways of thinking and acting and create new attitudes and ideas, devise and refine new behavioral routines, and create new social structures that will help to sustain the change over time. The process will also include a reflective component (or feedback loop) that allows participants to consider how things are going and to make changes when needed.

Perhaps the most important feature of the change process is that it should promote reflection, learning, and adaptability. People will be experimenting with new ideas and attitudes. They will be trying to think about their work and their colleagues in new ways. They will also be experimenting with new behaviors and with new social structures that will help to shift them away from the old way of being and toward new ways of thinking and acting. Learning takes time, and learners usually make errors when learning new ideas and skills. The interventionist's implementation process must permit errors to occur. People should not be punished or humiliated when they make mistakes. Instead, a process must be created that can help people to acknowledge, accept, and learn from their mistakes, and to make adjustments and keep moving forward.

For some people, transforming a system of thought, behavior, and social structures will be as difficult as learning to play a complicated game like golf or chess. It will take many months, and it will often be discouraging. The people engaged in the change process will make mistakes. To succeed, they will need to experience support and encouragement. They will need to create motivation within themselves. The job of the interventionist is to facilitate a process that helps participants to create these experiences.

When you work with a small system – a work team or a single department within an organization – it can be relatively easy to keep an eye on what is happening and to see with your own eyes the gradual transformation of the system. When working on a large-scale change, however, one that involves numerous people who are located in different cities, and that includes intervention targets at a variety of system levels, the process can span several years, and you may only get intermittent glimpses of the transformational process.

A few years ago, I worked with a group of aphasia researchers from Canada, the United States, Australia, South Africa, and the United Kingdom.[5] Aphasia is a disorder that is sometimes experienced by people who have suffered a stroke. Certain parts of the brain become damaged in ways that make it difficult for aphasia sufferers to communicate through language. Speaking becomes difficult. Conversational fluency can be replaced by a disjointed way of speaking. Sometimes people with aphasia insert incorrect words, or even made-up words, into their sentences. Approximately 2 million Americans are currently living with aphasia, and about 80,000 new cases are diagnosed each year.[6] More than 350,000 people in the United Kingdom, 100,000 Canadians, 80,000 Australians, and 16,000 New Zealanders are believed to be living with aphasia.[7]

Until recently, the most common way of treating aphasia was to offer therapy through a speech-language pathologist (SLP). The treatment involved a limited number of sessions with an SLP that were intended to restore some verbal functioning to the person with the condition. This consisted of work to improve pronunciation and the fluency of speech.

The aphasia researchers whom I worked with felt that these conventional approaches were limiting. They supported the traditional SLP therapies, and also believed that an appropriate goal for the treatment of aphasia would be to help the person with aphasia to participate as fully as possible in all of the activities of life. They conceived of a social approach to aphasia that would look not just at verbal functionality but also at ways to overcome stigma, and ways to become connected to and active with family, friends, and the broader community. Traditional SLP therapy would often be part of this approach, and there would also be efforts to learn new communication techniques and to regain a sense of confidence and well-being and an ability to enjoy life.

When I was first getting to know these researchers, one of them told me that this new approach to aphasia treatment derived in part from a particular experience that many therapists had while working with clients. The therapist would get to know the client and would offer the series of therapeutic sessions that the client's insurer was willing to pay for. Then, at the end of the treatments, while saying goodbye to each other, the person with aphasia would say something like, "Thank you for making me feel like a human being again," or "Thank you for giving me back my self-respect." Interestingly, these heartfelt expressions of gratitude would be made even when the treatments had little effect on restoring the person's ability to communicate verbally. From the client's perspective, the success of the therapy often had more to do with the relationship that had been formed with the therapist, and with a general sense of confidence and well-being, than with a restored ability to correctly pronounce certain words.

These researchers, most of whom were also SLPs who worked with clients with aphasia, were determined to change the world of aphasia care. In the status quo, insurers would pay only for a certain number of traditional speech therapy sessions. They would not pay for any other form of therapy that might allow the person with aphasia to recapture some joy and connectedness in life. Many physicians and therapists who worked with stroke victims also believed that their remit was restricted to the health condition, consisting of a conglomeration of physical symptoms, and their work focused exclusively on the treatment of these physical symptoms.

The aphasia researchers who approached me wanted to create a situation in which researchers, scientists, and policy makers would think more about the human being who was living with aphasia, what this person's life was like, and about how innovative treatments could be devised and offered to improve this person's quality of life. They wanted insurers to realize that treatment should include ways of helping people to resume their participation in all that life has to offer. They wanted researchers to start investigating approaches that would promote a greater quality of life for people with aphasia. They wanted health policy makers to take a person-centered view of aphasia, and to provide funding to train health care providers in new techniques for communicating with and caring for people with aphasia.

Because they were research scientists as well as practitioners, and because they wanted to influence other scientists, senior practitioners, and policy makers, they believed that it was essential to assemble and use scientific evidence (and, to a lesser extent, evidence derived from expert practitioners) that supported the importance and usefulness of social approaches to the treatment of aphasia. This was likely to be challenging. The researchers and practitioners who supported the status quo tended to value quantitative research, especially the so-called gold standard, which consists of research conducted through experimental designs and randomized control trials (RCTs).

However, the aphasia researchers who favored the social approach to treatment were unaware of any published RCTs that would help them to make their case, and they were also unsure of whether it would be feasible to carry out an RCT that would show the value of a social approach. The improvement that would support the usefulness of a social approach was not an improvement in functionality that could be quantified and measured. Instead, it was more of an attitude toward life and an appreciation of an ability to participate in certain valued activities. The supporting evidence so far tended to consist of qualitative data that included interviews and focus groups with people with aphasia and their families in which they described their positive attitudes toward the social treatments they had experienced. Some scientists would tend to dismiss this. A person's attitude does not necessarily correspond to a reality in the objective world.

Our initial intervention design included several components and activities and was intended to begin the process of influencing the attitudes and priorities of researchers and clinicians who worked with people with aphasia. My role was to design, coordinate, and facilitate the process. I began by working with three aphasia researchers to create and distribute a package of pre-reading materials for the fifteen participants. There was then an open email exchange among participants in which they discussed the strengths and weaknesses of the materials included in the pre-reading package. Then participants gathered in Toronto for a two-day facilitated session where they discussed the current situation, identified key areas requiring attention and approaches for filling the evidence gaps, and created a plan for collaborative action in the ensuing months. At the end of the two-day session, they also participated in a conference in which SLPs and others interested in aphasia treatment gathered for professional development sessions and a facilitated Conversation Café process to continue the discussion of how things could be improved. After the in-person meetings, I helped the participants to create a report that served as a call to action for those who support the growing movement to endorse social approaches to treating aphasia.

The think tank session included a presentation by a health economist to help participants understand the values of the people (especially senior policy makers) whom they were hoping to influence, and a presentation by someone with expertise in knowledge translation to help them understand the processes through which new health innovations gradually make their way into policy and practice. They engaged in numerous discussions that resulted in agreement on six goals that could help them to bring about the changes that they desired, and action plans for achieving the goals.

The action plans included work assignments and deadlines for the participants.

Think tank participants continued to work together for about four years. They exchanged emails, they lobbied influential people and organizations, and they held private and public meetings at conferences in different parts of the United States. I continued to support their efforts, acting as a designer and facilitator whose role was to help them to form new or better relationships within and across professional communities, and to help them to help others to reframe the way they thought about the treatment of people living with aphasia. The initial goal was to change mindsets. Think tank participants believed that when this goal was accomplished it would become possible to change behavior and to begin to change social structures – for example, to change the coverage rules in health insurance policies.

One unique aspect of this case is that it was an intervention nested within an intervention.

Think tank participants were intervening in the world of aphasia research and treatment. They wanted to alter existing mindsets and to change behavior and supporting structures. They wanted to help people to see that the most useful way to think about supporting people with aphasia was to think about helping these people to participate fully (or as fully as possible) in all that life has to offer. Treatment was not just about overcoming the physical constraints of aphasia. It was also about overcoming the social constraints and helping people to live full and meaningful lives.

My role was in part to act as an intervention coach, helping think tank participants to design and implement an intervention process. However, in addition to this I was also often in the stance of an interventionist. My client system included think tank participants and those with whom they interacted and whom they sought to influence over the four years when we worked together. My primary task was to ensure that we all worked with each other, and that the think tank participants did not fall into the stance of *doing things to* those whom they sought to influence.

I was engaged in my balancing act, judging when to assert my own views and when to inquire into the views of others, and I encouraged think tank participants to do the same. Think tank participants recognized this issue as we worked together, and as we prepared for a conference session planned for the third year of the process, they considered how best to manage it. Here is an excerpt from the journal that I kept during the project:

> One significant reservation that was expressed by attendees at the November meeting was that the conference session, if one was held, must not simply involve the social approach people trying to win the other side over, or trying to persuade the impairment people that the social approach is better in some way. The worry stemmed in part from a recent conference in Europe, which was intended to foster collaboration across paradigms, but which only heightened the divide. It also stemmed from a concern that perhaps some TT participants were more interested in winning "buy-in" (a phrase that was used occasionally) from the impairment proponents, rather than engaging in a process of mutual inquiry and true collaboration.

In the end, we agreed that we would be transparent about our intentions. The invitation that went out to potential participants included these words: "This meeting is an outgrowth of a 'think tank' that was held in Toronto in 2007 where attendees identified gaps in aphasia research relative to measuring treatment outcomes. The meeting objective is to contribute to a process to close this gap. It is hoped that the long-term result will be greater collaboration among researchers interested in impairment and/or participation outcomes." That was, indeed, the intention of the think tank participants, and they accepted the likelihood that an inquiry process would produce results that they could not entirely anticipate. It was likely that the impairment proponents would have their own ideas and aspirations, and that these would need to be considered and included if a collaboration was to emerge.

Even in the language that was used one can see the gap that existed between the two camps. My think tank participants thought of the other side as the "impairment proponents," unintentionally implying by this wording that they were advocates or proponents for impairment. But of course this is not how the "impairment proponents" thought of themselves at all. They were pragmatic scientists and therapists who focused on the physical symptoms of the condition because here they were dealing with something concrete and measurable. The notion of participating fully in life was highly subjective and resisted measurement except through unreliable methods such as self-reports.

Nonetheless, these traditionalists felt compassion toward people who lived with aphasia, and wanted to help. We anticipated that thirty people would attend the conference session. Instead, sixty people showed up. One think tank participant started things off with a plenary address that focused on an aphasia treatment model that could encompass the treatment of physical conditions as well as approaches to encourage a full participation in life.[8] This was followed by an Open Space discussion that allowed people to suggest small-group discussion topics, after which six groups were formed and discussions took place.[9] Initially there was some apparent disengagement by a few people, but soon all participants were engaged in the discussions. At the end of the session, two tables stayed together for another fifteen minutes, continuing their discussions – and most participants remained in the room, clustering together to talk. The session closed with a full plenary discussion which led to a general acknowledgment that an all-encompassing treatment model was useful but that it would take some time for people to become comfortable with the new model and to test its accuracy and efficacy. After we closed the session, several participants approached me to say that this work represented a good start on a more inclusive and collaborative approach to aphasia-related research and practice.

The aphasia think tank process was a long-term, complex intervention. Think tank participants wanted me to help them to remain in an appropriate collaborative stance as they attempted to mobilize interest in new approaches to aphasia care. They wanted to create a coalition of people associated with both the new and traditional approaches to care who would then begin to influence the attitudes of leaders in aphasia care and research around the world. They wanted to influence individuals, care teams, research teams, health delivery organizations (from family practices to hospitals), health insurers, and health systems.

Precise outcomes could not be predicted in advance. My role was to design and influence *how* they would go about pursuing improvements. My deliverable was the process that they used to work with each other and with a growing coalition of stakeholders over the four years that we spent together. Although I also helped to design events and to produce documents such as agendas, session minutes, and reports, my primary responsibility was to create and implement a process that would help the group to keep building their coalition and exerting influence.

During the implementation and evaluation phase, the interventionist manages the container – the process.

Create a Reflective, Adaptive Process

The most important advice that I can offer about effective implementation processes is this: whatever model or method you use, make sure that it allows participants to gather data about what is happening as implementation moves forward, to reflect together on the meaning of the data, to conduct the appropriate analysis of the data, to revise implementation plans and approaches when needed, and to keep moving forward.

Implementation thus resembles a process of learning through experience. It is a process of trial and error, in which errors are expected and are not the occasion for punishment and humiliation. We try something. If it fails to produce the desired result, we look at what happened, we reconsider our assumptions, we formulate new hypotheses, we design new experiments, and we keep going.

Human beings learn their way through periods of social change. Years ago, the great Canadian communications scholar Marshal McLuhan speculated that one day we would all "learn a living."[10] Throughout the 1990s, when the speed of technological innovation increased and rapid change became the norm in almost all organizational contexts, the truth of McLuhan's prophesy became apparent. To remain effective in a world where individual people, organizations, markets, and societies are changing in fast, unpredictable ways, rapid learning and adaptability become necessary core competencies.

The practical implications of this are that processes to implement change must include a reflective component. That is why I have focused this chapter on implementation and evaluation. The two are bound up together. As we implement our proposed changes, we evaluate our own process and the results that we are encountering. Are things proceeding as expected, or are we producing unanticipated and unwelcome reactions? Is our theory of action – our theory that certain actions will produce predictable results – being proven incorrect? What assumptions and theories do we need to reconsider? How might we revise our plan in order to keep moving toward the outcomes that we desire?

Implementation thus can resemble the "plan, do, study, act" (PDSA) cycle that is favored by many who work in the area of quality assurance and continuous improvement.[11] This approach involves a cycle consisting of four stages. The "plan" stage involves identifying a target for the change effort and agreeing on steps to bring about the change. The "do" stage involves taking action to carry out the steps. The "study" stage involves examining what happened when the actions were taken, and the "act" stage sees the participants making revisions to the approach that then feeds into a new iteration of the cycle. Most practitioners believe that the PDSA should be used on a small and contained scale and the cycle should be used iteratively to move forward with an intervention in a complex social environment. The limited scale may encourage participants to experiment with new approaches, and it facilitates the gathering of data to inform learning.

Many of the structured change methods that have been devised over the years – for example, Search Conference, Appreciative Inquiry, Deliberative Dialogue, Future Search, and Preferred Futuring – include components that call for participants to reflect together on what they are experiencing in their organization.[12] If you are new to the field of human systems intervention, you may find it helpful to rely on "recipes" such as these when you first launch your practice.[13] Over time, as you experience more client situations and you continue to read reports of social science research in planned change and experiential reports by expert practitioners, you will gain the confidence needed to develop unique designs that are tailored solely to the needs and capacity of your client.

Over the past twenty-five years I have worked with colleagues, clients, and students to devise and test reflective processes for bringing about change. I have drawn on the PDSA model, and also on structured change processes described by Beer and Eisenstat,[14] by

Chris Argyris,[15] and by Michael Patton.[16] Because I design processes that are tailored to the needs and capacity of individual clients, I cannot present a single model here as the one preferred approach that I recommend. Instead, I offer the following eight principles for you to consider when you work with a client to implement an intervention and bring about change.

1. Do not get drawn into the task. Stay with the process.

The implementation and evaluation phase is a time when work is carried out and when progress is measured in relation to deadlines and deliverables. If you are like me, your need to act with integrity may push you try to make sure that tasks are accomplished and outcomes are achieved. What's more, members of your client system may ask you to pitch in and become directly involved in some of the implementation efforts.

Be careful about this. Remember that you are *not* responsible for implementing changes to resolve the problematic situation. You are responsible for assuring the integrity of the process that facilitates change. If you find yourself accepting responsibility for tasks that properly belong with system members, you may be colluding with the existing patterns that hold this system in place.

2. Be real about what is happening.

Do not hide or shy away from problems and mistakes. If unanticipated obstacles arise, or if some people become discouraged, do not pretend that you did not notice. Sharing what you have noticed and are confused about is one of the key interventions that you will make during the implementation process. This type of intervention takes the following form.[17] First, you state what you observed and ask for confirmation. For example:

"Earlier you all agreed that for these changes to succeed you have to accept the fact that each of you depends on the others, and that each work unit depends on work accomplished by other work units. You are interdependent. But just now, when you were describing the norms that you will need to create if you are to succeed in the future, several of you said that one important norm is that each individual should have the freedom to operate in a way that is unencumbered by others. Have I got that right?"

Then share the inference you have drawn from your observation, and ask what others think:

"You recognize the need for interdependence and more collaboration within and across the units. But some of you don't want others to interfere with your work or with your decisions. This strikes me as a contradiction. Does anybody else see it that way? Or am I misunderstanding something?"

Finally, if most people affirm your observation and your inference, ask what needs to be done:

"It sounds like everybody does support the need for interdependence and collaboration, but people have different views about what this means. How do you want to sort this out?"

When you notice a contradiction between what people say they value or they intend to do and what they are actually doing, consider pointing this out and asking some questions. If you notice something disrupting the implementation process, ask about it. The intervention can be as simple as a four-word interrogative sentence: *What is going on?*

3. Access craft knowledge from throughout the system.

I like the distinctions drawn by Patricia Pitcher in her theory of leadership.[18] She says that some leaders are technocrats who have mastered certain technologies (theories and methods) and who believe that leadership involves bringing these technical innovations to the work of a group. Other leaders are visionaries who can see a future that has yet to be achieved, and who encourage followers to strive for lofty goals. Still other leaders, however, are steeped in the craft that is practiced by the organization, and understand how the work has evolved and become entwined with the people who inhabit the organization. This craft knowledge derives from the tacit knowing that underlies the expertise of skilled practitioners. The interventions being implemented must somehow fit into the existing ways of knowing and acting, must inform them and possibly transform them, without disrupting things so thoroughly that the system is destroyed. People who know the ropes must be part of the conversation, and their misgivings must be taken seriously.

Interventions tend to be more successful when you do things with people rather than to people. This does not mean that you should get "buy-in" or "input." These can be insulting terms. When you seek buy-in or input, you are putting a tick-mark on a checklist of things that you have been told that you are supposed to do. You already have everything figured out (or so you think), and now you want to manipulate and persuade people so they will cooperate with you.

Doing things *with* people means being genuinely, authentically open to the ideas and contributions of others. It is a stance that recognizes that people in workplaces and communities have created ways of being that are at least in some fashion productive and coherent and that allow them to survive and carry on. They have created ways of thinking, acting, and structuring that create and sustain something of value for them. You do things with people to demonstrate that you respect the valuing that lies within their current patterns, that you want to understand their worlds, and that you want to work with them to seek beneficial improvements.

While the idea of working collaboratively and inclusively with others may appeal to our liberal and democratic values, there is also a hard-nosed reason for taking this approach. Planned change requires that we access all available and relevant knowledge about the human system that needs to change, and that we use this knowledge to design an intervention process that corresponds to the affordances and constraints that characterize this social reality. This knowledge does not reside solely in the heads of a few organizational leaders, or on the pages of a strategic plan, or in the minds of a handful of senior professionals. It is embodied in the skilled practitioners who are doing the work of the organization at all levels and in all locations. I advocate a democratic and participative approach to change not just because it appeals to my sense of fairness. I advocate a participative approach because it is the most effective way of ensuring that change moves forward and produces useful and sustainable results.

Your process must be as inclusive and participative as possible. Not all system members will join the coalition that supports the change. The recalcitrant members should be listened to and treated fairly, and they should be told the consequences of their refusal to cooperate. If they are treated fairly, there is a good chance that many will prove themselves to be among the "late majority" or the "laggards" identified by Everett Rogers, and they will start to cooperate once the success of the change efforts becomes apparent.[19] A few may be unable to adapt to the new patterns that have been created, and they may choose to exit from the system.

A participative approach usually takes more time than a top-down approach. More meetings and discussions will be needed, and plans may need to be revised several times as new perspectives and ideas are added to the mix. This additional time is often needed to assure success.

4. Use the self as an instrument of change.

Throughout this book I have argued that an intervention into a human system is a balancing act. The interventionist balances the formal intervention plan that is intended to produce desirable changes with emergent planning that evolves over time as the intervener learns more about the functioning of the human system. An intervention is thus a search for a desired outcome rather than the imposition of a predetermined outcome.

An intervention into a human system is made up of numerous actions that are intended to produce specific results. These actions are taken by the interventionist and are often intended to encourage system members to pause, to notice, and then to reflect together on the meaning of what they are doing. When the interventionist implements an intervention with an action, usually the action involves saying something. The interventionist interrupts the pattern that is unfolding among system members by making a statement that draws attention to the pattern. The interventionist is using herself as an instrument to bring about a change in the patterns of the client system.

The use of self as an instrument of change should be understood in two ways. First, I use myself as an instrument to measure (or notice) what is occurring in the group. I do this by paying attention to what is going on, by remembering the discoveries that were made during the exploration phase and the feedback and decision phase, and by considering whether the problematic situation is manifesting itself in the room where system members have gathered. I also do this by noticing my own reactions to what is occurring in the group. Am I experiencing certain emotions? Am I engaged, or is my attention wandering? Do others seem to be having similar reactions? What might these reactions tell us about the way in which the group is working together? Are these reactions part of the patterns that produce the problematic situation and, if they are, should I bring this to the attention of system members?

The second way that I use myself as an instrument of change is by designing and implementing actions to interrupt the pattern that is occurring at this moment, and to draw attention to the pattern so its meaning and importance can be considered. My intervention consists of my own behavior, usually verbal behavior.

Intervening in a human system is essentially interpersonal. It is a contact sport. You yourself are the primary tool that you use to help the client to bring about change.

5. Be straight with people.

Since your interventions will usually take the form of communication acts, and since much of your work will focus on helping people to act in ways that are consistent with their intentions, it is important that you model this behavior by speaking in ways that are direct and straightforward.

When you want to find something out, ask a question. When you disagree with something that was just said, say that you disagree, and explain why. When you have an alternative perspective to share, share it.

I say this because I have noticed that people often communicate in indirect and tricky ways. In the example shown in table 7.1, Ken disagrees with Beth's opinion on a subject. Instead of saying in a direct and straightforward manner that he disagrees, Ken instead asks an indirect question.

Table 7.1. Saying one thing and thinking another

Speaker	What they say	What they think
Beth:	Okay, so the suggestion is that Laurie is going to take notes during the session. Noah and I will facilitate. And then Ken will keep track of what is happening in the room and will let us know if an intervention is needed. Is everyone okay with this?	*We need to be clear on our roles or we could create confusion and annoy the client.*
Ken:	Yeah ... So, are you planning to do one of your theory lectures at the start of the session? We just need to be careful about the time.	*Beth loves the sound of her own voice. Here she is with a bunch of role assignments that marginalize me and put her at center stage. I can just see her dominating things with her favorite theories and not leaving enough time for discussion.*
Beth:	Well, we had talked about giving them some information on how to handle disagreements in a productive manner. I could whip something up on conflict management if you guys think it would be useful.	*What's Ken getting at? Was that a dig? Or does he think that the client needs some theory? I'd better be careful how I reply.*
Ken:	Yeah, maybe. As long as it doesn't take too long.	*Oh God. Here we go. She's probably going to show them about forty slides on conflict management before we even start to look at their data. This will take all morning and will bore them to tears.*

Teams and groups that have developed dysfunctional patterns often engage in this sort of indirect communication. People say one thing when they mean something else. Instead of making a clear assertion that presents an alternative point of view, people ask sneaky questions or make passive-aggressive comments. This in turn provokes more caution and fancy verbal footwork, and pretty soon you have a conversation that conceals more than it reveals about what is going on in the room.

You, the interventionist, must not contribute to this. You must communicate in a direct and straightforward manner with your clients.

6. Remember you are working *with* people.

Through my work as an interventionist over a career that now spans more than thirty years, I have learned that a project's goals are intimately related to the process of working to achieve those goals, and that a focus on the nuts and bolts of an organization's design must not obscure the fact that when you are working in and for an organization you are always working with people. Everybody is having their own unique and contextual experience of the change process. While the interventionist may be excited at the prospect of meeting a tight deadline, members of the client system may be worried about failure, frustrated by not being listened to, angry that a valued colleague has been transferred, or hurt because a favorite idea was ignored.

During implementation it can be easy to think only of what your client is trying to accomplish – changing norms, altering workflows, revising incentive systems, and so on. Sometimes we forget that a human system is brought to life by the people who inhabit it. This means that the implementation process will almost certainly be characterized by the emotions and conflicts that are present wherever people gather. You are not working with machines or robots; you are working with people. Some of these people may be having important and difficult experiences as the process unfolds, and you may be unaware of what they are going through. Be human, and recognize the humanity of others. Notice what is happening. If someone becomes silent in a meeting, if one person repeatedly interrupts another person, if you see people rolling their eyes – pay attention. Give opportunities to people to participate in the process.

Open doors, but do not push people through. Support, but do not take sides. Part of your work is to try to help members of the client system to remain engaged in the process. You are not a therapist (though some people may find it helpful or affirming to talk to you), but you do have responsibilities. Things can be messy and uncomfortable. Your job is to remain observant and to help people through the difficulties that often arise.

Check in with the groups that you work with. Ask them, "How do you feel about what we accomplished today? Can we make things better? Does anybody have any worries they would like to put on the table?"

Check in with individuals. If you noticed someone being unusually quiet, ask about it: "I don't think you said more than one or two things at the meeting today. Your contributions are usually so important for helping the group to move forward. Is anything wrong?" If you saw someone rolling their eyes, ask about it: "You seemed frustrated when Kelly went over the budget justification at the progress meeting this morning. Is there something that you are concerned about?"

It is appropriate for the interventionist to create opportunities for system members to confront the dysfunctional elements of their patterns. However, I often find myself recalling the old adage: *You can lead a horse to water but you cannot make him drink.* Sometimes system members do not wish to publicly discuss a troubling issue or concern. Sometimes the system's power dynamics may make an open discussion of a difficult issue unsafe for members. Because of this, the interventionist can point out doorways that might lead to change, but should not push anybody through the doorway. If system members hesitate or retreat, this is not necessarily a reflection of the interventionist's skill.

Take action to make visible that which is invisible. Keep the conversation moving along productive lines. Your finger is constantly taking the pulse of this human system, so you can judge whether affordances are opening up pathways toward the client's goals or constraints are closing in.

7. Be vigilant about collusion.

Although it is important that the interventionist employ her empathy to remain aware of what is going on with the individuals who make up the client system, it is also important to maintain the boundary between interventionist and client.

Several years ago, a colleague and I were consulting with a large hospital system that was experiencing some dysfunctional and distressing patterns, including bullying and harassment. My colleague spent considerable time with the different clinical and administrative work units, and on one occasion was told about the approach of a unit director to bringing new people into the unit. If the new hire was not able to adapt to the unit's culture and routines within a few weeks, then the director would summon the person into her office. She would have a brief, blunt conversation with the new hire, ending with the words "Fit in or f*** off."

That crude statement represents the cold and relentless logic that underlies a human system. The system demands that you fit into the existing patterns of thought, action, and structuring or you will be expelled. You must accept many of the existing assumptions and ideas that inform behavior. You must fit into the existing patterns of task and social behavior that bring the system to life. And you must conform to most of the structural pressures that hold the system in place. You must find a role that conforms to the prevailing reality of the place.

Interventionists also feel this pressure. We are pressured to take sides in existing disputes. We are encouraged to accept existing assumptions about how life works in this organization. We are told that the organization's structural elements are necessary and non-negotiable. The system wants us to fit in or f*** off.

But an interventionist must resist this pressure. An interventionist stands on the boundary that separates the human system from its environment and observes the patterns that allow this group to create integrity – in the sense of wholeness, soundness, resilience.

Do not take sides. Allow yourself to feel compassion for members of the client system, but do not allow this compassion to slide into uncritical sympathy. Use the techniques described in chapter 5 (in the discussion of the participant observer) to maintain your professional distance from the system that has asked for your help.

8. Phase yourself out.

If the client is able to resolve or ameliorate the problematic situation that you are helping them with, and if you have been able to remain effective by staying in a participant-observer stance, it is likely that you will begin to feel redundant as the implementation and evaluation phase moves forward. Your role diminishes over time. At a project update meeting you may think to yourself, "There is nothing useful that I can contribute to this conversation. They are doing fine without me."

This often means that the process is working well. Your goal has been to help the client system to stretch its affordances and to push back its constraints so it can tackle the problematic situation. Although you focused attention on the specific issues that the client described to you, your approach has been to help the client to create new and expanded problem-solving and learning capacity. This capacity becomes part of the client system. At some point in the process, they may very well no longer need your help.

If early in the implementation process the client says that they no longer need you, and if you are skeptical that they have been able to create new capacity in so short a time, you may wish to consider whether you are encountering client resistance. Sometimes this simply means that some system members are starting to feel threatened by the likely consequences that will be produced by the change process. When this happens, I pay close attention to what is happening in the room. If I notice behaviors that are consistent with patterns identified during the exploration and sensemaking activities, I will make an emergent intervention to draw those patterns to the attention of participants. Then I will ask if they are certain that they have solved all of their problems. Usually, they will acknowledge that more work needs to be done, and we will continue to work together on implementation. Sometimes they continue to insist that my work is complete. I take this to indicate that the client's existing capacity is insufficient to continue with this work, and I thank them for allowing me to work with them, and I exit from the system.

Some consultants like to encourage dependency in clients. When I first began my consulting business, I read several articles about how to create and maintain a successful consulting practice, and I often encountered advice to the effect that a good consultant makes clients dependent on his expertise. About five years before writing this chapter, a colleague and I were consulting to a large government organization, and we encountered another organization development (OD) consultant who was also working with this client on a different contract. In an unsubtle manner, this consultant warned us to not mess up her effort to sell a large system-change intervention to the client. She had been working on this sale for many months, she told us, and we had better not say anything that could undermine her. I understand this consultant's desire to win contracts and to maintain a steady income. We all have bills to pay. However, I have no sympathy with efforts to sell organizations or people things that they do not need, and I question the ethics of an OD consultant who acts in ways that could threaten a client's ability to act independently and effectively.

What's more, I have found that encouraging client resilience and capacity does not mean that the client will not want to work with me again in the future. My practice has been to try to be real with clients, to do what I said I would do, to be flexible when situations change or new information becomes available, to finish things, and to be courteous. I create processes that allow members of the client system to practice new behaviors and develop new skills, so they will have more capacity when I exit from the system.

My experience has been that clients like this. They enjoy working with a consultant who is cheerful and professional; they like to learn new ways of thinking and acting; and they appreciate being left with a sense of being bigger than when the project began.

Almost all of my consulting work has come from either repeat business or referrals. When I phase myself out, it seems that I am also creating the conditions needed to secure the next piece of business from the network of contacts that this client belongs to.

Transformational Change Takes Time

Regardless of the size of the group that you are working with, transformational change takes time. People need time to set aside cherished assumptions and beliefs, and to develop new ways of seeing and thinking about their worlds. They need time to abandon old habits and to develop new skills and behavioral routines. They also need time to reconsider existing social structures and to design, test, and implement new structures that can support the new ideas and behaviors that they are putting in place.

When I first became interested in organizational transformation, I recall being told by people who claimed to have expertise in culture change that it usually takes about three years to change an organization's culture. I have been able to find no reliable and verifiable predictions of the length of time needed for transformational change in the management or social science literature. Anecdotal accounts on the internet often continue to suggest that it can take around three years to create a fundamentally new culture in an organization.

We should be cautious about attributing too much weight to these personal predictions. Nonetheless, it seems to me that one might posit two propositions that could provide interim guidance until empirical research on this subject yields reliable and replicable findings.

Proposition One: Transformational change involving changes to the way a group of people think, act, and structure their activities will require a substantial investment in time. We are talking months, not days. Sometimes we may be talking years, not months.

Proposition Two: It will usually be the case that the transformation of a relatively small, intact group or team could take less time than the transformation of a large and complex organization.

I am writing this book primarily for those who intend to act as interventionists. I anticipate that my readers will help clients to design processes of planned change and will then help clients to implement those plans. When considering the length of time needed to help a client to change its existing patterns, I want to make two points.

First, make sure that your project plan includes sufficient time for the client system's core team to experience the change process. This means that a contract that focuses on changing an intransigent problematic situation will generally require about six months from start to finish.

Second, interventionists might find that they have a healthy perspective on their own work and contribution if they think of their efforts as falling into broader, longer-lasting change processes. My contribution will occur over a period of six months, but it is likely that the client system will continue to work on the change process for a much longer period. Even if during my participation we make only modest progress toward identifying and solving problems and creating new capacity, it is possible that my efforts will contribute to the creation of new insights and resolve among some influential system members, and these contributions may bear fruit only months after I leave the system.

My advice to the new interventionist is this. Do not be discouraged. Keep learning. Keep climbing down out of the stands and putting yourself in the action on the playing field. Chances are you are making a bigger contribution than you realize.

Ensuring That Positive Changes Are Sustained

Some books and articles on organizational change conclude with a discussion on how to embed the changes in the organization's culture or on how to ensure that positive changes are sustained over time.

There is, however, a contradiction here. We are concerned with creating a greater capacity in a client organization. We want the organization to become more effective and agile in responding to intractable challenges. This implies fluidity, an ability to challenge the organization's existing attitudes and norms and standard ways of thinking. It almost sounds as though some scholars and expert practitioners of organizational change want us to conclude the change process by laying the groundwork for the next set of problems. We create a new stasis that will end up needing to be broken apart as new challenges emerge.

I want to suggest an alternative way of thinking about the ultimate goal of organizational change. Remember that the *balancing acts* approach is concerned with intractable problems and adaptive challenges. In a world characterized by seemingly endless technological upheaval, by global competition, and by the mass movement of peoples with their diverse cultures and ways of seeing the world into organizations in the United States, Canada, and elsewhere, it is reasonable to suggest that for the next several decades we can anticipate that our organizations will continue to face numerous unexpected adaptive challenges and will thus need an ever-present capacity to take on these challenges and thrive. Our goal is not to create a new status quo, a new stability that is impervious to a turbulent world. Our goal is to create organizations that are capable of maintaining some modicum of balance while coping with high levels of uncertainty.

I offer four suggestions.

First, *organizational change is granular, not monolithic.* We set off down the path toward the broad goal of our change initiative. However, as we gather information from people at different levels and in different divisions of the organization, we realize that this broad goal will need to be operationalized in many different ways among different groups and units. We speak as though we have one broad goal, but we come to realize that in fact there are fifty smaller goals that must be achieved. Following the processes described in this book, we may form fifty small project teams that work on a wide variety of local changes. Some teams experience progress while other teams become stalled. We help the teams to monitor their work; we see how things are going; we share ideas, perspectives, data, and insights. We regroup, revise, and try again. We create a vast process for learning and change throughout the organization, and we experience both successes and setbacks. Organizational change is not one big thing. It is many things – or, rather, it consists of many actions undertaken by many people, and it produces many results, some positive, some neutral, and some negative.

Second, *organizational change is complex, not binary.* Much discussion of change asserts that change results in success or failure.

There is a literature, highly contested, on this subject, and it tends to assert that change projects succeed or fail.[20] But if change really consists of numerous projects, numerous actions undertaken by many people, then the likelihood is that actions will succeed or fail to varying degrees and will also produce unexpected consequences, some of which will be positive and others negative. Assessing the success or failure of a change initiative can thus be enormously difficult. And expecting categorical success may be unrealistic.

Third, *the interventionist's goal is a verb, not a noun.* The interventionist is not trying to create a "thing." As I have said before in this book, the interventionist is concerned with "the how" and thus works to create and facilitate a process, a set of actions that unfold over time. Earlier in this chapter I described this by saying that the interventionist's deliverable is the *process.*

Fourth and finally, *by creating and facilitating an effective change process,* one that becomes spread throughout the organization in numerous undertakings carried out by many people in ways that could contribute positively to the goal of the change initiative, *the interventionist helps the client to develop a resilient and adaptive way of thinking.* That is, the interventionist helps to create a transformative mindset within the organization.[21] In a change process with a high level of stakeholder involvement, this mindset may be shared by many organizational members and may produce a new pattern of thought within the organization. Numerous organizational members are aware that their perspective on organizational phenomena is merely one way of seeing things, and that others may have equally legitimate and interesting perspectives on the same phenomena. They will know that to move forward when facing vexing situations, it is important to engage in a process of perspective sharing and to do so with an open mind. They will be curious about how their behavior impacts others, and they will be willing to speak up in a direct manner about how organizational situations and members are occurring for them.

The client wants to address a specific concern. The interventionist wants to help the client to address this concern and also to enhance its capacity to address all concerns. The interventionist wants to help the client to become better, stronger, smarter, and more resilient.

The deliverable is the process; numerous people are involved, and the process reflects (or contains) the end-state that is desired. We may not need to embed "change" in the culture. Through their participation in the project, organizational members have become that which they desire.

Evaluating the Process

This fourth phase of the intervention process is known as implementation and evaluation, and I will conclude the chapter by considering how the interventionist might evaluate the intervention.

For many people, the term "evaluation" implies performing measurements and then rendering judgment on the success of an endeavor. We evaluate the learning of students by administering examinations and assignments. We evaluate the performance of employees through a variety of systems that focus on the results produced by employees as they carry out their assigned duties. We evaluate the performance of a portfolio of investments by seeing whether they have increased or decreased in value and comparing this to the average performance of the relevant markets.

When it comes to interventions into human systems, many people want to know whether the intervention produced the desired results. Establishing the necessary chain of causation to demonstrate an intervention's success can be surprisingly difficult.[22] For many organizational leaders, an intervention is intended to bring about some change in the results produced by the work that takes place within the organization. An intervention may be intended to reduce costs associated with hiring and training new employees, or to reduce the operational costs of a customer call center, or to improve worker productivity in ways that increase a unit's profitability or improve the health and quality of life of residents in long-term care, and so on. This means that the intervention will need to be "received" by people who can influence the desired results. They will need to understand what is expected of them. They may need to alter the ways in which they think about their social world (by altering their existing attitudes, assumptions, mental models, etc.) and the ways in which they act while performing their work. They may also need to change the quality of their existing relationships with colleagues, subordinates, superiors, and other stakeholders, and also form new relationships. They may need to alter existing behavioral norms, and also understand and accept changes to explicit social structures such as policies. These changes must in turn produce the immediate effects envisaged by the intervention designers, which could include a reduction in the time it takes to train a new employee, or faster processing averages for units of work, or fewer errors detected through quality assurance programs, or a reduction in the rate of employee turnover on the production floor, and so on. And these changes must then produce the intended intermediate effects, which could include factors such as higher levels of employee engagement or more robust decision processes or progress achieved on the implementation of some strategic objectives. These changes in turn must then produce the final intended effects, which could include higher revenues, higher profits, reduced costs, improved health and quality of life, greater sales volumes, and so on.

Following this trail of causation is difficult. There are numerous points on the chain where confounding factors could arise, muddling the process and diminishing the expected results – even if the intervention process was implemented with skill and precision, and even if the initial effects were produced as intended.

My preference is to approach the evaluation of interventions in a developmental manner. This means first of all recognizing that each intervention represents a unique interaction between an intervention process and a target social context.[23] It is not so much that the intervention impacts upon and causes changes in the target social context. Rather, the intervention and the target social context come into contact with each other and interact with each other, producing unique effects that are attributable to the unique circumstances of this interaction.

Instead of using evaluation to measure the effect of the intervention, developmental evaluation is used to assure that an intervention has the desired effect.[24] Evaluation is used to adapt and develop the intervention as more is learned about the context and the surrounding environment.

Earlier I emphasized the importance of including a reflective component in the implementation process. This reflective component can be used to provide a home (as it were) to your developmental evaluation. Members of your client system may prefer to conduct this evaluation in an informal manner, with participants merely providing their observations on how things are going and then discussing how the intervention process might be improved. Some, however, might want to see the evaluation carried out in a more rigorous manner, with data gathered from intervention participants, organized and analyzed by the interventionist and possibly others, and then fed back to those who are participating in the intervention so they can make sense of the findings and consider how the intervention should be changed in order to ensure that it will achieve its desired effects.

At the conclusion of the intervention process, it can be helpful and informative to conduct a final evaluation of the overall intervention.

This sort of activity has been referred to as a project post-mortem or (borrowing a term from the military) an after-action review. The point of this final evaluative activity is to make explicit the most useful lessons that can be learned from the experience of this intervention. One way to structure this inquiry is to devise some questions that focus on what happened, how people experienced the process, what can explain the way that things turned out, and how things might have gone better. A group of people who participated in the process are gathered in a meeting room, and a facilitator (often the interventionist) leads them through the questions. Somebody is tasked with making detailed notes on the conversation, and key points are recorded on a white board or flip charts. At the end of the meeting, the key points are summarized, and people are asked if they agree. Then a list of "lessons learned" is created.

Summary

The purpose of the implementation and evaluation phase is to make changes to the current pattern of thinking, acting, and structuring in ways that resolve the problematic situation. The interventionist is concerned with *how* the changes are implemented more than with *what* is being implemented.

The interventionist's concern is thus with the change process. The process acts as a container for implementation activities and for the emotions that people experience as they encounter new and uncertain situations.

The process will include a reflective component (or feedback loop) that promotes learning and adaptability. People will be experimenting with new ideas, behaviors, and social structures that will help to shift them away from the old way of being and toward new ways of thinking and acting. Learning takes time, and learners usually make some errors. People should not be punished or humiliated when they make mistakes. Instead, the process should allow people to learn from mistakes and to make adjustments and keep moving forward.

I recommend eight principles to guide an interventionist during the implementation and evaluation phase.

1. Do not get drawn into the task. Stay with the process. You are responsible for assuring the integrity of the process that facilitates change.
2. Be real about what is happening. Acknowledge errors and mistakes, and ask questions that help participants to discuss their efforts. When appropriate, stop the action and ask: *What is going on?*
3. Access craft knowledge from throughout the system. Changes must fit into existing ways of knowing and acting without disrupting things so thoroughly that the system is destroyed.
4. Use the self as an instrument of change. Pay attention to your own emotions, and to the way that others are reacting to situations. Intervene by inserting yourself into conversations, drawing attention to what is happening in the room.
5. Be straight with people. When you want to find something out, ask a question. When you disagree, say that you disagree, and explain why. When you have an alternative perspective to share, share it. Be clear on what kind of statement is needed, and then produce a statement in the correct form.
6. Remember you are working with people. A human system is brought to life by the people who inhabit it, and implementation will be characterized by strong emotions and interpersonal conflict. Check in with individuals and groups, and try to help them to remain engaged productively in the implementation process.

7. Be vigilant about collusion. Maintain the boundary between interventionist and client. Do not take sides.
8. Phase yourself out. Your goal is to help the client stretch its affordances and push back its constraints so it can tackle the problematic situation. At some point in the process, the client may no longer need your help.

I recommend taking a developmental approach to evaluating the intervention. Instead of measuring the effect of the intervention, developmental evaluation assures that an intervention has the desired effect. It is used to adapt and develop the intervention as more is learned about the context and the surrounding environment.

CHAPTER EIGHT

The Ethics of Intervention

Ethical conduct is an important and sometimes controversial subject for all professionals. Lawyers, engineers, physicians, nurses, teachers, scientists, psychologists, journalists, and many others are bound by codes of conduct published by licensing bodies or professional organizations.

An interventionist does not belong to a distinct and well-defined professional group. Many interventionists are OD practitioners. Others are organizational and social psychologists, management consultants, organizational and community leaders, political and social activists, and social scientists who use collaborative research methods such as participative action research. Some are bound by distinct codes of professional conduct. Others are not.

An interventionist is likely to encounter ethical dilemmas in all of the intervention phases discussed in this book. These ethical dilemmas arise from the ways in which power is distributed and used within a social system, and from the never-ending challenge of finding the right balance between confrontation and compassion, participating and observing, asserting and inquiring, staying the course and changing course, all while helping a dynamic and complex client system to understand and resolve a problematic situation.

To provide some context for this discussion of ethical dilemmas, I begin with four tales from the field.

The First Tale: Caught in the Middle

Sandra was invited by the CEO of an urban health care center to help ameliorate some problems in the center's social system. The center operated a large urban hospital, a smaller rural hospital, a long-term-care facility, and five community outreach programs. The CEO had been hired one year earlier, and he had spent his first twelve months trying to understand the strengths and challenges of his organization. During that time, he had learned that middle managers and staff felt disempowered and unmotivated, and that many complained that some managers and colleagues were bullies.

Sandra met several times with the senior management team and was assured that they supported the CEO's desire to create a more empowered workforce and to put an end to the culture of bullying and harassment. She met with a cross-section of people from all levels of the organization and developed a process that would allow clinical and administrative units to share their experiences and perspectives and to develop plans for improvement. She also met with union leaders (for this was a unionized environment) and other influential members of the system to ask for their advice and support. The union leaders were initially suspicious, pointing to the many instances of bullying and harassment that had not been satisfactorily resolved; however, after watching Sandra's process move forward, they began to support her efforts.

Sandra met with more than sixty groups within the organization. She helped them to design customized inquiry processes, and she acted as a facilitator and coach. Initially, many people were wary of speaking openly during these sessions. Gradually, however, as Sandra continued to meet with people individually and in small groups, as she listened to and validated their experiences and worries, as she coached them about the small preliminary steps that they might take to see if it was safe to participate, and as several senior managers publicly stated their support for the process and their determination to create a more congenial and supportive workplace, the process gained momentum.

Then, without warning, the CEO was fired. Within a few weeks he was replaced by a new CEO. The new man asserted that the organization was in chaos and that he would clean things up. Within weeks he had fired three members of the senior leadership team and replaced them with people he had worked with in the past.

When Sandra attended her regular monthly briefing with the senior management team, the new CEO grilled her about her project. He asked about quantifiable measures that would prove that her work was making an important contribution to the organization. He asserted that charges that there was a culture of bullying in the workplace were preposterous. "These people are being coddled!" he asserted at one point. "That ends now. They have work to do, and they are going to do it."

Despite this unpromising discussion, Sandra was told to continue her work. When she met with the groups in the next few weeks, she found that they were continuing to identify and make improvements at their local levels, and they also were identifying some ideas about improved communication and workflows that needed to be approved by the senior management team. Sandra checked with two of the senior leaders who in the past had supported this process to see if they would help to present these ideas to the new CEO. Both vice-presidents were evasive. Perhaps, they said, it would be better to "wait and see what happens."

Sandra called me and asked if she could use me as a sounding board. We met for coffee, and she told me about what had been happening for the past few months. I asked a few questions, and Sandra did most of the talking. After an hour she summarized her dilemma. "No senior leader is willing to support this work. Even though the project has produced a more hopeful and cooperative atmosphere in the workplace, and the units have been instituting lots of improvements that make things more efficient and also improve the patient experience, the new CEO sees my work as his predecessor's project. He wants nothing to do with it. I am worried that he is letting it continue just so he can see who the troublemakers are, and he can sideline them or fire them. If I stay, people might get hurt. If I leave, the project will probably be canceled. I'd like to stay and keep trying, but I just can't see a way to make this work. I feel like I am being used."

The Second Tale: Espionage and the Interventionist

Connie was hired by the operations director for a large government organization. The director was establishing a new Organization Development Unit (ODU) that would provide assistance to teams that were leading change initiatives within the organization. Lots of change was planned for the coming years, and the ODU would play an important role.

Connie was excited to be part of something new. She had a graduate degree in organization development, and had more than fifteen years of experience working as an external OD consultant. She was excited about being part of an internal team and having the opportunity to see the lasting results of her work.

This excitement continued for about two months while Connie and her teammates set in place the processes and plans needed to support their work. Then the director called a meeting with the new unit. At the meeting he congratulated the team for its progress so far, and then made some comments about the change initiatives that would be announced in the next few weeks. He explained the biggest contribution that the ODU was expected to make.

"You're going to be meeting with lots of people, in all of our locations, and in all of our departments and units. You're going to find out who is prepared to cooperate with our plans and who is going to cause trouble. You are to bring this information back to me. I want to know who we can count on and who I need to watch out for."

Connie was shocked. She looked around the room to see how others were reacting to this statement. Most people had neutral looks on their faces. Vickie, however, was frowning, and exchanged a glance with Connie.

"Um, I just ..." Connie started to speak, and found that she was unsure of how to phrase her question. "I would like to clarify what you just said. When I speak to people about the work that we are going to do, usually there is an understanding that I am going to treat the conversation as confidential. I mean, that is a standard part of OD practice. I just don't know how this is going to work if we are supposed to tell you what people are saying."

The director stared at Connie for a moment. "This isn't kindergarten," he finally said. "This is the real world. We all have a responsibility to move forward with these strategic changes in a way that doesn't bankrupt us. There are bound to be some complainers and some resisters. I need to know who they are so we can make plans to deal with them. Anything else?"

Nobody else raised any questions or concerns about the director's approach.

When the meeting ended Connie retreated to her cubicle feeling shaken. The director wanted the OD team to be his spies. How could she possibly work in a place where she was ordered to spy on people?

The Third Tale: The Plagiarists

Connor was an organizational consultant who loved to use behavioral science theory to understand the patterns at work in social systems. He had a great fondness for doing research, for solving puzzles, and for tackling meaty problems. He was always on the lookout for consulting assignments that involved assessing the needs of a workforce, evaluating change-readiness, and creating plans for large initiatives.

Several years ago, he was invited to help the senior leaders of a large organization to achieve a better understanding of the concept of employee engagement and to develop a transformation plan to move the organization to a higher level of performance. Connor approached the assignment with relish. He conducted a thorough literature review of the relevant social science, he interviewed people throughout the organization, and he met regularly with one of the organization's senior vice-presidents and her most trusted director. After a few months, another consultant, named Viv, also started to participate in these meetings. Connor was told that Viv was a specialist who would be helping to implement the transformation plan.

Connor produced two comprehensive reports for the client, one titled *An Employee Engagement Framework for ABC Corporation*, and the other titled *Implementing Employee Engagement at ABC*. He received effusive thank-yous and compliments from many people, including the senior vice-president, the director, and Viv. Connor exited from the system on a high note.

A few years later, while conducting some research for another client, Connor happened upon two articles that had been published in professional journals by Viv, the director, and the senior vice-president. Both articles were about employee engagement and transformation. Curious, he read both of the articles from cover to cover. As he read, he experienced a growing sense of betrayal. He dug out the two reports that he had written, and compared them to the articles. Connor discovered that ideas, phrases, sentences, and even entire paragraphs had been cut out of his reports and pasted into these articles. Nowhere did the authors acknowledge that some of their work had been written by somebody else.

Connor reviewed his old contract with the corporation, and saw that he had turned over copyright of this material to the corporation.

His contract said that the corporation would own this copyright, and that nobody could use this material without written permission from the corporation. Connor also discovered that the laws concerning copyright and the social norms governing plagiarism are not the same thing. Plagiarism can occur without the violation of copyright.

Connor felt a growing sense of anger. His work had been stolen, and this was wrong. But the thieves were powerful people who would not want to be exposed. He found himself ruminating about this betrayal, and unsure of what he should do.

The Fourth Tale: Life in the Real World

Viv was a well-regarded and successful consultant. She worked exclusively with senior management teams and claimed to specialize in a variety of techniques that could be used to introduce changes into patterns of human behavior. In her marketing materials, she boasted that her work was often transformative.

She had a graduate degree in OD, which she prominently displayed on her website and business card. During her time in school, she had been immersed in the humanistic values that characterize the field of OD. She had been taught the importance of being collaborative and of working with people rather than helping managers to impose autocratic solutions onto employees.

After graduation, Viv had bumped head-first into the "real world." Over the years her education seemed increasingly idealistic and out of touch. In the real world, senior managers called the shots. To pull in lucrative and interesting assignments, it was important to ally herself with these senior managers and to encourage these managers to become dependent on her so she would be awarded more lucrative contracts down the road. Viv became adept at making her highly paid clients feel good, at helping them to develop and implement their plans, and at helping them to avoid blame when things went wrong.

After several years of building up her international practice, Viv was contacted by one of her favorite clients. She entered into the client system and discovered that while she had been off working on other projects, this client had formed an OD team. Most of the members of the OD team were new to the field of OD and had backgrounds in facilitation or human resource management. One person, however, had a graduate degree in OD (just like Viv), and said and did things that suggested that she still believed in the idealistic values and practices of a humanistic approach to OD.

Viv persuaded the senior vice-president who had brought her in that she should undertake a review of this new OD team to make sure that everybody was fitting in and working together effectively. When she interviewed the people with no background in OD, Viv asked questions that made them nervous, and then she calmed them down by saying that they shouldn't worry about their lack of experience, that she would mentor the group and help it find its footing. She took a different approach with the experienced OD practitioner. "You're not fitting in," she asserted. "And you're messing up all of the work that I have done with this client for the past five years. I am days away from clinching a new contract to do an appreciative inquiry process here. I won't allow you to screw up my work."

Viv reported her findings to the vice-president later that afternoon. Before the end of the day Viv saw a security guard escorting the experienced OD practitioner out of the office. The real world is full of winners and losers, Viv thought to herself, and she was going to remain a winner.

Democracy and Intent

I contend that an ethical approach to intervention requires that the interventionist adopt a democratic stance and act with intent. I make this contention based on my experience as an interventionist and on my research into and reflections on the ethics of intervention.

A democratic stance means that the interventionist seeks to understand how power is distributed in the client system and accords all members of the system the dignity and respect due to human beings. Power can be used to subvert, oppress, and coerce, and it can also be used to open up new ways of being – new ways of thinking, acting, and structuring. Power can oppress and power can liberate. Members of a client system can be treated as objects that are manipulated in order to achieve organizational objectives, or they can be treated as empowered individuals who might be mobilized in a joint effort to create improvement.

In the first two tales presented above, Sandra and Connie are attempting to create the conditions in which members of the client system can work together to open up new opportunities and new value. These endeavors prove inconsistent with a countervailing effort to use power to judge, control, penalize, and coerce. Think back to the discussion of intervention approaches presented in chapter 2. The normative-reeducative and interpretive-communicative strategies proposed by Sandra and Connie are quashed by the power-coercive strategies used by the CEO and the director.[1] After attempting to find a way out of their ethical dilemmas, both Sandra and Connie recognize that they must exit from these systems.

The third and fourth tales demonstrate some of the pernicious effects of unethical behavior. Intellectual property is stolen and dependency is encouraged so as to enhance the reputation and income of a few powerful individuals. The client system becomes a resource that is used to advance careers and to accrue personal advantages. The well-being and prosperity of the many thousands of others who work in the system are less important than the success of the few.

These four tales are based on real experiences that I have encountered in the systems where my colleagues and I have worked.

This chapter is a plea to readers to avoid the temptation to collude with those who dehumanize their colleagues and clients.[2] I begin the discussion by considering the oft-repeated admonition that an interventionist – like all people who work in a profession that provides help to others – must *do no harm*. I then consider the ethical dilemmas that arise in relation to the four balancing acts discussed in this book. Then I turn to what I believe is a useful ethical precept for an interventionist: *act with intent*. This is followed by some reflections on the ethical dilemmas that arise from the ways in which power is generally distributed and used in human systems. I conclude by reviewing specific examples of ethical dilemmas that practitioners and scholars suggest are commonly encountered.

Do No Harm!

The ethical principles of the American Psychological Association begin by stating that psychologists should work to benefit clients and to do no harm.[3] Some have suggested that this aphorism can be traced back to the ancient Hippocratic Oath that dictates the standards of behavior required of physicians, but this view is not without controversy.[4] Regardless of its origins, the admonition to do no harm permeates the practice of human systems interveners.

A set of ethical principles to govern the fields of organization and human systems development was created with support from the American Association for the Advancement of Science and the Illinois Institute of Technology's Center for the Study of Ethics in the Professions. The principles were established through consultations with numerous scholars and practitioners from a variety of countries. The first moral rule in the resulting Statement of Values and Ethics reads: "Do no harm."[5]

The code of professional conduct published by the Certified Management Consultants of Canada requires that certified members avoid work that could be detrimental to clients.[6] The Canadian Organization Development Institute and the International Organization Development Institute have published ethical codes that opt for a more positive phrasing of the principle, requiring that practitioners work in ways that serve the well-being and interests of clients and stakeholders.[7] In the United States, the Institute of Management Consultants' code of ethics also uses a positive phrasing, stating that the consultant must display competence, integrity, and professionalism (among other things) while working with clients.[8] The ethical code released by the Association of Change Management Professionals (ACMP) includes a duty of responsibility, stating that members must make decisions and take actions to safeguard a wide range of stakeholders.[9]

When my colleagues discuss ethical concerns related to the work of an interventionist with a client, the admonition to do no harm is the most common precept that is voiced. A few years ago, one of our student consulting teams was about to start working with their client when a bitter conflict broke out among team members. They reached out to faculty members, saying that their internal disarray made it impossible for them to work effectively with the client. I recall one of my faculty colleagues saying, "It is admirable that they grasped the importance of doing no harm to the client."

An interventionist often enters a client system when it is being held hostage by a problematic situation that is hidden and is producing distress. Client productivity may be impaired by the situation. Social relations may be strained. The system is probably unable to adapt to new circumstances arising in its environment. Harm is prevalent in the system before the interventionist arrives.

In this book I have conceived of the problematic situation as an adaptive challenge, a challenge for which there is no known

solution. There is no off-the-shelf technology, no prefabricated social arrangement, that can simply be imposed upon the client that
will resolve the problem and allow life to resume a more productive
and a happier course. Instead, the interventionist must help the client to engage in a search for new patterns of thought and behavior
and new structuring that might allow the problematic situation to
be framed in a way that suggests a feasible and useful solution. The
way forward resembles a process of trial and error. The interventionist and client formulate a theory of action and then test the efficacy of the theory by loosening some old assumptions, trying out
some new attitudes, experimenting with new behaviors, and altering the current structural arrangements. Invariably, because these
tests occur within the context of a complex human system that is by
its nature unpredictable, some tests will fail. Mistakes and errors are
inevitable, and that is why the intervention process must include
a reflective component that allows participants to monitor results,
reflect on errors, and make the appropriate adjustments.

But some also say that harm is inadmissible. I have found that
some interventionists are confounded by the inevitability of error
and the injunction to avoid harm. If we make mistakes, it might be
the case that some people will experience harm. I have known some
novice interventionists to conclude that it is best to avoid all assertive interventions. Instead, they focus entirely on creating psychological safety, and they hope that this will be enough to set in motion
a process of inquiry that results in positive and sustainable change.

This is not a productive way to think about ethics in the work
of a human systems intervener. Some interventionists interpret the
words "do no harm" to mean that they must produce no uncomfortable conversations or bring to the surface issues that may cause
members of the client system to experience negative emotions. I
have seen students become frozen in place, or become angry, anx-
ious, and confused, as they apply their learning with a client during

field assignments and try to comply with the unbending require-
ment to cause no harm.

The perplexing nature of this problem can be seen in the philosoph-
ical conundrum known as the trolley problem.[10] The trolley problem
is a moral puzzle used by philosophers to encourage students to delve
into the complexities surrounding a difficult moral choice. It goes like
this. A trolley is rushing out of control along a track. Ahead of the
trolley, five people are tied to the track and unable to escape. If it is
not stopped, the trolley will hit and almost certainly kill them. You are
nearby, standing next to a lever that controls a switch. If you pull the
lever, the trolley will be diverted onto a different track, thus saving
the five people. However, on this other track there is one person who
will be killed if you pull the lever. You have a stark and unavoidable
choice. You can do nothing, and five people will be killed. Alternatively, you can pull the lever, thus saving five people and killing one.

What should you do?

If you are an interventionist who is governed by an ethical code
stipulating that you must do no harm, then you are caught in an
intractable double bind. You are paralyzed, or your mind is scram-
bling to find a utilitarian solution. Causing harm to one person is
less harmful than causing harm to five people, so perhaps that will
be your solution.

Fortunately, the ethical dilemmas that arise in organizational consulting are usually considerably less urgent and fatal than the trolley
problem. A typical example is the dilemma of whether to confront
the client about a puzzling aspect of their behavioral pattern. You
have noticed the pattern, you believe that it is counterproductive
and may be related to the problematic situation that you have been
asked to help with, and you see it appear in the here and now while
you interact with members of the client system. You have an excellent opportunity to point it out. So far members of the client system
have for the most part presented themselves as emotionally mature

and rational. You decide to draw the behavior to the attention of the people in the room and invite them to consider whether this behavior is part of a larger pattern that might be constraining the system from moving forward.

I encountered this type of dilemma when working with a client system that aspired to develop a greater capacity for learning and adaptability. I had noticed that two members of the system had a tendency to raise controversial and emotionally charged issues just as a meeting was drawing to a close. There was no time to discuss the issue, but participants would leave the meeting with the issue on their minds, almost certainly meaning that private conversations would continue in hallways and offices. This created the potential for individuals and groups to create assumptions about each other and to fall into the trap of the fundamental attribution error.

I had met with this client on five occasions when the behavior appeared for the fourth time. I noticed the behavior, reflected on its surprising re-occurrence at the end of each meeting, and decided to take action.

"What is going on?" I asked. "This is the fourth time this has happened. Why? What is this about?"

I expected that people would ask me what I was referring to. I would explain, and then a discussion would ensue.

Instead, a stunned silence fell upon the group. Then one person began to cry.

System members confronted me about my abrasive manner. I was told that I had frightened some people. I was urged to behave in a more professional manner. A few system members disagreed with their colleagues, saying that they were not offended or upset by my intervention, and that they were curious to learn about my intention.

However, no system member asked me to explain my intention. The people in the room talked for several minutes, then said that they had said all that needed to be said, and we agreed on the date and time for our next meeting.

That was it.

I learned two things from this episode. First, I had touched a very sensitive spot. This tendency to raise touchy issues at the end of a meeting, without time to discuss or resolve the issue, was an important part of their behavioral pattern, and they were neither willing nor able to examine it. I resolved to continue to observe the occurrence of this behavior and see if I could determine how it interrelated with other aspects of their pattern. I noted that the behavior allowed them to raise touchy issues, creating the impression that they were honest and forthcoming and brave. It also prevented them from delving into and resolving touchy issues, allowing them to be safe from the uncertainty of confronting a difficult subject.

Second, the episode indicated that although they were adept at creating the impression in others that they were a mature and rational group, suggesting that they possessed a well-developed capacity to learn and solve problems together, they in fact may have possessed a limited capacity for learning. Not only did they not discuss the issue that had been raised by system members at the close of the meeting, but they also did not discuss the issue that I had raised. Instead, they made my raising of the issue into a new issue, and then they avoided this new issue by not asking me about it – even though some system members said that they were curious about why I had raised the issue, and even though I had pointed out that system members were saying they were curious about my intention but were not directly asking me to explain my intention.

I realized that I had more to learn about the patterns at work in this system, and that I should be careful of overestimating the system's capacity to deal effectively with an emergent intervention.

Did my intervention cause harm? Some might say it did. One participant wept. Others expressed dismay.

However, we then continued to work together for several months, and system members were eventually able to gain new insights into their current patterns and to experiment with new attitudes, behaviors, and structures.

I agree with those who say that the admonition to do no harm should be interpreted as a commitment to continuously learn and develop more skill. If I pay close attention to the words and actions of my clients, if I notice the intended and unintended consequences produced by specific interventions, if I continue to read the relevant social science and other publications that shed light on human behavior, if I continue to reflect together with clients and other skilled practitioners on the impact and meaning of my work, then I can hope to continuously create in myself more capacity to do no harm.

For an intervener, avoiding harm cannot be the same as avoiding risk. Intervening in human systems is a risky business. Recall the old adage: nothing ventured, nothing gained.

An intervener must balance the potential benefits and harms of action with the potential benefits and harms of inaction. And that, of course, brings us back to the balancing acts.

The Ethical Dilemmas of the Balancing Acts

An interventionist helps a client to explore, understand, and take action to resolve a problematic situation. Rarely can the interventionist know with certainty that his proposed actions will produce entirely beneficial results and that no unintended and harmful results might also be produced. Social change involves risk, and where there is risk there is always danger.

The four balancing acts that form the core of this book have to do with creating the conditions needed for members of a client system to take actions with the intent of creating beneficial changes.

Interventionists accept the paradox of creating safety to enable risk. They seek relationship while pushing back against the temptation to fit in and collude. They inquire into the client reality and occasionally assert their own views and interpretations in ways that might open up new realities for the client. They act on their stated intentions and occasionally depart from agreed-to plans to help clients to see how the problematic situation is showing up in the interactions that are currently taking place.

Table 8.1 highlights some of the risks associated with the four balancing acts. Some risks have to do with the relationship that the interventionist forms with members of the client system – the interventionist may be overly friendly or too distant. Other risks arise from the approaches that the interventionist uses – the interventionist may rely too much on the tasks, milestones, and deliverables identified in the formal project plan, or may be too cautious, overconfident, or even arrogant when intervening in the client's behavior patterns. Still other risks can arise when the interventionist fails to see how specific behaviors fit into the patterns that are the concern of this intervention process. Regardless of the direction in which these risks push the interventionist, the result is the same: the interventionist's actions are pushed away from the real target of the intervention, and the problematic situation remains untouched.

Falling prey to one of these risks could mean that the interventionist colludes with the existing power structure in a human system or adds to the confusion and uncertainty that afflict the client. There is no perfect stance or approach in this type of work. The interventionist engages in a constant struggle to achieve the best balance for the unfolding events that characterize the intervention process. Although perfection is unattainable, it is often possible for the interventionist to keep these risks at bay and to support the effectiveness of the intervention process and the well-being of the client system. This is done by acting with intent.

Table 8.1. The ethical risks of the balancing acts

The balancing act	The risks
Confrontation and compassion	• The interventionist is timid and cautious because she fears pushing the client beyond its present capacity to act, and thus creates the conditions for the client to remain stuck in a problematic and unproductive pattern. • The interventionist is overconfident and aggressive, and encourages the client to act in ways that are beyond the client's current level of capacity.
Participating and observing	• The interventionist allows himself to become close to and familiar with the client system, and thus is pulled into the existing patterns and loses the capacity to see and reveal the systemic nature of the problematic situation. • The interventionist is cautious and aloof, does not experience the unproductive patterns of thought and action, and produces a misdiagnosis of the factors that are producing the problematic situation.
Asserting and inquiring	• The interventionist worries about creating harm, and remains firmly in an inquiry stance despite the client's continuing inability to uncover and see the factors that create the problematic situation. • The interventionist is arrogant and overconfident, and pushes his own views on the client in ways that provoke defensiveness and resistance.
Staying the course and changing course	• The interventionist insists on following the agreed-to plan that was negotiated in the early stages of the work, despite new information that comes to light indicating that the client has misunderstood important facets of the problematic situation. • The interventionist becomes mesmerized by specific features of the client interaction pattern that are not related to the problematic situation and intervenes in relationships and patterns that distract effort and attention away from the project's original goals.

Act with Intent

From time to time, I meet someone who does the same sort of work that I do and who tells me that one of their key skills is that they are very good at reading people.

I am curious about statements such as this – "I am good at reading people," or "I like to start by creating a safe space," or "I like to be mindful of the emotional atmosphere in the client's workplace" – statements that sound good but that are also worryingly vague.

"How do you read people?" I might ask.

"Oh, it's not a technique," is the scoffing reply. "I just do it. I have this intuitive ability to read people and to *get* them and to understand what is going on."

One of the most useful pieces of information that I have picked up from the work of Chris Argyris is that members of an effective human group will tend to state inferences in ways that can be tested. When we are talking about something that exists, that has some manner of being in the world, then we ought to be able to talk about it in ways that allow us to get at that existing phenomenon or object. What is reading people? What is a safe space? How is a safe space created? What is an emotional atmosphere? How do I access and measure this atmosphere?

Too often my inquiries about the existential properties of these elusive phenomena are met with blank stares or with condescension. People use a faculty that they often term "intuition" to access these phenomena and are unable to provide empirical evidence to support the inferences that they derive from their intuitions.

Be careful not to fall into this trap. It is natural for an interventionist to experience a feeling that something important is happening while observing or interacting with members of the client system. However, these feelings should be accepted as merely preliminary indications that something interesting might be going on. We must be clear-headed and attentive. We must develop and use our abilities to see and hear what is happening around us, to recognize the patterns that characterize and shape a human group, to recognize that our inferences are hypotheses that must be tested and confirmed, and to put intensive effort into ensuring that we act with intent.

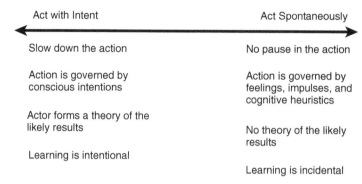

Figure 8.1. Acting with intent

Imagine a spectrum that runs from "act with intent" at one end through to "act spontaneously" at the other end (see figure 8.1). Acting spontaneously means that one takes action based on a gut feeling or an inarticulate impulse. One "feels" that a certain action is the one to use, and one then implements the action. Depending on the situation, this way of acting can be appropriate and useful. When playing a fast-paced game of ice hockey, where there is no time to work out a carefully formulated strategy as opposing players rush toward the puck and a teammate speeds toward the blue line, we act on the basis of our "reflection in action," as Donald Schön put it.[11] Cognitive processes clearly accompany all actions, and when we are in the midst of a fast-paced and unpredictable stream of interaction we rely on these situated and ingrained ways of thinking. In fact, becoming self-conscious in moments like this can be counterproductive. We may pause as we consider options, and the flow of action leaves us behind.

This rapid-form cognition in action is what Kahneman has referred to as System 1 cognition.[12] We possess a broad set of cognitive heuristics that allow us to rapidly settle on a course of action without having to resort to careful deliberation. Although Kahneman acknowledges that this form of rapid, situated cognition can be useful when the occasion warrants rapid responses, it can also produce serious flaws in human decision-making processes when it is misapplied.

At the other end of the spectrum, acting with intent means that we slow down our cognitive processes and consciously consider alternative courses of action and the possible results that could be produced by those actions. We take the time – perhaps only seconds – to formulate a hypothesis: if I perform action X, then result Y will be produced. We then perform the action and observe the results. If the anticipated result is produced, then we have created some evidence to support our hypothesis. If an unexpected result is produced, then we must go back to the drawing board and reconsider what might be going on in the client system.

Acting with intent means that I consciously formulate a plan to help the client. When I act with intent, I am consistent with the codes of conduct put forward by the Canadian Organization Development Institute, the International Organization Development Institute, the United States Institute of Management Consultants, and the Association of Change Management Professionals requiring that I act with integrity and that my actions safeguard and promote the well-being of clients. My actions are intended to help. I may act in ways that produce new information that sheds additional light on the client's problematic situation. I may also act in ways that open up new understanding for members of the client system and that nudge the client toward new patterns of thought, behavior, and structuring.

To act with intent, we sometimes need to literally slow down the flow of interaction in a client system. If I am attending a meeting of the client system and believe that I see the problematic situation appear in the room, I may need to interrupt the action by saying something like, "Just a moment, everyone." I then might need to have the self-possession that allows me to think for a moment while everyone turns to look at me. What intervention may be useful in this situation? What is my current assessment of the client's capacity? Should I ask a question or make an assertion?

Sometimes all that is needed is a simple statement of inquiry: "Do any of you have concerns about the proposal that you have been discussing for the past five minutes?" In a system that has started to develop the capacity to inquire into the factors that are producing the problematic situation, two or three participants may accept this invitation and begin the inquiry process. If participants are confused by your intervention, you might try a more explicit statement: "It occurred to me that this proposal may be inconsistent with some of the guiding principles that you discussed at our last meeting. What do others think?" If participants continue to be confused, it is a simple matter to acknowledge that you may be mistaken and to encourage people to continue with their discussion.

To act with intent, you form an intention and then you design and implement actions to carry out that intention. Acting with intent therefore requires that you act with integrity. The word *integrity* means to be unified and sound or coherent. When applied to a human being, the word implies that a person declares their intentions and then acts in ways that are consistent with the declaration – that the person "walks their talk." Many people think of integrity as a moral or normative matter: you are a "good person" when you exhibit integrity, and you are a "bad person" when you are out of integrity. However, it is possible (and useful) to regard integrity as a purely descriptive term, without moral connotations.[13] A person is either in or out of integrity, and it is likely – given the many competing priorities that we all face, and our packed schedules and the social pressures that act upon us – that from time to time we will all find ourselves out of integrity. When we are out of integrity, it is usually a simple matter to return to a state of integrity: we acknowledge to the relevant people that we have run into problems and are not able to fulfill our commitments or act on our previous intentions, and then we explain how we now intend to clean up the mess that we have created. An interventionist who adopts this view of integrity may find it easier to be honest and straightforward with clients and colleagues.

An interventionist's overall intent during the course of a lengthy intervention process is to design and implement actions that meet the requirements set forth in the agreement that was negotiated during the contracting phase and that may be further defined in the project charter. It is therefore important to ensure that the contract and charter provide a framework for action that is both effective and ethical. It is especially important to protect the interests of less powerful members of the client system. Your contract should make it clear that participation in the intervention process is voluntary, that people are permitted to choose their own level of participation, and that all interactions between you and members of the client system will be treated as confidential.

Ethical Dilemmas: A Compendium

To assist those who are new to the field of human systems intervention, I offer this short compendium of common ethical dilemmas. I developed the list on the basis of my own experience, the experience of colleagues with whom I routinely discuss the ethical pitfalls of intervention, and my reading of the texts that discuss the ethics of intervention.[14]

Here, then, are seven ethical dilemmas that an interventionist may encounter when working with a client system.

Coercion

Typically, an interventionist contracts with an organizational leader (or leaders), or with a person who has stature and power within the human system that is seeking help. Quite often, this powerful individual or group has determined on behalf of the system that change is needed, and they want the interventionist's help to create a process for moving forward with the initiative. Often the person will say, "We need to get buy-in from our people." This suggests that you are being invited to help a leadership group to do *things to* people rather than to do *things with* people.

In effect, members of the human system are to be coerced – coaxed, persuaded, influenced, manipulated – into participating in the change process. The leaders will often stipulate that people participate in meetings, discussions, interviews, or focus groups. They are expected to cooperate, to provide data, to allow their awareness to be raised, to accept education, and to cooperate with the intentions of the powerful system leaders.

To acquiesce in this type of agenda is to objectify the members of the system. They are to be manipulated as though they were mere objects or cogs within a mechanical system. One way or another, they must fall into line with the plans of the all-knowing, all-powerful leaders.

The espoused paradigm for social organization in much of the world is derived from democratic principles. Citizens elect their governments, and they expect to be consulted on important decisions that affect the way in which human life is organized and conducted within their societies. Many of us participate in processes to elect national, regional, and municipal representatives, and the language that is used here – we say that we elect our representatives, not our leaders – is telling. Those whom we elect are expected to take our aspirations and concerns forward into the deliberative forums that we have created.

To an increasing extent, these principles are also applied to the organizations that we create to conduct the business of the private, public, and nonprofit sectors. Although much organizational life remains essentially autocratic, the flaws in the existing system – which allow unethical people who have accumulated power and wealth to manipulate social and economic systems for their own benefit – are increasingly apparent. Moreover, research shows that employees often work harder and are more motivated to contribute to the work when they are treated like valued members of a team rather than as replaceable parts of a machine. Consequently, there is a growing demand for safeguards to protect us from unethical behavior and for norms and mechanisms that create new distributions of power within organizations. Governments enact regulations to ensure that competitive pressures within vital industries do not undermine the need to bolster the safety and well-being of the public. Boards of directors protect broad institutional interests and have the power to hire and dismiss organizational leaders. The growth in specialized domains of knowledge has created a need to share decision-making power with those who are in the best position to make timely and appropriate decisions. The findings of social science on toxic phenomena such as groupthink and confirmation bias have convinced many people of the need to encourage viewpoint diversity in decision-making contexts and on leadership teams.

In the late nineteenth century, Frederick Taylor's scientific management was the governing principle for how industrial organizations should be designed and operated. Employees were part of the machinery of the workplace. Social relations were to be minimized. Technological innovation and the logic of science would be used to squeeze more and more productivity out of organizational infrastructure. In the early twenty-first century, however, we are more likely to talk about the importance of a supportive and adaptive organizational culture than to consider the usefulness of a time and motion study. An organization's social dimension is seen as a vital factor in shaping employee behavior, and leaders are increasingly likely to focus their energy on creating the conditions that nurture and release the talents and energies of employees. More and more leaders are willing to set aside the old coercive mechanisms of the past and to experiment with new democratic methods.

I do not automatically reject a contract with a system in which organizational leaders coerce system members to cooperate and fall into line.

My decision to accept or reject the contract depends on two criteria. First, is the leadership team (assuming that this is who contacted me) espousing a desire to move toward a less coercive state? For example, leaders might have realized that performance could be improved if employees were more committed to the organization and were more fully engaged in the activities of the workplace. Although to begin with these leaders may be wondering how they can create this state of affairs merely by influencing and manipulating their employees, rather than by calling upon their employees' ability to make free and informed choices, my preliminary discussions could indicate that several leaders are open to considering new ideas and new approaches.

Second, will it be possible for me to mitigate the coercive forces in the system through the process that I put in place? For example, the system leaders might require that employees participate in interviews with me. However, will I be able to provide a reasonable guarantee of confidentiality to those who show up for an interview? Will I be able to conduct the interview in private? Does my contract and project charter allow me to treat interview data as confidential, and to conceal the identities of people who made specific statements? Will I be able to share the results of the exploration phase with all system members?

If I believe that system members are at least espousing a desire to move toward a more democratic and collaborative way of operating, and if it seems possible for me to create a process that mitigates the coercive forces that currently operate within the system, then I may accept the contract.

Manipulating Data

Interventionists are sometimes expected to manipulate the data gathered during the exploration phase so the findings support a predetermined diagnosis or point of view.

This dilemma sometimes comes to light during the contracting phase. Your contact client tells you that she wants to implement a particular program in the organization, but her superior has insisted that she put together an evidence-based justification for the program. She invites you to assemble the evidence that she needs and then to help her design and implement the program.

When the dilemma presents itself in this manner, it is often simple to resolve. I ask my client how she will feel if the evidence does not support her plans but instead suggests that the status quo is preferable or that some other intervention is needed. I push this line of questioning until I am satisfied that I understand the client's position. If she intends to accept the findings of the exploration process and is willing to abandon her plans if the data point us elsewhere, then I will likely move forward with the contract. If she tells me that my job is to find evidence to support her plans and that my contract will not include finding contrary evidence, then I will likely decline.

The situation is trickier when the client reveals her expectations only when the exploration phase is drawing to a close. One of my staff and I once worked with a large financial services organization on an extensive data-gathering process, and as we were organizing and analyzing our findings, we met with our contracting client to discuss the best way to organize the findings. During the course of our discussion, we described some of the more significant data points, and our client reacted with dismay. She insisted that certain findings be concealed, other findings be emphasized, and some assertions that were absent from our findings be presented as though they had turned up in the data. We refused. The result was a difficult conversation that failed to reach a conclusion that was satisfactory to our client. We completed our work and presented a final report, and the client then terminated our contract. I had expected to present the findings at a discussion session with organizational leaders from across the country, but she prevented this from happening. I had carried out work with this client for more than a decade, but this was our last contract.

Scapegoating

Sometimes members of a client system tend to look for individuals or groups to blame for the organization's problems. This phenomenon of scapegoating occurs so often that we must conclude that it is a natural human tendency to associate collective successes and failures with specific individuals or groups. Systems thinking requires that we set aside this tendency.

When I first contract with a client to investigate a problematic situation within a human system, I discuss the importance of finding a system-level solution. I explicitly state that we often tend to affix blame to one or two people and that this is generally not an effective way to resolve a problem that is arising from the current configuration of a dynamic system. If one person exits from the system and a new person arrives, that new person will be pulled into the patterns that are producing the current problems, and the problems will survive. Instead of identifying and firing the culprit, our focus should be on identifying the patterns that are producing the problem and then finding ways to alter these patterns.

Sometimes I use the dramaturgical metaphor that can be found in the work of Erving Goffman and William Kahn.[15] The human system is staging a performance, and thus the system has cast individual system members into certain roles. These individuals dutifully play their roles each day as they interact with other system members. Some people may play the role of heroes, while others play the role of villains, and still others play small supporting roles. The villains, however, are merely responding in a particular way to the situation that they are presented with, and if we can alter that situation then almost assuredly their behavior will also change.

This framing of the project is often sufficient to persuade my contact client to see how our process unfolds. They may be curious to see how the analysis could reveal a systemic pattern that lies beneath the level of individual actions. They may be somewhat removed from the emotionality and conflicts that are arising from the problematic situation, and thus the idea that they could resolve the problems without triggering difficult processes to terminate unpopular employees might be welcome.

Nonetheless, at the end of the day it is the client system that will take action. Even if your process is designed to avoid blaming individuals for the system's problems, it is possible that some people will feel blamed. It is also possible that the tendency to associate the existing problems with a specific individual is too entrenched to overcome. Your responsibility is to try to keep the focus at a system level and to keep out of – and when possible to mitigate – the blaming dynamics that are present in the system.

The Ends Justify the Means

Sometimes an interventionist might believe that the goal of an interesting project is inherently worthwhile, and then with this in mind may collude with unethical or questionable activities during the exploration or implementation process. The ends justify the means, and thus I will help these leaders to coerce and manipulate their employees.

This is unacceptable.

When using an intervention process to help a client system to resolve an adaptive problem, it is incorrect to say that the ends justify the means. Rather, the means anticipate the ends.

It is almost always the case that the interventionist's process – for collecting data, for organizing and feeding data back to the system, for designing and implementing a program to bring about beneficial change – must mirror the end state that the client is working toward. The intervention process becomes an incubator or a school for creating the new attitudes, behaviors, and structuring that characterize the new way of being desired by members of the client system. If the goal includes more collaboration, then the process should create more collaboration. If the end state includes participative decision making, then the process should see the emergence of participative decision making. If the end state includes a higher level of employee commitment to the enterprise, then the intervention process should allow participants to create the conditions needed for enhanced commitment and should encourage participants to demonstrate this commitment through the work they contribute to the initiative.

Using force or compulsion to create freedom of choice is a tricky business, and I have never seen it succeed.

Competence Issues

An interventionist should accept work that she is competent to carry out and should decline work that she is not competent to carry out.

Suppose a client asks you to help them with a project, and the client says that they have determined that the best process to use is a well-known large change process – let's say it is the World Café process. Suppose the client's rationale for selecting this process is sound, and suppose you have no experience in using the World Café. You must decline this work.

Suppose, however, the client says that they are not worried that you have no experience in using the World Café. The client says that their existing relationship with you is important, and that the people who would be participating have indicated that they would like you to facilitate the process. The client asks if you could educate yourself about this process. In that case, you might investigate the World Café method and determine how you could prepare yourself to lead this client engagement. You might then describe to the client how you could prepare yourself for this work and also explicitly discuss the benefits and the constraints of having you act as the process facilitator under these conditions. If the client still wants you to accept the contract, and if you are prepared to undertake the preparations that you have described, then you may conclude that you have appropriately mitigated this ethical risk.

However, it is never acceptable to mislead a client into thinking that you have competencies that you in fact do not have.

Fostering Dependency

The interventionist's consulting stance described in these pages, which is consistent with the process consulting approach described most fully by Edgar Schein, intends to foster and enhance the capacity and capability of client systems.[16] Our methods create independence rather than dependence.

This contrasts with the stance taken by some management consultants, who explicitly try to create dependent or symbiotic relationships with clients. They want to secure a reliable long-term revenue source, and so while they may emphasize the importance of client success, they also try to contribute to this success by allowing the client to become dependent upon their expertise. Although this is an explicit strategy followed by some management consultants, some commentators have pointed out that this approach can sometimes privilege short-term gains over long-term strategic advantages.[17]

An interventionist who helps clients to resolve adaptive problems is necessarily concerned with the development of new capacity. The presence of the adaptive problem is to be explained in part by the client's current inability to frame the problem in a way that allows it to be resolved and their inability to take effective action to resolve the problem. To be helpful, the interventionist must help the client system to create the needed new abilities.

I can see no reason for an interventionist to fear this approach. Contemporary organizations and communities have no shortage of challenges, and the pace of technological and social change shows no signs of slowing down. The fact that you basically work yourself out of a job with each consulting assignment does not mean that there soon will be no more jobs for you to do. On the contrary, with each new project you demonstrate again your commitment to the well-being and capacity of your clients, thus laying the groundwork for a healthy and ongoing relationship based on respect and competence rather than a draining and debilitating relationship based on dependence and exploitation.

The interventionist functions in a manner that resembles an effective teacher. As George Steiner once wrote, the teacher's calling is both worthy and profound: "To awaken in another human being powers, dreams beyond one's own; to induce in others a love for that which one loves; to make of one's inward present their future; that is a threefold adventure like no other."[18]

Stealing Ideas, Approaches, Techniques, and Tools

An interventionist must resist the temptation to steal ideas, approaches, techniques, and tools without appropriately acknowledging the source. Our field is now replete with the findings of science and with techniques and methods that were developed and shared by skilled practitioners. In an era in which many people are persuaded that understanding and action should be informed by reliable evidence generated through scientific investigation and expert practice, there seems to be little downside in honestly acknowledging that one's own methods rest firmly on a solid scientific and expert foundation.

It is wrong to present as one's own proprietary method a technique that in fact is derived from the work of another. It is wrong to take material from reports or publications and present it to clients or to the public as one's own.

How can you help a client to solve problems and generate new capacity when your own stance is without integrity and is steeped in dishonesty? We may like to think of ourselves as sophisticated humans of the new century – people who pursue our self-actualization in increasingly original ways – and that we live in a postmodern age where we use terms such as "post-truth" and "truthiness," but surely we can still recognize that some statements are dishonest and some actions are unethical. Presenting somebody else's work as your own is unethical and dishonest.

Summary

Intervening into human systems to help clients to resolve adaptive problems is inherently risky. The interventionist and the client are stepping into unknown territory. Errors are likely, and it is possible that the client system may experience some harm.

It is important that the interventionist be committed to continuous learning and to improving her practice, so that the interventionist is continuously creating new capacity to protect and help the client and minimize harm. It is also important for the interventionist to act with intent. To act with intent, the interventionist slows down the action that is occurring in the client system and forms a theory about what is going on and about the actions that might produce beneficial change. The result is an intentional approach to learning and improvement, such that the interventionist can be said to be acting with intent rather than acting on the basis of impulse or vague intuitions.

Certain ethical dilemmas frequently arise in the work of an interventionist. Some client systems use coercion and manipulation to force compliance, and others expect the interventionist to assist them to manipulate data into supporting predetermined conclusions. Some client systems prefer to scapegoat specific individuals by blaming them for systemic problems, and others believe that worthy goals can justify the use of unethical processes during an intervention. Interventionists may occasionally be tempted to accept work that they are not competent to perform, or to encourage a client to become dependent on them in order to secure a long-term revenue stream. Others may be tempted to steal ideas or techniques. To maintain an ethical and effective practice, the interventionist must avoid these temptations and pitfalls.

CHAPTER NINE

Changing the Future of Planned Change

In the preceding chapters, I have discussed some lessons that I have derived from more than thirty years of consulting and fifteen years of research. I have argued that social change is about changing the way people think about their social experience, how they act in their social milieu, and how structures are created and sustained to promote stability and valued outcomes. In my view, social scientists like me do not seek the truth about social change. Instead, we attempt to map the territory of social experience. We will never, in my opinion, have a final, settled map of the territory known as human social experience, but we might nonetheless hope to become better mapmakers.[1]

I conclude by reviewing some of the more generative ways that we might think about social change. Then I describe how an interventionist might bring this thinking into action.

Generative Ways of Thinking about Change

To be an effective intervener into human systems, I must have a way of thinking about change that supports and releases my effectiveness. How, then, do people think about change? I suggest five propositions.

Proposition 1: Adaptive change is needed to transform complex human systems.

Over the past six decades, scholars and practitioners have often asserted that there are two basic, distinct ways of thinking about and acting on social change. Michael Beer and Nitin Nohria distinguish between Theory E change led by top-down leaders who develop and execute a plan to alter organizational strategies, systems, and structures, and Theory O change mobilized by collaborative leaders who use a flexible and participative process to transform organizational culture.[2] Douglas McGregor presented us with Theory X, which assumes that people tend to respond largely to financial incentives and often need to be managed through careful supervision and control, and Theory Y, which assumes that people are self-motivated, especially when they are given opportunities to participate in organizational decision making.[3] Chris Argyris wrote articles and books about two opposing theories of action, Model I and Model II, which roughly correspond to more controlling versus more collaborative approaches to leadership and change.[4] Heifetz and Linsky argue that organizational leaders are confronted with technical and adaptive changes.[5] Technical change is needed when the problems we face have known solutions, and the leader's task is to call on experts who know how to solve the problem. Adaptive change is a foray into the unknown, a search for solutions to novel problems that are not fully understood and that require experimentation, exploration, and the mobilization of numerous points of view.

The literature on change is full of distinctions of this sort. On the one hand there is the desire to control and predict; on the other there is the desire to collaborate and explore. It looks as if we have a choice to make. Will we predict and control, or will we negotiate and adapt?

Each human system – whether it is a corporate division, a small business, a government department, a nonprofit agency, a sports team, a school – is unique. Each is composed of a unique collection of individual human beings with their unique life experiences and predispositions. Each has its primary and secondary tasks, its culture, technologies, sense of purpose, sets of procedures, and physical location and infrastructure. Each is acted upon by a unique set of outside forces, and in turn acts upon its environment as it seeks to fulfill its purpose. Each is characterized by a unique configuration of affordances and constraints that open up opportunities and possibilities and also impose boundaries and limitations. In short, a human system is not a simple phenomenon whose functioning is determined by a limited number of linear causal forces. Instead, a human system is *overdetermined* – that is, its functioning is the product of a complex web of interactions and influences that often make it impossible to quickly diagnose or explain the persistent dilemmas and challenges that are encountered by system members.

When a human system is confronted with a challenge that persists over time, that appears resistant to the obvious remedies, and that is experienced differently by different system members, then it is likely that a successful change effort will be more adaptive than technical. Interventionists and system members will need to search for a solution. They will need to form and test hypotheses that allow them to learn more about the challenge, and they may need to question their own assumptions about the nature and operation of their social world.

Proposition 2: Change is situated in unique local circumstances.

The case for an adaptive approach to change derives in part from the realization that change is essentially a local, situated phenomenon. The meaning of this assertion can be seen by considering the way in which an experienced physician arrives at a treatment for a patient. Doctors know that evidence-based treatments often need to be individualized, depending on the health and circumstances of the patient. Each patient is unique. Some have allergies, some have multiple medical conditions and are taking several medications, and some are not able to easily visit a therapist or a pharmacist. A good doctor will take all of this into consideration when prescribing a treatment that is tailored to the circumstances of the unique individual who is seated on the examining table.

An intervener faces the same dilemma. Each human collective is unique. The administrative, clinical, and occupational hierarchies in a big urban teaching hospital differ from the hierarchy in an automobile factory. The culture of an insurance company in Hartford will differ from the culture of a video game producer in Vancouver. An intervention that works in one social milieu might be transferred to a different social milieu where it is then implemented with *fidelity* – that is, in precisely the same way that it was implemented in the first milieu – and yet the second implementation may fail. A good idea in one place may be a bad idea in another. Thus, interventions must almost always be tailored to the unique circumstances of a particular social milieu.

Proposition 3: Change is guided by theories of action.

When we attempt to bring about social change, we do so on the basis of a theory of action. We theorize that action X will produce result Y. For example, a public health official's theory of action might be, *If I provide education about the health risks associated with obesity, more people will engage in exercise and will consume healthy foods.* A chief financial officer's theory of action might be, *If I explain how my company's new order entry system can increase our revenue and provide greater job security and better year-end bonuses, more employees will fill out the order entry screens correctly.*

Our theories of action concerning planned social change are based on assumptions about the causes of human behavior. In the past, many have looked to personality, power, reason, self-interest, and cultural norms as determinants of behavior. Many social psychologists now suggest that human behavior arises out of the social situations that people encounter and that to alter behavior we need to understand and influence situational factors. Finally, some have pointed out that human beings make sense of situations through learned and innate cognitive structures and procedures, and these procedures sometimes lead people to arrive at erroneous conclusions that produce unfortunate courses of action.

I have distilled these ideas and arguments into two statements. The first is a paraphrase of a simple statement proposed by Zaffron and Logan: How people act correlates with how the situation that they are acting in occurs to them.[6] Behavior does not correlate with the situation in itself. Behavior does not correlate with the absolute truth of the situation. Behavior correlates with human thought processes, with how the situation occurs in the mind of the person who is acting in that situation. Behavior correlates with thought.

The second statement has to do with the nature of this thinking. Human thinking is both rational and, borrowing the term from Keith Stanovich, dysrational.[7] This takes into account that how a person acts is often mediated by the defensive routines that the individual has created for himself, and by the defensive routines that have been created by the groups to which the individual belongs. It also takes in the fact that our actions often arise from the heuristics that govern our thinking and acting rather than from reflective or rational thought.

Proposition 4: Defensive behavioral routines will resist efforts to bring about change.

Scholars and practitioners such as Chris Argyris and Erving Goffman have provided a strong foundation of theory and research to account for the pervasiveness of individual and collective defensive routines.[8] My point is that the theory of action that underlies an intervention might be quite sensible, and yet it might be derailed by defensive forces that are not apparent to the intervener.

In part this defensiveness arises from the fact that human thought is structured and organized through mindsets or mental models. We all have our favorite explanations and theories that allow us to see a coherent world. Some may believe that bosses are duplicitous, that middle managers are lazy, or that customer service representatives are uncaring. Others might believe that teamwork and collaboration produce the best results, and that a cultural transformation is more likely to succeed when employees are given opportunities to discuss their fears and aspirations. We all possess theories like this, and we often internalize them into mental models that over time we believe correspond to the underlying structure or order of our social world.[9] These theories play an active role as we scan our surroundings and take in data. They lead us to filter out disconfirming data and to pay most attention to data that support our preferred way of seeing things.

Social psychology has revealed many of the roots that lie beneath this thorny tree of defensiveness. Confirmation bias is the tendency to find and interpret evidence that supports our existing beliefs.[10] The anchoring effect shows that we tend to overemphasize the importance of information gathered early in an inquiry or investigation and de-emphasize information that has turned up later.[11] Cognitive dissonance shows that when people experience an uncomfortable disconfirmation of a deeply held belief, they sometimes refuse to abandon their belief and instead will concoct explanations that allow them to disconfirm the new evidence.[12] These tendencies may make it difficult for proponents of social change to appropriately appraise new evidence and ideas.

Nisbett and Ross have asserted that "The most general and encompassing ... theory of human behavior ... is the assumption that behavior is caused primarily by the enduring and consistent dispositions of the actor, as opposed to the particular characteristics of the situation to which the actor responds."[13] This fundamental attribution error leads us to ignore situational factors that are usually more significant than disposition in explaining behavior. Other social psychologists have conducted research that confirms that much human behavior is situational. Solomon Asch convincingly demonstrated that peer pressure can often lead people to support judgments and opinions that they know to be false.[14] Stanley Milgram's "Obedience to Authority" experiments and Philip Zimbardo's "Stanford Prison Experiment" confirm these findings.[15]

Over the past few decades, cognitive science and neuroscience have revealed numerous heuristics that can interfere with sober, rational judgment, and social psychology has produced a mountain of evidence showing that behavior correlates with situations rather than dispositions. This growing body of work that reveals the phenomenon often labeled as "fast thinking" has not yet been adequately integrated into the theory and practice of social change.[16] This work shows that we humans may not be as rational as we suppose.

Proposition 5: A human system is a pattern of thought, action, and structuring.

Here once again is the model that I propose in this book (figure 9.1).

This model offers a way to think about and approach the functioning of a human system. The system consists of an intertwined pattern of thought, pattern of behavior, and the structuring that arises from and supports these patterns. This, for me, is the basic map. It gives me a flexible way of thinking about any human system that has asked for help in bringing about beneficial change. As I enter into the system and begin interacting with system members,

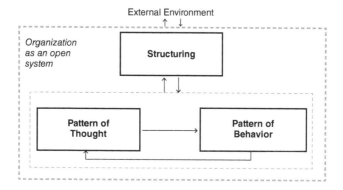

Figure 9.1. A human system as a pattern of thought, behavior, and structuring

I can observe the behaviors; I can begin to see some of the structuring; and I can ask about the thinking – about the aspirations, goals, strategic objectives, culture – and compare these statements with what I observe. As I reveal the full, rich dynamic that brings this framework to life in this system, I am looking for the affordances and constraints that arise from the dynamic.

The point of this map is to allow the framework to expand, to be fleshed out with the unique reality of this client system, so the researcher, the consultant, and the system members can all see the system's pattern of thought, pattern of behavior, and structuring, and how these elements interact with each other and produce a coherent and functional, and perhaps also dysfunctional, whole. Chapter 6 presented some examples of interaction maps that depict an often messy web of influence that produces a somewhat stable equilibrium consisting of a pattern of thought, behavior, and structuring. The point is not to reduce the richness of experience in this system down to an abstract and essential core. Rather, the point is to expand the basic model so we can identify the patterns that are brought to life through interactions within this system and thus identify the constraints that are producing the problematic situation that is limiting the system's performance, as well as possible intervention targets that could nudge the system to a new and more productive equilibrium.

Look back at the elements in figure 9.1 within the embedded dotted-line box, the pattern of thought and pattern of behavior. Remember my paraphrase of Zaffron and Logan: How people act correlates with how the situation that they are acting in occurs to them. The pattern of thought takes in how the situation is occurring for the people in the system. It may include their goals and aspirations, their beliefs about the work that they do and about each other, their expertise or tacit knowledge. I say this is a pattern of thought because for each individual system member, their thinking tends to be organized by the mindsets, the mental models and heuristics, that characterize their cognitive experience; and for the collective as well, the thinking will tend to coalesce into a pattern. This does not mean that everyone is thinking the same thing. It means that the thinking that occurs in the system will arrange itself into a coherent and more-or-less stable pattern.

The pattern of thought correlates with the pattern of behavior. The way in which people experience this behavior and the results produced by it can influence their thinking. We are capable of changing our minds. New thinking can lead to new ways of acting.

This model also recognizes that structuring is an integral part of any human system and that it arises naturally from the patterns that human beings inevitably create. Structuring arises from, and then in turn influences and supports, the patterns that we create. In some cases, working only on the pattern of thought and behavior may fail to produce sustainable change because the compelling force of a system's structuring will push the behaviors back into the previous routines. Similarly, in some cases working only on a system's structuring may fail to produce sustainable change because the compelling force of a system's pattern causality will undermine and overturn efforts to create change through structure.

So far, I have been talking about ways to think about social change. Now I want to consider what we might do about this.

What Is a Helpful Way to Act on This Thinking?

A pragmatic view of knowledge is implicit in the work of Lewin, Argyris, and Schein: knowledge is for action. This epistemological position links to an important principle for human systems interveners. When I work with a client, I am helping that client to conduct a search, and the purpose of this search is to yield a useful way of responding to an adaptive challenge – a challenge that has no known or correct solution but that might be responded to in a variety of ways, depending on the client's capacity and on the values and preferences of the people who have a stake in the challenge. Our work is a search for new knowledge that will then allow system members to produce new behaviors. I act as a guide on this search, but not in the sense that I know where we are going and am familiar with our destination. Rather, I know something about venturing into the unknown, and I have some skill at creating new knowledge by mapping a new and unknown territory.

As we conduct the search, we – the intervener and the client – must remain in the stance of the searcher. I must help my client to achieve this stance. I must help to create the conditions needed for us to conduct the search. I think of this as working *on* the context rather than *in* the context.

Remember that the situation is occurring for the client *in context*, and that this correlates with the behaviors that the client is able to produce. My job is to help the client to alter their context.[17]

Helping the client to create a new context for experiencing their challenges is not like helping somebody to learn a recipe and cook a meal. It is not like executing a procedure. It is more like remaining in an attitude, a stance, that may allow the client to see something that they have not been able to see before.

When I try to create the conditions for a person or a group of people to achieve something new – for instance, when I am creating the conditions for my undergraduate students to learn or for my client to understand what is making it difficult for them to implement their strategic plan – when I am trying to create these conditions, I often see myself as balancing a set of competing priorities. I want to foster independence and provide support. I want to respect the system's fragility and help system members to take a risk.

To create the conditions needed for a client to engage in a productive search, the intervener must perform the four balancing acts that we have been discussing throughout this book.

Balancing Confrontation with Compassion

The first balancing act sees the intervener balancing the need to challenge and at times push the client toward success with the need to create safety and to show compassion for the client. The intervener is confrontational *and* compassionate.

On the one hand, we have the importance of the helping relationship and of the need to create and maintain psychological safety. Members of the client system are in a troubled state. They are worried and uncertain. On the other hand, there is the need to support members of the client system as they experiment with new ideas, new interpretations, new behaviors, and new structuring. To change things, the client must act.

When thinking about this balancing act, I like the contrast that one can discern between the ideas and approaches of Edgar Schein and those of Chris Argyris. Schein is the proponent of the helping relationship and humble inquiry. He believes that one is confronting the client when one merely expresses an opinion. If the consultant can create the conditions for psychological safety – which Carl Rogers defined as unconditional positive regard, congruence, and empathy toward the client – then the client will enter into a state that allows for learning and change.[18] The consultant need only ask questions. Schein talks about using pure inquiry and exploratory diagnostic inquiry to help the client see things differently. This new way of seeing will release new behaviors.

I believe that Schein is quite right to emphasize the importance of the helping relationship and of the need to create the conditions for safety. In the disciplines of clinical and counseling psychology there is considerable research that supports the contention that the single biggest factor that "causes" positive change in clients is the person of the therapist.[19] It seems that much change is relational.

At the same time, however, we have the inescapable need for action. For things to change, people need to do things. Feeling safe is not enough. Out of psychological safety must emerge the willingness to experiment with new behaviors. And for this to happen, sometimes the consultant must show the client things that were previously hidden and be firm in the face of client ambivalence.

This is why Chris Argyris suggests that while some leaders, consultants, and scholars place a high value on harmonious relationships, to achieve organizational excellence it can be important to create competence, learning, and justice.[20] Argyris reminds us that it is almost always necessary for the consultant to confront the client with disturbing facts. If the consultant is overly concerned with making the client feel good, it may become difficult to intervene. Argyris emphasizes the need to "create conditions of psychological success"[21] that involve open-mindedness, self-confidence, and competence, and that are achieved when a person takes personal responsibility for attaining goals.[22]

We must balance the goodwill and validation of psychological safety with the competence and risk taking of psychological success. The intervener must balance confrontation with compassion.

Balancing the Planned with the Emergent

In the second balancing act, the intervener balances the need to engage in planned and intentional activity with the need to be open to the emergent and unexpected. The intervener stays the course *and* changes course.

This is one of the most difficult things for an intervener to grasp, and I think it fair to say that during my work as a consultant on large projects, one of the main causes of failure was the unwillingness or inability of those undertaking a change initiative to take in new and unexpected information and to make the necessary course corrections. We do need a plan to begin with. We have to know where to put down our foot when we take the first step. We begin with a theory of action – a theory concerning what actions are needed in these circumstances to bring about the changes that we require.

However, when we are intervening in a complex social system – and all human systems are complex – then it is usually not possible for us to predict the future. Our initial theories of action are almost always based on incomplete or inaccurate information. We are going to need to learn more about the client system as we do our work; and we are almost certainly going to find that we are making mistakes and that we are uncovering new information. We are going to need to revise and refine the intervention plan as we move forward.

For me, one way to think about this is to recognize that the problem is in the room. Whenever I am with the client, interacting with one person, a few people, or a large group, the problem that we are working on is there with us, showing up in our interactions.

When the client and I begin to work together, we talk about the problem or challenge or opportunity that will be our focus as a thing-like phenomenon that is out there somewhere in the organization. We are going to work on that thing. We meet together in a boardroom and we talk about the problem. We fill white boards and flip chart sheets with our bullet-point ideas about the problem and what is to be done about it. It is out there somewhere.

But the skilled intervener knows that this is not true. If systems thinking is correct, if group dynamics are real, then the problem must, by definition, be with us in the room. It is showing up in the pattern of thought and pattern of behavior that characterize this group and is present with us as we work together in the room. It is showing up in the structuring that supports our efforts. It is there in the affordances and constraints that characterize our way of working together in the "here and now."

And this means that I do not need to wait to intervene until the moment prescribed by the formal intervention plan. I do not need to think of the intervention as a sort of safari that we are all going to go on when we leave the boardroom and venture out into the organization.

Instead, as I become skilled in seeing the problem show up in the patterns in the room, and as I become more confident of my abilities, I can intervene in the moment. I can say," I am noticing X, Y, and Z. Are others noticing this?" And if they are, I might say, "This looks like an example of the situation that we have been discussing for the past hour. Do others see it that way?" And if enough people say yes, I might ask, "What would you like to do about it?" And then, with humility and courage, we might set aside the formal plan and tackle the problem as it presents itself in the room as we are working.

Balancing Participation with Observation

The third balancing act calls for the intervener to balance the need to become part of the client system with the need to remain distinct and apart. The intervener participates *and* observes.

Pattern causality acts like a gravitational force at work in the social field. You step into the client system and, possibly without realizing it, you are caught by this gravitational force. The system is pulling you in. If you allow yourself to be pulled into the patterns at work in this system, you are no longer in a position to be helpful. Though this may sound eerie or mysterious, be assured that it is real. Human beings are social animals, and it is in our nature to find ways to fit into human groups. Goffman's theory of impression management, Argyris's and Schön's theory of defensive routines, and many articles and books in the fields of social, evolutionary, and moral psychology help to explain this phenomenon. It has been my experience that this is sometimes a difficult subject for people to discuss. We all experience the phenomenon and understand it, but we nearly always feel compelled to assert that it does not apply to us. "Not me. Oh gosh no, I am always very honest and straight. I never worry about my reputation. I just do my thing."

Don't believe it.

The client system will try to pull us in. We need to get close enough to do our job, but we must ensure that we are not immersed in the dynamics that are producing the problem that we are there to help resolve.

You need to get close, but not too close. You need to be friendly and helpful, but not too friendly.

Watch for these warning signs. Are you taking sides? Are you starting to think that there are good guys and bad guys in the system? This can sometimes be an indication that the system is pulling you in. To guard against this danger, I often try to persuade myself that this human system is putting on a play, and that all of the people I meet are terrific people who have been cast in their various roles. After all, social psychology tells us that their behavior is rising up out of the situation and should not be attributed to some bone-deep disposition. So, if some people are doing things that trouble or irritate me, and if I notice that others are also troubled, I do not participate in the blaming and the gossip.

Collusion, transference, projective identification, emotional contagion – there are many theories that offer explanations for this phenomenon. When a human person or group comes into relationship with another human person or group, there is a negotiation, a coupling that occurs to allow the relationships to be sustained. We tune ourselves to each other. I take on some of you and you take on some of me.

This is the sort of thing that Watzlawick and colleagues were getting at when they described the pragmatics of human communication.[23] Their description of the explicit and implicit nature of human communication is apt. I state my message explicitly, and I also make an implicit claim about the nature of our relationship and of this shared situation. You reply with your explicit message, and you make your implicit claim. Back and forth we go, exchanging information and ideas aloud, and silently negotiating our relationship. If this is accurate, then members of the client system will always be making their silent appeals to us, reeling us in to their orbit.

Balancing Assertion with Inquiry

The fourth and final balancing act requires that the intervener balance the inclination to tell the client the solution to client problems with the need to create the conditions in which members of the client system can discover the answers for themselves. The intervener asserts *and* inquires.

As Edgar Schein says, "One of the most important functions of process consultation is to make visible that which is invisible … The first step in making things visible … is … to create the conditions that will motivate the client to see more deeply …"[24]

I love what Schein says here. We must create the conditions in which the situation may occur for the client in a new way, implying that this new way of seeing and knowing may then correlate with behaviors that were previously inaccessible to the client. If I am able to be appropriately confrontational *and* compassionate, if I am able to stay the course *and* change course, if I am willing to balance my participation in *and* my observation of the client system, then together the client and I may be able to produce a map that reveals what was previously hidden, that makes the invisible visible for the first time.

So together we engage in the process of creating this new map. The client and I discuss what questions should be asked, and I participate in that discussion. I make my assertions. The client and I together participate in the data-gathering activities, usually interviews, and data emerge from the conversations that we create together. This means that the client and I are talking about things, we are gathering and agreeing on facts, we are considering interpretations and possibilities, we are considering hypotheses. From time to time, I notice the problem in the room, and I ask questions about it, and the client then displays their capacity to confront what is hidden, and also creates new capacity. By the time I bring the data back to members of the system, first in an unpolished but organized form, and then gathered into a maplike drawing derived from the many conversations that we have had, the client has already begun to transform.

Adding to Our Mapmaking Capacity

I have shared with you my current thinking about planned social change, and about what I think is a useful way to bring that thinking into action. There remains a great deal of work to be done.

I am troubled by the lack of skill I observe in framing problems as problems that can be solved. It seems to me that we are experiencing something of a crisis in problem framing these days, and evidence of this can be found in how we are reacting to the big challenges facing humans today – climate change, population growth, bloated and ineffective health systems, ongoing violent conflict, the ravages of a global pandemic, political polarization, and so on. Donald Schön has provided a lucid description of how an expert practitioner seeks to understand the affordances and constraints of a problematic situation by engaging in a sort of conversation with the problem, searching for a framing of the problem that points us toward a solution.[25] Knowledge is for action, and thus we value the act of solving the problem as much as we value the elegance and accuracy of the diagnosis.

However, this may leave us trapped in our existing mindsets that are preventing us from seeing important facets of the problematic situation. It may also leave us at the mercy of the heuristics and cognitive shortcuts that prevent us from fully understanding the way in which a complex human system is producing unwanted and limiting patterns. We need an actionable understanding of the process of framing problems that maintains the pragmatism needed by people who are facing important and intractable challenges and that also helps us to reduce the errors produced by our cognitive apparatus.

More work needs to focus on our inability to move knowledge into action. Why are there not more learning organizations? We need to improve our ability to hear and understand the perspectives, experiences, and ideas of others, especially people with whom we disagree. We need more explanations for the incongruence of intention and action – for the knowing-doing gap – and interventions to help us address these challenges. We need to continue to investigate the factors that contribute to our inability to see, understand, explain, and act on hidden dysfunctions within our social systems.

We need to integrate the recent findings of cognitive psychology and neuroscience and behavioral economics into the field of human systems intervention. This work has hardly begun, and it is urgently needed.

Finally, instead of settling on a few questions and an all-encompassing reductive theory of social change, we need to get better at defining the best processes for searching out ideas and answers within unique social situations, and we need to get better at persuading others that it is the way of searching for answers, and not the answer itself, that should be our central concern.

Notes

Part One: Thinking about Change

1 Beer and Nohria (2000).
2 McGregor (2006).
3 Likert (1967).
4 Argyris explains this distinction in many of his publications. Try Argyris (1993).
5 Heifetz and Linsky (2002).

1 Terms of Art

1 My slide was based on the work of Smith (2002), whose review of published accounts of organizational change initiatives yielded an overall average success rate of 33 per cent. More recent studies confirm that the success rate of organizational change initiatives may run between 30 per cent and 40 per cent (Stouten, Rousseau, & De Cremer 2018). However, these numbers are controversial. For example, Hughes (2011) reviewed five instances of the claim that organizational change faces a failure rate of about 70 per cent, and argued that there is no reliable empirical evidence to support this claim. More recently, Jones, Firth, Hannibal, and Ogunseyin (2019) looked at 200 reflective case studies produced by mature business students in the United Kingdom, and found that 72.5 per cent of the cases recounted successful change initiatives. We cannot settle this dispute here, but I think it worth noting that although a special 2011 issue of the *Journal of Change Management* suggested reasons for some healthy skepticism about the oft-repeated claims of a 70 per cent failure rate, in the introduction to the issue the editor wrote "it would be wrong to deny that

many organizations do seem to struggle to implement change successfully" (Burnes 2011, 446).

2 For a useful discussion of the competing priorities faced by family doctors,
and how this influences their clinical decisions, see Gabbay and Le May (2011).

3 For more on the concept of fidelity, see Ansari, Fiss, and Zajac (2010).

4 Schein (1999) makes this suggestion on page 17 of his now-classic book on
process consulting.

5 Virtually all of Chris Argyris's books deal with his notion of a theory of action (for example: Argyris 1993, 2010). Typically, he claims that we all possess
such a theory, and that it is often the case that people in organizations have
an *espoused* theory of action (that is, if you ask them about the intentions
that underlie their actions, they will describe to you certain principles that
they claim give rise to their actions) and a *theory-in-use* (that is, the theory of
action that you can infer by observing them act in the organization, and that
often differs in important ways from their espoused theory). In other words,
Argyris says that people often say one thing and do another. The field of program evaluation often refers to the program theory, or the theory of action,
that underlies the design of a program to bring about change. The theory of
action can often be depicted as a logic model illustrating the causal connec-
tions between actions taken via the program and the outcomes produced by
those actions. See Patton's (2015) discussion of program models and theories
of change to get an idea of how the concept is used by evaluators.

6 For a useful review of Frederick Taylor's scientific approach to management, which called for the strict control of distracting social factors in the
workplace, see Clegg and Dunkerley (1980) and Schwartzman (1993).

7 The work that can best be called the classic presentation of the Hawthorne
Experiments is Roethlisberger and Dickson (2003). Elton Mayo's 1949
work offers the perspective of the Harvard researcher who joined the research team in the late 1920s. For an early social psychology interpretation
of the research results, see Homans (1950).

8 The well-known forming-storming theory of group development was
first presented by Bruce Tuckman (1965). For a more recent perspective on
group development theory, see Bushe and Coetzer (2007). For an attempt
to review and synthesize the numerous theories of group development that
were created in the second half of the twentieth century, see G. Smith (2001).

9 Many consider the standard text on culture to be Schein (2004).

10 These subjects are covered well, and with reference to the Hawthorne experiments, by Homans (1950). For a more recent treatment of group phenomena see Smith and Berg (1987).

11 One of the Hawthorne experiments showed how supportive leadership and a collaborative atmosphere produced cooperation and greater productivity, and another showed how employee distrust of management intentions resulted in the development of implicit norms to keep productivity low. Homans (1950) provides a useful discussion of these results.

12 The term "group dynamics" first appeared in Kurt Lewin's 1939 article. An excellent account of how the term came into being can be found in Marrow (1969). Excellent overviews of the subject of group dynamics can be found in Fisher and Ellis (1990) and in Smith and Berg (1987). Recently some interesting work has focused on the sensemaking patterns that are evident in groups as they collectively construct an understanding of their shared reality. See Thurlow and Mills (2009), and especially Weick, Sutcliffe, and Obstfeld (2005).

13 Senge (1990).

14 See page 169 of Lewin (1951).

15 An interesting discussion of the tendency of human beings to see things in terms of causation can be found on page 74 of Kahneman (2011). See also Taleb (2010).

16 The definitive source on realistic evaluation is Pawson and Tilley (1997).

17 I have read that a better translation of his actual words would be "no plan of operations extends with any certainty beyond the first contact with the main hostile force." See page 92 of von Moltke (1993), translated by Daniel J. Hughes and Harry Bell.

18 Pawson and Tilley (1997) have a useful discussion of the trials and tribulations faced by program evaluators. Ansari, Fiss, and Zajac (2010) provide a useful discussion of fidelity in relation to the diffusion of corporate practices across social boundaries. A good discussion of the use of fidelity in program evaluation can be found in Fixsen and colleagues (2005, 2007). For an interesting case illustration of the tensions between fidelity and adaptability during implementation, see Aarons and colleagues (2012).

19 Realistic evaluation is covered well in Pawson and Tilley (1997). For discussions of developmental evaluation, see Patton (2011), Conklin and colleagues (2015), and Rey, Tremblay, and Brousselle (2013).

2 Doing Things *to* People and Doing Things *with* People

1 Our research is reported in Hart and Conklin (2006).

2 Waddell (1995).

3 The quotation appears on page 4 of Bennis, Benne, and Chin (1985).

4　Chin and Benne (1985).

5　Daniels and Dewine (1991).

6　The idea here is that conscious human agents create or construct social facts. This process of construction occurs through social interaction, where groups of people talk and interact in ways that bring social facts, including organizations and institutions, into existence. The Statue of Liberty is not a social fact. It is a distinct and real physical object. The meaning of the physical object known as the Statue of Liberty, however, is a social fact that is constructed by human beings through their thoughts and interactions. Some see the statue as a symbol of freedom. Others might see it as a symbol of American imperialism. The argument in this book includes the suggestion that when we want to bring about change involving social facts, we need to invoke the processes through which these facts come into being. That is to say, our change process must involve human thinking, behavior, and structuring. For readers who would like to delve into the literature on the construction of social reality, I recommend Berger and Luckmann (1966), Goffman (1959), and Searle (1995).

7　A concise treatment of dialogic OD can be found in Bushe and Marshak (2015).

8　See page 409 of Bushe and Marshak (2015).

9　An interesting discussion of pattern causality can be found in Argyris (1993). The advocates of dialogic OD have made a useful contribution by emphasizing the importance of meaning-making patterns in organizations, in part by teasing out some of the implications from the work of Argyris (with help from his colleague Donald Schön) and also from the work of Karl Weick on organizational sensemaking. Readers interested in these ideas and their practical applications may consult Argyris, Putnam, and Smith (1985) and Weick (1995, 2009).

10　See page 410 of Bushe and Marshak (2015).

11　Michael Stauffacher and colleagues (2008) have shown how stakeholders can be involved in different ways at different times during an initiative, and that the overall collaboration can be designed in ways that allow participants to learn together.

12　The argument that follows draws on the work of Frank Dumont (1993), who considered how these cognitive errors might negatively affect the clinical reasoning of a psychotherapist. Many of Dumont's arguments apply equally well to the errors that change agents may make while working with organizational clients. Other excellent sources on the subject include Kahneman (2011), Taleb (2010), and Haidt (2012).

13　Hume (1969/1739).

14 Watzlawick (1976) gave an early account of this phenomenon. This is essentially the same dilemma that Chris Argyris (1983) attempts to resolve with his ladder of inference. We take in the raw data through our senses, and as we consider it, we invariably create layers of meaning and interpretation by contexting the data against our past experiences and acquired knowledge. While this is happening, we often continue to think that we are merely observing and contemplating the facts of the situation, when in fact different witnesses to the same situation are all now dealing with a different set of facts.

15 Quite a few theorists and researchers have commented on this phenomenon. Carol Dweck (2006), for example, has looked at personal development and success in terms of generative and constraining "mindsets." Gabbay and Le May (2011) have studied the extent to which innovations are able to enter into a primary care practice's "mindlines." Argyris (2010) and Senge (1990) have both considered the extent to which mental models orient us toward the social world, and Argyris (2010), Bartunek (1984), and Bartunek and Moch (1987) have suggested that double-loop or transformational learning is needed to challenge existing mental models. Kegan and Lahey (2009) suggest that certain big assumptions (that we are often unaware of) tend to constrain the way we think and act when faced with difficult situations. Finally, Festinger (1957) and more recent researchers have shown that our need to minimize cognitive dissonance plays tricks with our reasoning, leading us to be more likely to confirm existing beliefs and to disregard evidence that could challenge such beliefs. All of this indicates that we keep a map of the social world in our mind, and we constantly reference this map as we encounter the situations of daily life. The map tends to anchor us to our existing way of seeing things and being in the world and makes it difficult for us to behold new possibilities and territories in our social environment.

16 See the discussion in Nickerson (1998).

17 See page 202 of Dumont (1993).

18 Festinger (1957).

19 See page 98 of Kahneman (2011).

20 Kahneman (2011) provides a useful summary of this research.

21 See page 199 of Dumont (1993).

22 See page 31 of Nisbett and Ross (1980).

23 Nisbett and Ross (1980, 31).

24 Kahn (2003).

25 Asch (1955).

26 My account here relies on Milgram's own report of the experiments (1974), and on Blass's excellent intellectual biography of Milgram (Blass, 2004).
27 See page 31 of Milgram (1974).
28 Blass (2009).
29 Burger (2009).

3 Searching for Answers

1 I am drawing on Schön's ideas on problem framing here (Schön 1983).
2 I particularly like the distinction elaborated by Heifetz and Linsky (2002) in this regard. Also useful are Argyris and Schön's (1978) discussion of single- and double-loop learning, and Bartunek's (1984) and Bartunek and Moch's (1987) work on levels of transformative learning and change.
3 Some readers may find it useful to relate this distinction between technical and adaptive problems to the distinction offered by Karl Popper in his essay "Of Clouds and Clocks: An Approach to the Problem of Rationality and the Freedom of Man" (Popper 1972).
4 See page 31 of Kegan and Lahey (2009).
5 See Barley (1996) and Barley and Bechky (1994).
6 The project is reported in an article published by Troy Hartley, who acted as the academic partner and facilitator for the process (Hartley 2006).
7 For a useful discussion of the importance of thought (mental models, schemata, attitudes, beliefs), behaviors, and social structures in transformational change, see Argyris and Schön (1978), Bartunek (1984), and Bartunek and Moch (1987).
8 For our purposes, *social structure* refers to the structuring that arises from patterns of thought and action that are characteristic of a social milieu. These patterns are widely recognized and accepted as part of the existing status quo. A social structure can be rather small and contained, such as a group norm that helps to shape the behavior of a particular project team. A social structure can also be monolithic and widespread, such as the rules that govern democratic elections in a state, province, or nation. When we are concerned with organizational change, the social structures that will tend to concern us include the formalized rules and procedures in an organization, such as the organization's published vision, mission, values, and strategic plan, as well as its standard operating procedures, job descriptions, organizational chart, performance appraisal system, professional development plans, and other documented policies and procedures that are used in the daily routines of the organization. The social structures will also include the informal ways of operating that are part

of the cultures of operating units and occupational groups, such as the norms about how much information subordinates will share with superiors, the ways in which interpersonal conflicts are handled, the way time is managed (Are deadlines of paramount importance, or are they elastic? Do meetings begin on time? Do people remain at work until their work is complete, or do they leave promptly at quitting time?), and the way internal and external clients are treated (with respect, with derision, with compassion and attention, with benign neglect?).

9 Statistics Canada, *Annual demographic estimates: Canada, provinces and territories, 2020*. Downloaded on 6 April 2021, from https://www150.statcan.gc.ca/n1/pub/91-215-x/91-215-x2020001-eng.htm.

10 These projections were obtained from the Statistics Canada website on 16 February 2017: http://www.statcan.gc.ca/pub/91-520-x/2010001/part-partie3-eng.htm.

11 Statistics Canada, *Population projections for Canada, provinces and territories (2009-2036)*. (Cat. No. 91-520 XIE).

12 I retrieved this information from the Alzheimer Society of Canada website on 12 November 2015. http://www.alzheimer.ca/en/About-dementia/What-is-dementia/Dementia-numbers.

13 Gutmanis and colleagues (2015).

14 Gino and Staats (2015).

15 Schön (1983).

16 Gino and Staats (2015, 114–15).

17 In his work on dialogue, William Isaacs (1999) has suggested that conversations can be designed to allow people to think together in productive ways.

18 I developed this model on the basis of the research into social change that I have conducted over the past decade, and also on the basis of my consulting experience. I was also influenced by the work of action scientists and by the published work of scholars interested in transformational learning and change. In particular, I refer readers to Argyris and Schön (1978), Bartunek (1984), and Bartunek and Moch (1987).

19 Zaffron and Logan (2009).

20 The presence of a pattern of thought is not meant to suggest that all people in an organization have the same opinions, ideas, assumptions, and goals about their work and workplace. Some research shows that managers and employees may have very different ideas about their organizations (Smircich and Chesser 1981), and a recent case study has dramatically illustrated how differing patterns of thought and behavior among senior leaders and middle managers can produce serious dysfunction in an organization (Vuori and Huy 2016).

21 The field of action science posits the existence of a social force termed "pattern causality." Pattern causality suggests that a collective human behavioral pattern, a group dynamic, sustains itself through processes of self-regulation. System members are "regulated" into conforming with the pattern, and newcomers who enter the system are pulled into conformity with the pattern. The importance of this notion of pattern causality is that it challenges the idea held by some that all social change can be accomplished by modifying the social structures that contain and influence behavior. Action science indicates that changing social structure *will not necessarily* produce sustainable behavior change. Pattern causality acts like a gravitational force at work in the social field. You step into the client system and, possibly without realizing it, you are caught by this gravitational force. The system is pulling you in. Human beings are social animals, and it is in our nature to find ways to fit into human groups. See Argyris, Putnam, and Smith (1985) and Goffman (1959).

Part Two: The Doing of Change

1 See for example, Kotter (2007, 2012).
2 For example, Hughes (2016).
3 Stouten, Rousseau, and De Cremer (2018).

4 Creating a Contract with Your Client

1 In a watershed essay Lewin (1947) uses the term "freezing" for the third stage in his process, but most commentators have substituted the term "refreezing." For a recent and comprehensive review of the Lewin model, see Bartunek and Woodman (2015). Cummings, Bridgman, and Brown (2016) offer a contrary view when they argue that Lewin is not responsible for the creation of this three-step model, suggesting that the theory was developed only after he died. Their argument is intriguing and will be of interest to scholars. Nonetheless, it is certainly the case that in his 1947 essay Lewin included a brief section entitled "Changing at Three Steps: Unfreezing, Moving, and Freezing of Group Standards" (34). Although he did not elaborate these ideas into a comprehensive theory, many subsequent scholars and practitioners regard this as a formative moment in theorizing about planned change.
2 See page 35 of Lewin (1947).
3 Bridges (1991).
4 Kotter (2012).

5 Block (2011).
6 Kolb (1984).
7 See for example Langley and colleagues (2009).
8 Some readers may wish to know how big an experiential base I rely on. I did not keep a record of the number of consulting engagements I carried out up to the time of writing this book, so I am going to have to perform a calculation based on certain assumptions. First, I operated a busy consulting practice, which became a consultancy with fourteen employees at its peak, for twenty years. On average, I estimate that I was directly involved in six consulting engagements per year (this, I think, is conservative). Then for six more years I worked as an academic and research scientist, and also worked on about two consulting contracts per year. If this is reasonably correct, then my experience is based on direct participation (usually as the principal consultant) in at least 132 consulting engagements. Some projects would be relatively brief, perhaps involving some facilitation and sensemaking activities and lasting about one month. Others were major cultural and process transformation projects that continued for several years.
9 Combs and Gonzalez (1971, 204).
10 Argyris 2006, 161.
11 I have altered some details of this engagement to protect the identity of the organization and of the people who participated in this process. Nonetheless, this story accurately reports the mishaps in our contracting process.
12 For an interesting discussion of these different views, see Macey and Schneider (2008).
13 See Kahn and Fellows (2013), and also Macey and Schneider (2008).
14 This is the idea that underlies the service excellence framework recommended by some public sector researchers (for example, Heintzman and Marson 2005).
15 I try to create a project structure that allows for collaboration and interaction. I have found that most clients agree to the following approach. First, we create a "core team" of client system members who will act as the project leaders and who will be my primary contacts during the intervention process. A core team can consist of from three to seven people, and should include representatives from the core areas who have a stake in the problematic situation. A core team may meet as often as once a week, will participate in most project activities, and will act as the body that makes decisions or recommendations concerning the project. Second, we create an "advisory group" that links the project to all internal and external stakeholder groups who have information to contribute to the effort, and who may exert influence that could affect the project's success. This is sometimes a larger group

with from twelve to twenty-four members, who meet from three to four times over the course of the project. The advisory group provides advice on the project approach. They also help to interpret findings and design approaches, and they can often assist with the spread and scaling of the intervention in the case of large organizations or systems.

16 Through my consulting experience, and through my own experience as an organizational leader, I have learned that it is increasingly unpopular today to talk about superiors and subordinates in organizations. People prefer to talk about teamwork and collaboration, and to suggest that power differentials are becoming less important in today's fast-moving, technology-infused organizations. I urge readers to be cautious about believing these cheery claims about organizational democracy. As I write this chapter, a colleague and I are consulting to a large, national nonprofit organization known for the excellent work that it does to provide services to disadvantaged and suffering segments of the population. We heard the usual words about teamwork and collaboration as we entered this organization to begin our work, but within a few weeks we had accumulated a mounting pile of evidence that this organization was in fact a traditional hierarchy with power centered at the top, and with fiefdoms of functional power and influence creating silos throughout the organization. As Chris Argyris might have said, the espoused theory of these organizational leaders was that power and decision rights were shared among superiors and subordinates (so much so that the terms "superiors" and "subordinates" were anathema to our client), but their theory-in-use saw the centralization of decision making and the exercise of unilateral control by organizational leaders.

17 Edgar Schein (2006) proposes a more complex view of the client that includes six types of client: contact clients, intermediate clients, primary clients, unwitting clients, indirect clients, and ultimate clients. I encourage readers to take a look at Schein's model and to use it if this level of detail is useful. For me, I have usually found it sufficient to distinguish between the client who holds power and authority over the system and over the contract and those who are to a greater or lesser extent implicated in the problematic situation that we are concerned with.

5 Exploring the Client System

1 Marilyn Taylor (1986) suggests a simple and useful model for understanding the emotional reactions of learners as they acquire new knowledge and skills. Some former students and I described how this discomfort can be experienced by graduate students (Conklin, Kyle, and Robertson 2012).

2 Taylor (1986).

3 Conklin (2010a).

4 I should add that I did not necessarily always believe the two people who repeatedly phoned me during this consulting engagement. That is to say, I did not treat what they told me as the "true facts" of the situation. Rather, I accepted their descriptions and concerns as their perspectives about what was going on. Generally, when people whisper their views to me out of earshot of others, I find that they are usually pinning the blame for things on one or two of their colleagues. Leslie doesn't know how to collaborate with customers. John is stuck in the old paradigm. Sheri is too risk averse for this organization. I notice that there is a quality of "you and I know better" to these intimate disclosures. I try to pay attention to what is happening. People are whispering behind other people's backs. That may be one of the patterns that characterize this workplace. I listen. I indicate that I understand what they are saying, but I am careful to avoid agreeing with my unsought confidant(e). I continue to gather data.

5 I derive this idea of making that which exists only in one's subjective experience into an object that can be examined and acted upon from Robert Kegan's subject-object theory (Kegan 1994). An application of the theory to individual and organizational change can be found in Kegan and Lahey (2009).

6 Readers interested in this phenomenon may wish to consult the work of Kahn (2004), Moylan (1994), and Petriglieri and Wood (2003).

7 Dumont and Fitzpatrick (2001).

8 Varda Mann-Feder (2002) offers a useful summary of the forms of collusion in her discussion of use of self among youth workers.

9 William Kahn (2004) provides an account of a consulting engagement in which this very sort of collusion took hold.

10 Moylan (1994).

11 An excellent general text on qualitative methods is Michael Patton's popular and useful text (*Qualitative Research & Evaluation Methods*, 2015). In some ways, an intervention into a human system can resemble an action research project. Action research is an approach to research originally developed by Kurt Lewin that involves close collaboration between researchers and research subjects. The classic text on action research (and very thorough, at more than 700 pages) is by Reason and Bradbury (2008). Less extensive works are also available (for example, McNiff and Whitehead 2011). Krueger and Casey (2009) have written an excellent text on focus groups. An interventionist is often trying to gather data to create a map or model of the client system, showing how the problematic situation

is preventing the system from achieving goals or acting on intentions. A well-regarded qualitative text about the construction of models or theories on the basis of qualitative data is Glaser and Strauss's original description of grounded theory (Glaser and Strauss, 1967).

12 Conklin (2010b).

13 Conklin (2010b).

14 In fact, Ohanian (2008) published an entire book about Einstein's more notable errors.

15 After Clinton's defeat in the 2016 presidential election, political pundits were quick to itemize a variety of errors made by her before and during the campaign. Some argue that one of Churchill's most egregious errors was his assessment and handling of Gandhi and the question of Indian independence. Others like to hold up the Gallipoli campaign during the First World War as Churchill's most famous blunder. Gandhi has been accused of bungling on a number of issues as he attempted to steer India toward independence. In an interview with Alex Haley that was published in 1965, Dr. Martin Luther King, Jr., probably the most revered historical figure in the civil rights movement, candidly discussed a number of errors that he believed he had made. Arguably, the most effective people (including people who live in your neighborhood as well as world historic figures like Churchill, Gandhi, and Dr. King) have the ability to own up to their mistakes and to learn from them.

16 For example, see Kolb (1984) and Mumford (1997).

17 See Conklin (2010a) and Macintosh-Murray (2007).

18 Patton (2011).

6 Making Sense of Things

1 Some OD scholars claim that diagnostic approaches based on problem solving tend to generate "negative energy" within human systems and are less effective than positive or dialogic approaches that focus more on strengths and emerging opportunities (for example, see the first chapter of Bunker and Alban 2006). Dialogic and large group approaches are important and useful innovations, and their ongoing development should be encouraged and studied. I also believe that diagnostic approaches are important and valuable. Lewin's force field analysis is a method for revealing the countervailing forces that facilitate and impede a change initiative, and the usefulness of this diagnostic technique has been commented on many times (for example, see Grimshaw and colleagues 2012, and also the endorsement by Kahneman 1992). The balancing acts approach

is a diagnostic frame that includes dialogic elements. The approach considers the intractable challenge that the organization is contending with, and seeks to understand, mitigate, and if possible resolve the challenge through a structured yet flexible and reflective process that combines the strengths of problem solving and dialogue. The approach recognizes and works with the complexity of human systems and recommends a process of perspective sharing and dialogue as people think together about challenges, opportunities, and ways to move forward.

I also suggest that more research is needed to distinguish and appraise the merits and drawbacks of diagnostic, dialogic, large group, and positive approaches to organizational change. For example, to what extent might the findings of Tversky and Kahneman (see Kahneman 2011) on how humans typically appraise gains and losses be pertinent for positive versus diagnostic approaches to organizational change? Might one argue that positive approaches seek to capitalize on strengths, on areas where the organization is currently "winning," whereas problem-solving approaches seek to mitigate or transform areas where problems are undermining organizational performance, areas where the organization is currently "losing"? People experience different emotional responses to actions that could produce gains or losses. They are cautious when considering a gain (a bird in the hand is worth two in the bush) but are more prone to risk taking when trying to avoid a loss (fortune favors the bold). Does this mean that some people experiencing a positive approach are likely to be satisfied with small wins, while some people engaging in a problem-solving approach are more likely to pursue transformative change?

2 Argyris (1990).
3 Kegan and Lahey (2009).
4 The "anchoring effect" shows that we tend to overemphasize the importance of information gathered early in an inquiry or investigation and de-emphasize information that turns up later. Cognitive dissonance shows that when people experience an uncomfortable disconfirmation of a deeply held belief, they sometimes refuse to abandon their belief and instead will concoct explanations that allow them to disconfirm the new evidence. These tendencies may make it difficult for interventionists and clients to appropriately appraise new evidence and ideas. See Kahneman (2011).
5 Kegan and Lahey (2009) offer a comprehensive technique for surfacing hidden assumptions in a social milieu.
6 Kahn (2015) provides a useful discussion of assessing client capacity.
7 Isaacs (1999).

8 For a useful summary of scapegoating theory, see the chapter on prejudice in Aronson (2012).
9 Lieberson and O'Connor (1972) were among the first to advance this argument from a sociological perspective in 1972. Although the debate continues, many scholars would agree that the impact of a CEO on firm performance is mediated by several factors, and a charismatic CEO is not a sufficient condition for firm success (Clark, Murphy, and Singer 2013; Collingwood 2009; Fitza 2017; and Thomas 1994).
10 See for example Dixon (2007), Eagle and Newton (1981), Gemmill (1989), Keyton (1999), and Kline (1997).
11 This is consistent with the findings from Kurt Lewin's leadership experiments with children's hobby clubs at the University of Iowa in the 1930s (Lewin, Lippitt, and White 1939; White and Lippitt 1960). These experiments allowed the researchers to observe the effects of three different leadership styles – democratic, autocratic, and laissez-faire – on the behavior of children in the clubs. One finding showed that autocratic leadership often produced a scapegoating effect, and that the child singled out for blame and punishment was usually a reasonably strong and confident child who was prominent in the group but was not the most powerful member of the group. Perhaps the child at the top of the pecking order determined that the scapegoated child was a threat, and thus directed the animosity of members in this direction.
12 If you want to explore this matter further, you might refer to Clark and Myers (2007), Frost (2004), LaBier (2000), and McLain Smith (2008).
13 Compton and colleagues (2005) and Grant and colleagues (2004).
14 Ross and Nisbett (2011).
15 Edmondson (2012).
16 Edmondson (2008) and Edmondson and Lei (2014).
17 Fixsen and colleagues (2005).
18 Ansari, Fiss, and Zajac (2010).
19 Grol (2001) and Grol and Grimshaw (2003).
20 Kothari and Wathen (2013).
21 Greenhalgh and Wieringa (2011).
22 Some scholars have recently been considering the importance of stress and resilience during periods of organizational change. This work suggests that it is important for people to come together to discuss and make sense of these distressing experiences, engaging in a "relational pause" that allows people to clear the air and then focus once again on their task responsibilities. See for example Kahn (2019), Kahn and colleagues (2018), and Barton and Kahn (2019).

23   Stanfield (2000) provides a thorough treatment of ORID conversations.
24   For a discussion of the ladder of inference, see Argyris (1982).

7 Implementing and Evaluating the Intervention

1   These ideas derive from the work of D.W. Winnicott, who argued that the development of a child depends on the creation of stable and supportive "holding environments" that provide a safe haven within an uncertain environment. William Kahn (2005) points out that this notion has been applied to many areas of human experience, explaining that "individuals, across their lives, will at times require places in which they can safely experience and work through difficulties" (10). Amado and Ambrose (2001) have applied these ideas to the field of organizational change and argue that change processes often benefit when a "transitional object" is available that can provide the anchoring and stability that people need when they contend with new and uncertain situations. I am suggesting here that the formal intervention plan, with its lists of activities, milestones, deliverables, and responsibilities, acts as a transitional object during an intervention process, and the interventionist must help client system members to hold onto this object with a light grip. As new information comes to light, it is likely that the plan will need to be revised.
2   Argyris (1990).
3   Kegan and Lahey (2009).
4   Kahneman, Lovallo, and Sibony (2011). See also Lovallo and Sibony (2006) and Lovallo and Sibony (2010).
5   This work is described in Simmons-Mackie, Conklin, and Kagan (2008) and Kagan and colleagues (2010).
6   These and other statistics about the prevalence of aphasia can be found on websites such as www.aphasia.org and www.nidcd.nih.gov/health /aphasia. A good source of information about aphasia and ways of communicating with people living with the condition is Toronto's Aphasia Institute: www.aphasia.ca.
7   Figures for the occurrence of aphasia in the United Kingdom are from the Stroke Association's website, https://www.stroke.org.uk/finding -support/aphasia-and-communicating. Canadian numbers are from the Aphasia Institute's website: http://www.aphasia.ca/home-page/about -aphasia/what-is-aphasia/. New Zealand information can be found on the website of the Aphasia New Zealand Charitable Trust: http://www .aphasia.org.nz/public/. The Australian figures were found in Code and Petheram (2011).

8   This derived in part from a definition provided by the World Health Organization: World Health Organization (2001).
9   See Owen (2007) for a description of the open space method.
10 McLuhan and Leonard (1967).
11 A useful general description of the PDSA cycle in quality improvement can be found in Langley and colleagues (2009).
12 Most of these methods are discussed in *The Change Handbook*, edited by Holman, Devane, and Cady (2007). For an account of Preferred Futuring, see Lippitt (1998). Another useful source is Bunker and Alban (2006).
13 Putnam (1991) offers some interesting thoughts on how an approach based on "recipes" can be helpful for novices who are learning a new theory of action.
14 Beer and Eisenstat (1996).
15 Argyris (1993).
16 Patton (2011).
17 Roger Schwarz (2017) presents a model for intervening in a client system that involves three diagnostic steps and three intervention steps. My example here is a simplified version of Schwarz's approach.
18 Pitcher (1996).
19 Rogers (2003).
20 See: Hughes (2011), Jones and colleagues (2019), M.E. Smith (2002), and Stouten, Rousseau, and De Cremer (2018).
21 Bunker and Alban (2006) make a similar claim when they write that as a large group process to bring about organizational change comes to an end people can be disappointed: "the quality of insight, interaction, and problem solving that had occurred during the kick-off meeting disappeared" (315). What excited people was not just the content of the change process but the experience of being part of the process. Some participants hoped that this quality might become part of the way that work would be carried out in the future and were disappointed when this turned out not to be the case. Collaboration and engagement faded away.
22 The opening chapters of Pawson and Tilley's *Realistic Evaluation* provide a fine summary of these difficulties (Pawson and Tilley 1997).
23 This is the claim made by advocates of realistic evaluation (Pawson and Tilley 1997), who say that a program or intervention (which they term a "mechanism") interacts with the population or organization where it is applied (the "context") to produce some set of effects (the "outcome"). The emphasis here directs our attention to the nature of the interaction rather

than to a chain of causation. The context is just as likely to cause changes in the mechanism as the mechanism is to cause changes in the context.
24 Patton (2011).

8 The Ethics of Intervention

1 See Chin and Benne (1985) and Daniels and Dewine (1991).
2 Readers will find a thorough discussion of the dehumanization that results from moral disengagement in Bandura (2016). A fascinating study of the phenomenon that stems from reflections on the Stanford Prison Experiment can be found in Zimbardo (2007).
3 At the time of writing this could be found on the website of the American Psychological Association at this url: http://www.apa.org/ethics/code/.
4 Cedric Smith (2005) provides a useful review of the history of the dictum and shows that the prevalent use of the admonition to avoid harm is a relatively modern innovation. He quotes an American doctor, Lewis Stimson, writing in 1879: "The maxim that our first duty is to do no harm – *primum non nocere* – is not intended to reduce us to the rank of simple spectators; it is to stimulate us to attain greater accuracy in diagnosis, greater skill in treatment, and quicker perception of indications" (373). If this is correct, the primary intent has to do with continuous learning and development. The interventionist is to continue to develop her understanding and skill. Later Smith quotes Lou Lasagna, a pharmacy scientist, who in 1967 wrote, "to observe this advice [that is, do no harm] literally is to deny important therapy to everyone, since only inert nostrums can be guaranteed to do no harm. It is more reasonable to ask doctors to balance the potential gains against the possible harm: would that we could only quantify these probabilities more precisely" (375)! Lasagna's wording is instructive. One might take it to suggest that when possible we should resolve ethical quandaries by relying on probabilistic or statistical reasoning rather than on gut feelings. Ethical practice, then, will involve yet another balancing act: the balancing of the likelihood that an intervention will produce benefits against the possibility that it will produce harm.
5 See page 377 of Gellerman, Frankel, and Ladenson (1990).
6 At the time of writing the association's code of conduct could be found at this url: http://www.cmc-canada.ca/cmccacdesignation /codeofprofessionalconduct.
7 At the time of writing the Organization Development Institute's code was available online at: http://www.theodinstitute.org/od-library

/code_of_ethics.htm. The Canadian affiliate's code of ethics was found at this url: http://www.codicanada.com/?page_id=87.

8 At the time of writing the IMC USA code of ethics was at this url: http://www.imcusa.org/?page=ETHICSCODE.

9 At the time of writing the ACMP code of ethics and professional conduct could be found at http://www.acmpglobal.org/?page=CodeEthics.

10 An excellent and comprehensive treatment of the trolley problem in its many forms can be found in Edmonds (2013).

11 Schön (1983).

12 Kahneman (2011).

13 The creators of the ontological leadership course have written extensively about this. See for example Erhard, Jensen, and Zafron (2008).

14 The following works were especially useful: Benne (1964), Bermant and Warwick (1985), and Gellerman, Frankel, and Ladenson (1990).

15 See Goffman (1959) and Kahn (2015).

16 Schein (1999).

17 See Hamel (1998) and Witzel (2016).

18 This passage is in the Afterward of Steiner (2005, 183–4).

9 Changing the Future of Planned Change

1 I am saying that in my view there is no universal truth about social change that will allow humans to design and implement change processes that unfold exactly as planned, producing the desired positive benefits and not producing any negative and unintended outcomes. To think otherwise is to engage in utopian thinking. Humans and human systems are too variable, too complex, and too emergent to allow for a perfect, problem-free implementation of change. Nonetheless, we can become better at noticing the affordances and constraints of specific social milieus, and we can become more intentional and adaptive as we take steps to understand and overcome the problems that confront us.

2 Beer and Nohria (2000).

3 McGregor (2006).

4 Argyris (1993).

5 Heifetz and Linsky (2002).

6 Zaffron and Logan (2009).

7 Stanovich (1994).

8 Argyris (1990) and Goffman (1959).

9 Argyris (2010); Bartunek (1984); Bartunek and Moch (1987); Dweck (2006); Festinger (1957); Gabbay and Le May (2011); Kegan and Lahey (2009); Senge (1990).

10 Nickerson (1998).
11 Dumont (1993) and Tversky and Kahneman (1974).
12 Festinger (1957).
13 See page 31 of Nisbett and Ross (1980).
14 Asch (1955).
15 Milgram (1974) and Zimbardo (2007).
16 Dumont (1993); Haidt (2012); and Taleb (2010).
17 I am indebted here to the applied phenomenology of the team that created the ontological/phenomenological model of leadership, including Werner Erhard, Michael Jensen, Steve Zaffron, and Kari Granger. Interested readers can download materials related to this approach from the Social Science Research Network (SSRN). For example: https://papers.ssrn.com /sol3/papers.cfm?abstract_id=1263835.
18 See the explanation in Raskin, Rogers, and Witty (2014).
19 Mahoney (1991).
20 Argyris (1990).
21 Argyris (2006), 182.
22 Argyris (1964). See also Christensen (2008), 13.
23 Watzlawick, Bavelas, and Jackson (1967).
24 See pages 84–5 of Schein (1999).
25 Schön (1983).

References

Aarons, G.A., Green, A.E., Palinkas, L.A., Self-Brown, S., Whitaker, D.J., Lutzker, J.R., et al. (2012). Dynamic adaptation process to implement an evidence-based child maltreatment intervention. *Implementation Science, 7*(1), 32. https://doi.org/10.1186/1748-5908-7-32.

Amado, G., & Ambrose, A. (Eds.). (2001). *The transitional approach to change.* London: Karnac Books.

Ansari, S.M., Fiss, P.C., & Zajac, E.J. (2010). Made to fit: How practices vary as they diffuse. *Academy of Management Review, 35*(1), 67–92. https://doi.org/10.5465/amr.35.1.zok67.

Argyris, C. (1964). *Integrating the individual and the organization.* New York: Wiley.

Argyris, C. (1982). The executive mind and double loop learning. *Organizational Dynamics* (Autumn), 5–22. https://doi.org/10.1016/0090-2616(82)90002-X.

Argyris, C. (1983). Action science and intervention. *The Journal of Applied Behavioral Science, 19*(2), 115–40. https://doi.org/10.1177/002188638301900204.

Argyris, C. (1990). *Overcoming organizational defenses: Facilitating organizational learning.* Boston: Allyn and Bacon.

Argyris, C. (1991). Teaching smart people how to learn. *Harvard Business Review* (May-June), 99–110. doi NA.

Argyris, C. (1993). *Knowledge for action: A guide to overcoming barriers to organizational change.* San Francisco: Jossey-Bass.

Argyris, C. (2006). Effective intervention activity. In J.V. Gallos (Ed.), *Organization development,* 158–84. San Francisco: Jossey-Bass.

Argyris, C. (2010). *Organizational traps: Leadership, culture, organizational design.* Oxford: Oxford University Press.

Argyris, C., Putnam, R., & Smith, D.M. (1985). *Action science.* San Francisco: Jossey-Bass.

Argyris, C., & Schön, D.A. (1978). *Organizational learning: A theory of action perspective*. Reading, MA: Addison-Wesley Publishing Company.

Aronson, E. (2012). *The social animal*. New York: Worth Publishers.

Asch, S.E. (1955). Opinions and social pressure. *Scientific American, 193*(5), 31–5. https://doi.org/10.1038/scientificamerican1155-31.

Bandura, A. (2016). *Moral disengagement: How people do harm and live with themselves*. New York: Worth Publishers.

Barley, S.R. (1996). Technicians in the workplace: Ethnographic evidence for bringing work into organizational studies. *Administrative Science Quarterly, 41*(3), 404–41. https://doi.org/10.2307/2393937.

Barley, S.R., & Bechky, B.A. (1994). In the backrooms of science: The work of technicians in science labs. *Work and Occupations, 21*(1), 85–126. https://doi.org/10.1177/0730888494021001004.

Barton, M.A., & Kahn, W.A. (2019). Group resilience: The place and meaning of relational pauses. *Organization Studies, 40*(9), 1409–29. https://doi.org/10.1177/0170840618782294.

Bartunek, J.M. (1984). Changing interpretive schemes and organizational restructuring: The example of a religious order. *Administrative Science Quarterly, 29*, 356–72. https://doi.org/10.2307/2393029.

Bartunek, J.M., & Moch, M.K. (1987). First-order, second-order, and third-order change and organization development interventions: A cognitive approach. *The Journal of Applied Behavioral Science, 23*(4), 483–500. https://doi.org/10.1177/002188638702300404.

Bartunek, J.M., & Woodman, R.W. (2015). Beyond Lewin: Toward a temporal approximation of organization development and change. *Annual Review of Organizational Psychology and Organizational Behavior, 2*, 157–82. https://doi.org/10.1146/annurev-orgpsych-032414-111353.

Beer, M., & Eisenstat, R.A. (1996). Developing an organization capable of implementing strategy and learning. *Human Relations, 49*(5), 597–619. https://doi.org/10.1177/001872679604900504.

Beer, M., & Nohria, N. (Eds.). (2000). *Breaking the code of change*. Boston: Harvard Business School Press.

Benne, K.D. (1964). Democratic ethics and human engineering. In W.G. Bennis, K.D. Benne, & R. Chin (Eds.), *The planning of change: Readings in the applied behavioral sciences*, 141–8. New York: Holt, Rinehart and Winston.

Bennis, W.G., Benne, K.D., & Chin, R. (Eds.). (1985). *The planning of change*. New York: Holt, Rinehart and Winston.

Berger, P.L., & Luckmann, T. (1966). *The social construction of reality: A treatise in the sociology of knowledge*. London: Penguin Books.

Bermant, G., & Warwick, D.P. (1985). The ethics of social intervention: Power, freedom and accountability. In W.G. Bennis, K.D. Benne, & R. Chin (Eds.),

The planning of change, 4th ed., 449–70. Fort Worth, TX: Harcourt Brace Jovanovich College Publishers.

Blass, T. (2004). *The man who shocked the world: The life and legacy of Stanley Milgram.* New York: Basic Books.

Blass, T. (2009). From New Haven to Santa Clara: A historical perspective on the Milgram obedience experiments. *American Psychologist, 64*(1), 37–45. https://doi.org/10.1037/a0014434.

Block, P. (2011). *Flawless consulting: A guide to getting your expertise used,* 3rd ed. San Francisco: Pfeiffer.

Bridges, W. (1991). *Managing transitions: Making the most of change.* Reading, MA: Addison-Wesley.

Bunker, B.B., & Alban, B.T. (2006). *The handbook of large group methods: Creating systemic change in organizations and communities.* San Francisco: Jossey-Bass.

Burger, J.M. (2009). Replicating Milgram: Would people still obey today? *The American Psychologist, 64*(1), 1–11. https://doi.org/10.1037/a0010932.

Burnes, B. (2011). Introduction: Why does change fail, and what can we do about it? *Journal of Change Management, 11*(4), 445–50. https://doi.org/10.1080/14697017.2011.630507.

Bushe, G.R., & Coetzer, G.H. (2007). Group development and team effectiveness: Using cognitive representations to measure group development and predict task performance and group viability. *The Journal of Applied Behavioral Science, 43*(2), 184–212. https://doi.org/10.1177/0021886306298892.

Bushe, G.R., & Marshak, R.J. (2015). The dialogic organization development approach to transformation and change. In W. Rothwell, J. Stravros, & R. Sullivan (Eds.), *Practicing organization development,* 4th ed., 407–18. San Francisco: Wiley.

Chin, R., & Benne, K.D. (1985). General strategies for effecting changes in human systems. In W.G. Bennis, K.D. Benne, & R. Chin (Eds.), *The planning of change,* 22–45. New York: Holt, Rinehart and Winston.

Christensen, K. (2008). Thought leader interview: Chris Argyris. *Rotman Magazine* (Winter), 10–13.

Clark, J.R., Murphy, C., & Singer, S.J. (2013). When do leaders matter? Ownership, governance and the influence of CEOs on firm performance. *The Leadership Quarterly, 25*(2), 358–72. https://doi.org/10.1016/j.leaqua.2013.09.004.

Clark, S., & Myers, M. (2007). *Managing difficult conversations at work.* Kemble, Glos.: Management Books.

Clegg, S., & Dunkerley, D. (1980). *Organization, class and control.* London: Routledge & Kegan Paul.

Code, C., & Petheram, B. (2011). Delivering for aphasia. *International Journal of Speech-Language Pathology*, 13(1), 3–10. https://doi.org/10.3109/17549507.2010.520090.

Collingwood, H. (2009). Do CEOs matter? *The Atlantic* (June 2009), 9–14. doi NA.

Combs, A.W., & Gonzalez, D.M. (1971). *Helping relationships: Basic concepts for the helping professions*. Needham Heights, MA: Allyn and Bacon.

Compton, W.M., Conway, K.P., Stinson, F.S., Colliver, J.D., & Grant, B.F. (2005). Prevalence, correlates, and comorbidity of DSM-IV antisocial personality syndromes and alcohol and specific drug use disorders in the United States: Results from the National Epidemiologic Survey on Alcohol and Related Conditions. *The Journal of Clinical Psychiatry*, 66(6), 677–85. https://doi.org/10.4088/JCP.v66n0602.

Conklin, J. (2010a). Learning in the wild. *Action Learning: Research and Practice*, 7(2), 151–66. https://doi.org/10.1080/14767333.2010.488327.

Conklin, J. (2010b). Resisting change or preserving value: A case study in a health organization. *The International Journal of Knowledge, Culture, & Change Management*, 10(1), 481–93. https://doi.org/10.18848/1447-9524/CGP/v10i01/49907.

Conklin, J., Farrell, B., Ward, N., McCarthy, L., Irving, H., & Raman-Wilms, L. (2015). Developmental evaluation as a strategy to enhance the uptake and use of deprescribing guidelines: Protocol for a multiple case study. *Implementation Science*, 10(1), 91. https://doi.org/10.1186/s13012-015-0279-0.

Conklin, J., Kyle, T., & Robertson, C. (2012). The essential transformation: How masters students make sense and learn through transformative change. *Management Learning*, 44(2), 161–78. https://doi.org/10.1177/1350507612439279.

Cummings, S., Bridgman, T., & Brown, K.G. (2016). Unfreezing change as three steps: Rethinking Kurt Lewin's legacy for change management. *Human Relations*, 69(1), 33–60. https://doi.org/10.1177/0018726715577707.

Daniels, T.D., & Dewine, S. (1991). Communication process as target and tool for consultancy intervention: Rethinking a hackneyed theme. *Journal of Educational & Psychological Consultation*, 2(4), 303–22. https://doi.org/10.1207/s1532768xjepc0204_1.

Dixon, R. (2007). Scapegoating. *Journal of School Violence*, 6(4), 81–103. https://doi.org/10.1300/J202v06n04_05.

Dumont, F. (1993). Inferential heuristics in clinical problem formulation: Selective review of their strengths and weaknesses. *Professional Psychology:*

Research and Practice, 24(2), 196–205. https://doi.org/10.1037/0735 -7028.24.2.196.

Dumont, F., & Fitzpatrick, M. (2001). The real relationship: Schemas, stereotypes, and personal history. *Psychotherapy*, 38(1), 12–20. https://doi .org/10.1037/0033-3204.38.1.12.

Dweck, C.S. (2006). *Mindset: The new psychology of success*. New York: Ballantine Books.

Eagle, J., & Newton, P.M. (1981). Scapegoating in small groups: An organizational approach. *Human Relations*, 34(4), 283–301. https://doi .org/10.1177/001872678103400403.

Edmonds, D. (2013). *Would you kill the fat man?* Princeton, NJ: Princeton University Press.

Edmondson, A.C. (2008). The competitive imperative of learning. *Harvard Business Review* (August), 60–7. doi NA.

Edmondson, A.C. (2012). Teamwork on the fly. *Harvard Business Review* (April), 72–81. doi NA.

Edmondson, A.C., & Lei, Z. (2014). Psychological safety: The history, renaissance, and future of an interpersonal construct. *Annual Review of Organizational Psychology and Organizational Behavior*, 1, 23–43. https://doi .org/10.1146/annurev-orgpsych-031413-091305.

Erhard, W.H., Jensen, M.C., & Zaffron, S. (2008). Integrity: A positive model that incorporates the normative phenomena of morality, ethics and legality. *Social Science Research Network* (23 March), 1–124. http://doi.org/10.2139 /ssrn.920625.

Festinger, L. (1957). *A theory of cognitive dissonance*. Redwood City, CA: Stanford University Press.

Fisher, B.A., & Ellis, D.G. (1990). *Small group decision making: Communication and the group process*. New York: McGraw-Hill.

Fitza, M.A. (2017). How much do CEOs really matter? *Strategic Management Journal*, 38(3), 802–11. https://doi.org/10.1002/smj.2597.

Fixsen, D.L., Blase, K.A., Timbers, G.D., & Wolf, M.M. (2007). In search of program implementation: 792 replications of the teaching-family model. *The Behavior Analyst Today*, 8(1), 96–110. https://doi.org/10.1037/h0100104.

Fixsen, D.L., Naoom, S.F., Blase, K.A, Friedman, R.M., & Wallace, F. (2005). *Implementation research: A synthesis of the literature*. University of South Florida, Louis de la Parte Florida Mental Health Institute, The National Implementation Research Network (FMHI Publication #231), Tampa, FL.

Frost, P.J. (2004). Handling toxic emotions. *Organizational Dynamics*, 33(2), 111–27. https://doi.org/10.1016/j.orgdyn.2004.01.001.

Gabbay, J., & Le May, A. (2011). *Practice-based evidence for healthcare: Clinical mindlines*. London: Routledge.

Gellerman, W., Frankel, M.S., & Ladenson, R.F. (1990). *Values and ethics in organization and human systems development: Responding to dilemmas in professional life*. San Francisco: Jossey-Bass Publishers.

Gemmill, G. (1989). The dynamics of scapegoating in small groups. *Small Group Research, 20*(4), 406–18. https://doi.org/10.1177/104649648902000402.

Gino, B.Y.F., & Staats, B. (2015). Why organizations don't learn. *Harvard Business Review* (November), 111–18. doi NA.

Glaser, B.G., & Strauss, A.L. (1967). *The discovery of grounded theory: Strategies for qualitative research*. New Brunswick, NJ: Transaction Publishers.

Goffman, E. (1959). *The presentation of self in everyday life*. New York: Doubleday.

Grant, B.F., Hasin, D.S., Stinson, F.S., Dawson, D.A., Chou, S.P., Ruan, W.J., & Pickering, R.P. (2004). Prevalence, correlates, and disability of personality disorders in the United States: Results from the National Epidemiologic Survey on Alcohol and Related Conditions. *The Journal of Clinical Psychiatry, 65*(7), 948–58. https://doi.org/10.4088/JCP.v65n0711.

Greenhalgh, T., & Wieringa, S. (2011). Is it time to drop the "knowledge translation" metaphor? A critical literature review. *Journal of the Royal Society of Medicine, 104*, 501–9. https://doi.org/10.1258/jrsm.2011.110285.

Grimshaw, J.M., Eccles, M.P., Lavis, J.N., Hill, S.J., & Squires, J.E. (2012). Knowledge translation of research findings. *Implementation Science, 7*(1). https://doi.org/10.1186/1748-5908-7-50.

Grol, R. (2001). Successes and failures in the implementation of evidence-based guidelines for clinical practice. *Medical Care, 39*(8 Suppl 2), II46–54. https://doi.org/10.1097/00005650-200108002-00003.

Grol, R., & Grimshaw, J. (2003). Research into practice I. From best evidence to best practice: Effective implementation of change in patients' care. *Lancet, 362*, 1225–30. https://doi.org/10.1016/S0140-6736(03)14546-1.

Gutmanis, I., Snyder, M., Harvey, D., Hillier, L.M., & LeClair, J.K. (2015). Health care redesign for responsive behaviours – The Behavioural Supports Ontario experience: Lessons learned and keys to success. *Canadian Journal of Community Mental Health, 34*(1), 45–63. https://doi.org/10.7870/cjcmh-2015-001.

Haidt, J. (2012). *The righteous mind: Why good people are divided by politics and religion*. New York: Pantheon.

Hamel, G. (1998). Strategy emergence. *Executive Excellence, 15*(12), 3–4. doi NA.

Hart, H., & Conklin, J. (2006). Toward a meaningful model for technical communication. *Technical Communication, 53*(4), 395–415. doi NA.

Hartley, T.W. (2006). Public perception and participation in water reuse. *Desalination, 187*(1–3), 115–26. https://doi.org/10.1016/j.desal.2005.04.072.

Heifetz, R.A., & Linsky, M. (2002). *Leadership on the line: Staying alive through the dangers of leading.* Boston: Harvard Business School Press.

Heintzman, R., & Marson, B. (2005). People, service and trust: Is there a public sector service value chain? *International Review of Administrative Sciences, 71*(4), 549–75. https://doi.org/10.1177/0020852305059599.

Homans, G.C. (1950). *The human group.* New York: Harcourt, Brace & World, Inc.

Hughes, M. (2011). Do 70 per cent of all organizational change initiatives really fail? *Journal of Change Management, 11*(4), 451–64. https://doi.org/10.1080/14697017.2011.630506.

Hughes, M. (2016). Leading changes: Why transformation explanations fail. *Leadership, 12*(4), 449–69. https://doi.org/10.1177/1742715015571393.

Hume, D. (1969/1739). *A treatise of human nature.* London: Penguin.

Isaacs, W. (1999). *Dialogue: The art of thinking together.* New York: Doubleday.

Jones, J., Firth, J., Hannibal, C., & Ogunseyin, M. (2019). Factors contributing to organizational change success or failure: A qualitative meta-analysis of 200 reflective case studies. In R. Hamlin, A. Ellinger, & J. Jones (Eds.), *Evidence-based initiatives for organizational change and development,* 155–78. Hershey, PA: IGI Global.

Kagan, A., Simmons-Mackie, N., Gibson, J.B., Conklin, J., & Elman, R.J. (2010). Closing the evidence, research, and practice loop: Examples of knowledge transfer and exchange from the field of aphasia. *Aphasiology, 24*(4), 535–48. https://doi.org/10.1080/02687030902935959.

Kahn, W.A. (2003). The revelation of organizational trauma. *Journal of Applied Behavioral Science, 39*(4), 364–80. https://doi.org/10.1177/0021886303261954.

Kahn, W.A. (2004). Facilitating and undermining organizational change: A case study. *Journal of Applied Behavioral Science, 40*(1), 7–30. https://doi.org/10.1177/0021886304263845.

Kahn, W.A. (2005). *Holding fast: The struggle to create resilient caregiving organizations.* New York: Brunner-Routledge.

Kahn, W.A. (2015). *The ostrich effect: Solving destructive patterns at work.* New York: Routledge.

Kahn, W.A. (2019). Dynamics and implications of distress organizing. *Academy of Management Journal, 62*(5), 1471–97. https://doi.org/10.5465/amj.2016.0319.

Kahn, W.A., Barton, M., Fisher, C., Heaphy, E., Reid, E., & Rouse, E. (2018). The geography of strain: Organizational resilience as a function of intergroup relations. *Academy of Management Review, 43*(3), 509–29. https://doi.org/10.5465/amr.2016.0004.

Kahn, W.A., & Fellows, S. (2013). Employee engagement and meaningful work. In B.J. Dik, Z.S. Byrne, & M.F. Steger (Eds.), *Purpose and meaning in the workplace*, 105–26. Washington, DC: American Psychological Association.

Kahneman, D. (1992). Reference points, anchors, norms, and mixed feelings. *Organizational Behavior and Human Decision Processes, 51*(2), 296–312. https://doi.org/10.1016/0749-5978(92)90015-Y.

Kahneman, D. (2011). *Thinking fast and slow*. London: Penguin Books.

Kahneman, D., Lovallo, D.P., & Sibony, O. (2011). Before you make that big decision ... *Harvard Business Review, 89*(6), 50–60. doi NA.

Kegan, R. (1994). *In over our heads: The mental demands of modern life.* Cambridge, MA: Harvard University Press.

Kegan, R., & Lahey, L. (2009). *Immunity to change: How to overcome it and unlock the potential in yourself and your organization.* Boston: Harvard Business Press.

Keyton, J. (1999). Analyzing interaction patterns in dysfunctional teams. *Small Group Research, 30*(August), 491–518. https://doi.org/10.1177/104649649903000405.

Kline, W.B. (1997). Group as a whole dynamics and the "problem" member. In S.T. Gladding (Ed.), *New developments in group counseling*, 93–5. Greensboro, NC: ERIC Counseling and Student Services Clearinghouse.

Kolb, D. (1984). *Experiential learning: Experience as the source of learning and development.* Englewood Cliffs, NJ: Prentice-Hall.

Kothari, A., & Wathen, C.N. (2013). A critical second look at integrated knowledge translation. *Health Policy, 109*(2), 187–91. https://doi.org/10.1016/j.healthpol.2012.11.004.

Kotter, J.P. (2007). Leading change: Why transformation efforts fail. *Harvard Business Review, 86*, 96–103. https://doi.org/10.15358/9783800646159.

Kotter, J.P. (2012). *Leading change*. Cambridge, MA: Harvard Business Press.

Krueger, R.A., & Casey, M.A. (2009). *Focus groups: A practical guide for applied research*, 4th ed. Thousand Oaks, CA: Sage.

LaBier, D. (2000). *Modern madness: The hidden link between work and emotional conflict*. Lincoln, NE: Authors Guild Backinprint.com Edition.

Langley, G.J., Moen, R.D., Nolan, K.M., Nolan, T.W., Norman, C.L., & Provost, L.P. (2009). *The improvement guide*, 2nd ed. San Francisco: Jossey-Bass.

Lewin, K. (1939). Experiments in social space. *Harvard Educational Review, 9*, 21–32. doi NA.

Lewin, K. (1947). Frontiers in group dynamics: Concept, method and reality in social science: Social equilibria and social change. *Human Relations, 1*(5), 5–41. https://doi.org/10.1177/001872674700100103.

Lewin, K. (1951). Problems of research in social psychology. In D. Cartwright (Ed.), *Field theory in social science: Selected theoretical papers*, 155–69. New York: Harper & Row.

Lewin, K., Lippitt, R., & White, R.K. (1939). Patterns of aggressive behavior in experimentally created "social climates." *Journal of Social Psychology, 10*(2), 271–99. https://doi.org/10.1080/00224545.1939.9713366.

Lieberson, S., & Connor, J.F.O. (1972). Leadership and organizational performance: A study of large corporations. *American Sociological Review, 37*(2), 117–30. https://doi.org/10.2307/2094020.

Likert, R. (1967). *The human organization: Its management and value.* New York: McGraw-Hill.

Lippitt, L. (1998). *Preferred futuring.* San Francisco: Berrett-Koehler Publishers Inc.

Lovallo, D.P., & Sibony, O. (2006). Distortions and deceptions in strategic decisions. *McKinsey Quarterly* (1) (February), 18–29. doi NA.

Lovallo, D.P., & Sibony, O. (2010). The case for behavioral strategy. *McKinsey Quarterly* (2) (February), 1–14. doi NA.

Macey, W.H., & Schneider, B. (2008). The meaning of employee engagement. *Industrial and Organizational Psychology, 1*(1), 3–30. https://doi.org/10.1111/j.1754-9434.2007.0002.x.

Macintosh-Murray, A. (2007). Challenges of collaborative improvement in complex continuing care. *Healthcare Quarterly, 10*(2), 49–57. https://doi.org/10.12927/hcq..18795.

Mahoney, M.J. (1991). *Human change processes: The scientific foundations of psychotherapy.* New York: Basic Books.

Mann-Feder, V. (2002). The self as subject in child and youth care supervision. *Journal of Child and Youth Care, 15*(2), 1–7. doi NA.

Marrow, A.J. (1969). *The practical theorist: The life and work of Kurt Lewin.* New York: Basic Books.

Mayo, E. (1949). *The social problems of an industrial civilization.* London: Routledge & Kegan Paul.

McGregor, D. (2006). *The human side of management.* Annotated edition. Columbus, OH: McGraw-Hill.

McLain Smith, D. (2008). *Divide or conquer: How great teams turn conflict into strength.* New York: Portfolio.

McLuhan, M., & Leonard, G.B. (1967). The future of education: The class of 1989. *LOOK Magazine* (21 February), 23–5. doi NA.

McNiff, J., & Whitehead, J. (2011). *All you need to know about action research,* 2nd ed. Thousand Oaks, CA: SAGE Publications, Inc.

Milgram, S. (1974). *Obedience to authority.* New York: Harper.

Moylan, D. (1994). The dangers of contagion: Projective identification processes in institutions. In A. Obholzer & V.Z. Roberts (Eds.), *The unconscious at work*, 51–9. London: Routledge.

Mumford, A. (1997). The learning process. In M. Pedler (Ed.), *Action learning in practice*, 3rd ed., 229–42. Aldershot, Hants: Gower.

Nickerson, R.S. (1998). Confirmation bias: A ubiquitous phenomenon in many guises. *Review of General Psychology*, 2(2), 175–220. https://doi.org/10.1037/1089-2680.2.2.175.

Nisbett, R.E., & Ross, L. (1980). *Human inference: Strategies and shortcomings of social judgment*. New York: Prentice-Hall.

Ohanian, H.C. (2008). *Einstein's mistakes: The human failings of genius*. New York: W.W. Norton & Company.

Owen, H. (2007). Open space technology. In P. Holman, T. Devane, & S. Cady (Eds.), *The change handbook; The definitive resource on today's best methods for engaging whole systems*, 2nd ed., 133–48. San Francisco: Berrett-Koehler Publishers Inc.

Patton, M.Q. (2011). *Developmental evaluation: Applying complexity concepts to enhance innovation and use*. New York: The Guilford Press.

Patton, M.Q. (2015). *Qualitative research & evaluation methods*, 4th ed. Thousand Oaks, CA: SAGE Publications, Inc.

Pawson, R., & Tilley, N. (1997). *Realistic evaluation*. London: Sage Publications.

Petriglieri, G., & Wood, J.D. (2003). The invisible revealed: Collusion as an entry to the group unconscious. *Transactional Analysis Journal*, 33, 332–43. https://doi.org/10.1177/036215370303300408.

Pitcher, P. (1996). *Artists, craftsmen and technocrats: The dreams, realities and illusions of leadership*. Toronto: Stoddart Publishing Company.

Popper, K. (1972). *Objective knowledge*. Oxford: Oxford University Press.

Putnam, R. (1991). Recipes and reflective learning: "What would prevent you from saying it that way?" In D.A. Schon (Ed.), *The reflective turn: Case studies in and on educational practice*, 145–63. New York: Teachers College Press.

Raskin, N.J., Rogers, C.R., & Witty, M.C. (2014). Client-centered therapy. In D. Wedding & R.J. Corsini (Eds.), *Current psychotherapies*, 10th ed., 95–150. Belmont, CA: Brooks/Cole.

Reason, P., & Bradbury, H. (Eds.). (2008). *The Sage handbook of action research: Participative inquiry and practice*. Thousand Oaks, CA: Sage Publications, Inc.

Rey, L., Tremblay, M.C., & Brousselle, A. (2013). Managing tensions between evaluation and research: Illustrative cases of developmental evaluation in the context of research. *American Journal of Evaluation*, 35(1), 45–60. https://doi.org/10.1177/1098214013503698.

Roethlisberger, F.J., & Dickson, W.J. (2003). *Management and the worker.* London: Routledge.

Rogers, E.M. (2003). *Diffusion of innovations,* 5th ed. New York: Free Press.

Ross, L., & Nisbett, R.E. (2011). *The person and the situation.* London: Pinter & Martin.

Schein, E.H. (1999). *Process consultation revisited: Building the helping relationship.* Reading, MA: Addison-Wesley.

Schein, E.H. (2004). *Organizational culture and leadership.* San Francisco: Jossey-Bass.

Schein, E.H. (2006). The concept of "client" from a process consultation perspective: A guide for change agents. *Journal of Organizational Change Management, 10*(3), 202–16. https://doi.org/10.1108/09534819710171077.

Schön, D.A. (1983). *The reflective practitioner: How professionals think in action.* New York: Basic Books.

Schwartzman, H.B. (1993). *Ethnography in organizations.* Newbury Park, CA: Sage.

Schwarz, R. (2017). *The skilled facilitator,* 3rd ed. San Francisco: Jossey-Bass.

Searle, J.R. (1995). *The construction of social reality.* New York: Free Press.

Senge, P.M. (1990). *The fifth discipline: The art and practice of the learning organization.* New York: Doubleday.

Simmons-Mackie, N., Conklin, J., & Kagan, A. (2008). Think tank deliberates future directions for the social approach to aphasia. *Perspectives on Neurophysiology and Neurogenic Speech and Language Disorders, 18*(April), 24–32. https://doi.org/10.1044/nnsld18.1.24.

Smircich, L., & Chesser, R.J. (1981). Superiors' and subordinates' perceptions of performance: Beyond disagreement. *Academy of Management Journal, 24*(1), 198–205. https://doi.org/10.5465/255835.

Smith, C.M. (2005). Origin and uses of primum non nocere: Above all, do no harm! *Journal of Clinical Pharmacology, 45*(4), 371–7. https://doi.org/10.1177/0091270004273680.

Smith, G. (2001). Group development: A review of the literature and a commentary on future research directions. *Group Facilitation, 3,* 14–45. doi NA.

Smith, K.K., & Berg, D.N. (1987). *Paradoxes of group life: Understanding conflict, paralysis, and movement in group dynamics.* San Francisco: Jossey-Bass.

Smith, M.E. (2002). Success rates for different types of organizational change. *Performance Improvement, 41,* 26–33. https://doi.org/10.1002/pfi.4140410107.

Stanfield, R.B. (2000). *The art of the focused conversation.* Gabriola Island, BC: New Society Publishers.

Stanovich, K.E. (1994). An exchange: Reconceptualizing intelligence: Dysrationalia as an intuition pump. *Educational Researcher*, *23*(4), 11–22. https://doi.org/10.2307/1176257.

Stauffacher, M., Flüeler, T., Krütli, P., & Scholz, R.W. (2008). Analytic and dynamic approach to collaboration: A transdisciplinary case study on sustainable landscape development in a Swiss Prealpine region. *Systemic Practice and Action Research*, *21*(6), 409–22. https://doi.org/10.1007/s11213-008-9107-7.

Steiner, G. (2005). *Lessons of the masters*. Cambridge, MA: Harvard University Press.

Stouten, J., Rousseau, D.M., & De Cremer, D. (2018). Successful organizational change: Integrating the management practice and scholarly literatures. *Academy of Management Annals*, *12*(2), 752–88. https://doi.org/10.5465/annals.2016.0095.

Taleb, N.N. (2010). *The black swan: The impact of the highly improbable*. London: Penguin Books.

Taylor, M. (1986). Learning for self-direction in the classroom: The pattern of a transition process. *Studies in Higher Education*, *11*(1), 55–72. https://doi.org/10.1080/03075078612331378461.

Thomas, D. (1994). What to do with a lousy business. *Management Review*, *83*(6), 40–3. doi NA.

Thurlow, A., & Mills, J.H. (2009). Change, talk and sensemaking. *Journal of Organizational Change Management*, *22*(5), 459–79. https://doi.org/10.1108/09534810910983442.

Tuckman, B.W. (1965). Developmental sequence in small groups. *Psychological Bulletin*, *63*, 384–99. https://doi.org/10.1037/h0022100.

Tversky, A., & Kahneman, D. (1974). Judgment under uncertainty: Heuristics and biases. *Science*, *185*(4157), 1124–31.

von Moltke, H.G. (1993). *Moltke on the art of war: Selected writings*. New York: Presidio Press.

Vuori, T.O., & Huy, Q.N. (2016). Distributed attention and shared emotions in the innovation process: How Nokia lost the smartphone battle. *Administrative Science Quarterly*, *61*(1), 9–51. https://doi.org/10.1177/0001839215606951.

Waddell, C. (1995). Defining sustainable development: A case study in environmental communication. *Technical Communication Quarterly*, *4*(2), 201–16. https://doi.org/10.1080/10572259509364597.

Watzlawick, P. (1976). *How real is real? Communication, disinformation, confusion*. New York: Random House.

Watzlawick, P., Bavelas, J.B., & Jackson, D.D. (1967). *Pragmatics of human communication: A study of interactional patterns, pathologies, and paradoxes.* New York: W.W. Norton & Company.

Weick, K.E. (1995). *Sensemaking in organizations.* Thousand Oaks, CA: Sage Publications, Inc.

Weick, K.E. (2009). *Making sense of the organization: The impermanent organization, volume two.* Chichester: John Wiley & Sons, Ltd.

Weick, K.E., Sutcliffe, K.M., & Obstfeld, D. (2005). Organizing and the process of sensemaking. *Organization Science, 16*(4), 409–21. https://doi.org/10.1287/orsc.1050.0133.

White, R.K., & Lippitt, R. (1960). *Autocracy and democracy: An experimental inquiry.* New York: Harper & Brothers.

Witzel, M. (2016). *Management consultancy.* New York: Routledge. https://doi.org/10.4324/9781315756356.

World Health Organization. (2001). *International classification of functioning, disability and health (ICF).* Geneva: WHO, Marketing and Dissemination.

Zaffron, S., & Logan, D. (2009). *The three laws of performance.* San Francisco: Jossey-Bass.

Zimbardo, P. (2007). *The Lucifer effect: Understanding how good people turn evil.* New York: Random House.

Index

Endnotes, tables, and figures are indicated by a single letter after the page number: "n" for notes, "t" for tables, and "f" for figures.

action research, 323n11
adaptability, importance of, 235
adaptive problems, 59–74, 81, 97, 131. *See also* change, adaptive
advisory groups, 123t, 321n15
after-action review, 256–7
Alban, B.T., 328n21
Amado, G., & Ambrose, A., 327n1
anchoring effect, 47, 299, 325n4
aphasia, 227–30, 327nn6–7
Argyris, Chris: on client relationships, 100; on confrontation, 305; on defensiveness, 224; on inferences, 278; Model I and II, 5, 295; pattern causality, 41–2, 307–8, 316n9, 320n21. *See also* theories of action
Asch, Solomon, 52, 300
assumptions: avoiding anchoring effect, 184, 325n4; based on personal bias, 46–7, 317nn14–15; case histories, 104–9, 143–50; of managers, 4–5, 295; uncovering, 104–9, 117–21, 124, 125, 195. *See also* human reasoning; mindsets

authoritative change. *See* change, authoritative
authority figures, obedience to, 52–4
availability heuristic, 50–1

balancing acts: assertion and inquiry, 172–6, 206–7, 232, 271–3, 309–10; compassion and confrontation, 86, 97–9, 157–61, 304–5; critical balancing acts, ix–x, 171–2; ethical risks, 271–7, 277t, 282–93; intentionality and flexibility, 110, 172, 277–82; interventions as, ix–x, 3–8, 26–7, 86–90, 219–20; participation and observation, 137–43, 164, 246–7, 307–9; possible benefits vs harm, 271–5; staying the course and changing course, 219–24, 306–7
Beer, Michael, *Breaking the Code of Change*, 3–4, 5, 295
behavior. *See* human behavior
Benne, Kenneth, 37
Bennis, Warren, 37
blaming: each other, 124, 158, 199–200; fundamental attribution

error and, 51–2, 158, 203–5;
interventionists, 173–5; leaders,
114, 199–200, 326n10, 326n12;
responding to, 173–5, 203–4,
287–8; subordinates, 144–6, 147t,
149f. *See also* emotions
Block, Peter, 93, 94
Breaking the Code of Change (Beer &
Nitin), 3–4, 5, 295
Bridges, W., *Managing Transitions*, 93
Bunker, B.B., 328n21
Burger, Jerry, 54
Bushe, G.R., 41–3

case histories: caught in the middle
(Sarah), 261–3; changing course,
221–4; dealing with aphasia,
227–34; dealing with dementia,
73t; espionage (Connie), 263–4;
hidden assumptions, 104–9,
143–50; plagiarists (Connor &
Viv), 264–6; the real world (Viv),
266–7; touchy system members,
273–5; water recycling, 63–6
cause-and-effect thinking, 23–5
change, adaptive: as an attitude,
303–4; as democratic, 6–7, 35;
need for flexibility, 219–24, 306–7;
problems requiring, 59–74, 81, 97,
131, 295–6; reasons for choosing,
43; sustaining, 252–4. *See also*
change processes
change agents: change processes
and, 34f, 42f; moving too quickly,
73–4, 76; qualities of, 28, 29;
rationality of, 46–53, 55, 73–4, 76.
See also interventionists; system
leaders
change, authoritative: coercion and,
263–4, 282–6; failure of, 61–6; as

potentially unjust, 6–7; process of,
44–5; reasons for choosing, 43, 74
change frameworks, 8–9, 33–43,
69–72, 324n1. *See also* change
processes
Change Handbook, The (Owen),
328n12
change, obstacles to: client
resistance, 159–67, 173–4, 247–8,
298–300; lack of known solution,
59–66; patterns and structuring,
23–5, 68–9, 83–5, 137
change, planned: authoritative
vs adaptive, 3–7, 33–9, 42f,
102–4, 232–4; conceptions of,
10–16; discourse about, 4; level
of difficulty, 101–4, 102t; as local,
13, 31–2; models, 3–7, 33–43, 91–3,
320n1 (chap. 4); motivations for,
37, 43–4, 57; power involved in,
44–5; strategies for, 37–41, 42f, 43,
45–6, 59–60; theories of action and,
297–8; theories of, 3–4, 16, 54–5;
thinking about, 294–302, 330n1.
See also interventions
change processes: agreeing on,
126–31; balancing acts and, 89,
90t; change agents and, 34f, 42f; vs
content, 13; as deliverable, 224–34,
254; evaluating, 254–7; formal vs
emergent, 27–32, 34f, 42f, 60–9;
including system members in,
129–31, 187, 191–3, 239–41, 244–6;
as involving learning, 60–3, 226,
235; mirroring desired result, 128–
31, 130t, 289; time frame, 226–34,
240–1, 249–51. *See also* change
frameworks; interventions
change, transformational. *See*
change, adaptive

Chin, Robert, 37
clients: assessing capacity, 159–61,
    196–7; increasing capacity, 85, 129,
    197–9, 213–14, 247; respecting
    capacity of, 193, 195–9, 273–5;
    confidentiality, 128, 152, 155, 194t,
    264; dependence of, 247–9, 266,
    268, 290–1; gaining trust of, 126–8,
    140; relationships with, 97–104;
    resistance in, 159–67, 173–4, 247–8,
    298–300; types, 127, 322n17. *See also*
    human systems; system members
coercion: as strategy, 38–9, 42f, 43; by
    system leaders, 263–4, 282–6
cognitive dissonance, 47, 48–9, 51,
    299, 325n4
collaborative change. *See* change,
    adaptive
collusion, 138–43, 164–5, 237,
    246–7, 308
Combs, A.W., 98
competence issues, 289–90
conceptual frameworks. *See* change
    frameworks
confidentiality, 128, 152, 155, 194t,
    264
confirmation bias, 47, 48, 51, 299
continuous learning, 27, 275, 329n4
contracting phase, 97–133; agreeing
    on problem, 109–16; agreeing on
    process, 126–31; balancing act
    of, 97–8; ethical considerations,
    127–8, 282, 285–6; tasks of, 104–32;
    uncovering assumptions, 104–9,
    117–21, 124, 125, 195
conversation, creating meaning
    through, 41–2
core teams, 123t, 187, 210, 250,
    321n15
countertransference, 139

Daniels, Tom, 39–42
data: from emotional responses,
    140–1, 159–61, 163; emotional
    responses to, 172–3, 185; gathering,
    143–50, 152–5; interpreting,
    155–7; manipulation of, 286–7;
    organizing, 187, 188f, 189
data-gathering activities, 115–16,
    152–6, 184
defensive behavior, 173–4, 224,
    298–300
deliverables, 94, 122t, 129,
    224–34, 254
dementia, 69–71
developmental evaluation, 30, 168,
    256. *See also* evaluating
DeWine, Sue, 39–42
dialogic OD (organization
    development), 41–2, 316n9, 324n1
distress. *See* emotions
Dumont, Frank, 50–1, 316n12

emergence, x, 26–7, 43, 87
emergent interventions, 159–61
emergent planning, 27–31, 32
emotions: allowing expression
    of, 114, 202–3; anger, 108–9,
    142–3, 173–4, 207; arising in
    interventionist, 137, 142–3,
    163, 173–4, 241–2; as basis for
    human behavior, 46; projected
    on to interventionist, 139, 162;
    in response to data, 172–3, 185;
    in response to threats, 159–64; in
    response to uncertainty, 134–5,
    211–12, 326n23; as unavoidable,
    244, 271–2; as useful data, 140–1,
    159–61, 163. *See also* blaming
empirical-rational change strategy,
    37, 42f, 43, 45–6

employee engagement, differing views of, 117–20
ends and means, 288–9
environmental scans, 111–16, 125, 129, 131
ethics of intervention, 260–93; confidentiality, 128, 152, 155, 194t, 264; democratic approaches, 267–9, 283–5; "do no harm" dictum, 269–73, 275, 329n4; ethical dilemmas, 271–7, 282–92; harm/benefit assessments, 269–75, 277t; honesty, 127–8, 185, 237–8, 242–4; integrity, 281–2; unethical interventions, 248–9, 265–9; use of power, 267–8;
evaluating: change processes, 254–7; program evaluation, 25, 30, 168, 254–7, 328n23. See also implementation and evaluation phase
exploration phase, 134–70; balancing act of, 137–43; conclusion of, 184; creating space for reflection, 167–8; dealing with resistance, 162–7; emotional reactions to, 134–5; ethical considerations, 286–7; gathering data, 143–50, 152–5; interpreting data, 155–7; noticing emerging problems, 157–61; uncovering different perspectives, 143–50

feedback and decision phase, 171–216; action planning, 209–12; balancing act of, 172–6; checking in, 199; feedback sessions, 191–3, 194t, 195–207; preparing and presenting materials, 186–93, 194t; reflecting on results, 212–13;

respecting client capacity, 193, 195–9; showing the map, 175–6, 194t, 198; themes emerging in, 189–90, 189t. See also problem mapping
feedback sessions, 191–3, 194t, 195–207
Festinger, L., 48
fidelity, 13, 30, 297
focus groups, 152, 155, 156
formal planning, 27–30, 32, 87–9, 90t, 220–4, 327n1
framing. See change frameworks; problems, framing
freezing, 91–2, 320n1 (chap. 4)
fundamental attribution error, 51–2, 158, 203–5, 299–300

Gantt charts, 15
Gino, B.Y.F., 73, 78
Goffman, Erving, 287–8
Gonzalez, D.M., 98
group dynamics and norms, 17–20, 315n11. See also system patterns
groups. See focus groups; human groups

Hart, Hillary, 33
Hawthorne Experiments, 17, 315n11
Heifetz, R.A., 5, 295
helping relationships, 97–104. See also clients
heuristics, 49–51, 300
human behavior: in cases of dementia, 69–71; causes of, 51–4, 79–80; defensiveness, 173–4, 224, 298–300; effect of mindset and situation on, 51–4, 79–80, 203–5, 298; responsive behaviors, 70–1; scapegoating, 199–205, 287–8, 326n12; theories of, 4–5, 33–43,

45–6, 55. *See also* assumptions;
blaming
human emotions. *See* emotions
human groups: advisory groups,
123t, 321n15; dynamics and norms
of, 17–20, 315n11; focus groups,
152, 155, 156; human systems and,
17–19, 177. *See also* human systems
human reasoning: bias and,
46–8, 51, 299, 317nn14–15, 325n4;
cause-and-effect thinking, 23–5;
defensiveness and, 298–9; emotion
and, 46; "fast thinking," 300;
fundamental attribution error,
51–2, 158, 203–5, 299–300;
heuristics, 49–51; systems
thinking, 19, 287, 307; taking time
to think, 73–4, 76, 280–1; thinking
about planned change, 294–302.
See also assumptions; mindsets
human systems: affecting member
behavior, 51–4, 203–5; affordances
and constraints, 78, 136, 193,
195–6; complexity of, 22–7,
210–11; contradictions in, 175,
179, 180f, 181f, 224; defined, 26,
32, 210–11, 300–1; dependence of,
247–9, 266, 268, 290–1; differing
from groups, 17–19; dynamics
and norms of, 17–20, 315n11;
dysfunctional patterns in, 51–2,
179–81, 199–200, 242–3; external
environment affecting, 77, 77f,
182–3; hierarchical systems, 61–3,
126–7, 322n16; induction and
collusion, 138–43, 164–5, 237,
246–7, 308; levels of, 70t, 73t; as
overdetermined, 296; parts of, 20;
patterns of (*see* system patterns);
recognizing problems, 57–8; as

requiring adaptive change, 63–6,
295–6; resistance in, 159–67, 173–4,
247–8, 298–300; responding to
threats, 138–40, 162–5, 246–7,
287–8, 308. *See also* clients; system
members
Hume, David, 46

implementation and evaluation
phase, 217–59; balancing act
of, 219–24; creating reflective
processes, 234–49, 257–9;
deliverable of, 224–34, 254;
difficulty of, 219; program
evaluation, 25, 30, 168, 254–7,
328n23; sustaining change, 251–4;
time frame, 249–51
induction and collusion, 138–43,
164–5, 237, 246–7, 308
integrity, 281–2. *See also* ethics of
intervention
intellectual property theft, 264–6, 291–2
interpretive-communicative change
strategy, 39–41, 42f, 43
intervention phases, 91–7, 320n1
(chap. 4); contracting phase,
97–133; exploration phase, 134–70;
feedback and decision phase,
171–216; implementation and
evaluation phase, 217–59
intervention risks: ethical dilemmas,
271–7, 282–92; induction and
collusion, 138–43, 164–5, 237,
246–7, 308; power dynamics, 152
interventionists: acting with intent,
110, 172, 277–82, 279t; advice for,
98–100, 111–16, 237–49, 251–4;
client dependence on, 247–9,
266, 268, 290–1; client-specific
focus of, 14; compared to doctors,

11–13, 22–3; considering external
pressures, 182–3; dealing with
conflict, 108–9, 207; establishing
trust, 126–8, 140; getting blamed,
173–5; getting pulled into systems,
138–43, 164–5, 237, 246–7, 308;
as instruments of change, 241–2;
qualities of, x–13, 28, 29, 42;
types of, 260; using intuition,
277–9; using story and metaphor,
156–7, 189, 203, 287, 308; valuable
contributions of, 167–8, 237–8
interventions: as balancing acts, ix–x,
26–7, 86–90, 304–10; complexity of,
22–8, 25f, 55, 252–3; conceptions
of, 22–3, 26–30, 132–3; concluding,
247–9, 328n21; content vs process,
13; difficulty of, 89, 219; emergent
interventions, 159–61; emergent
planning, 27–31, 32; emergent vs
formal planning, 27–31, 32; ethics
of (see ethics of intervention);
evaluating, 254–7; as human
systems, 80; implementing,
209–12, 217–54; at multiple levels,
69–72; parts of, 28–9, 32; risk
mitigation, 123t; defining success,
217–18, 252–3; success rate of,
10–12, 93–4, 313n1 (chap. 1);
uniqueness of, 256, 296–7, 328n23;
use of power in, 44–5, 267–8; what
vs how, 13–14. See also balancing
acts; change processes
interviews, 115–16, 152–6

journaling, 142, 232
jumping to solutions, 57, 184

Kahn, William, 51–2, 287–8, 327n1
Kahneman, Daniel, 49, 224, 279–80

Kegan, Robert, 61, 175, 224, 323n5
Kotter, John, 88–9, 93

ladder of inference, 212–13
Lahey, L., 61, 175, 224
Lasagna, Lou, 329n4
late majority/laggards, 240
leaders. See system leaders
Lewin, Kurt, 19, 91, 320n1 (chap. 4),
  323n11, 324n1
Likert, Rensis, 12
Linsky, M., 5, 295
Logan, D., 79, 298, 302
Lovallo, D.P., 224

McGregor, Douglas, 4–5, 295
McLuhan, Marshal, 235
management: beliefs, 4–5, 295;
  practices, 113–14; systems, 5
mapping. See problem mapping
Marshak, R.J., 41–3
means and ends, 288–9
members. See system members
mental models. See mindsets
Milgram, Stanley, 52–4
mindsets: adaptive mindsets, 253,
  328n21; case history, 143–50;
  interfering with reasoning,
  47–53, 299–300, 317nn14–15; as
  unconscious, 136–7, 175. See also
  assumptions; human reasoning
  mistakes, 167–8, 324n15
Model I and II, 5, 295
Moyan, Deirdre, 141

Nisbett, R.E., 51, 205, 299–300
Nohria, Nitin, Breaking the Code of
  Change, 3–4, 5, 295
normative-reeducative change
  strategy, 37–8, 40, 42f, 43

organizational change. *See* change, planned

organizational leaders. *See* change agents; system leaders

organizations. *See* systems

ORID designs (Objective, Reflective, Interpretive, and Decisional), 195t, 212–13, 214t

overdetermination, 296

Owen, Harrison, *The Change Handbook*, 328n12

parallel process, 139–40

paralysis by analysis, 58

participative change. *See* change, adaptive

pattern causality, 41–2, 307–8, 316n9, 320n21

patterns. *See* system patterns

Patton, Michael, *Qualitative Research & Evaluation Methods*, 323n11

Pawson, R., 328n23

Pitcher, Patricia, 239

plagiarism, 264–6, 291–2

Plan-Do-Study-Act (PDSA) cycle, 96–7, 236–7

power, in interventions, 44–5, 267–8

power-coercive change strategy, 38–9, 42f, 43

predictive change. *See* change, authoritative

problem mapping: examples, 149f, 178–82, 183f; purpose of, 8–9, 136, 178, 183–4, 186; by system members, 198

problem solving, future of, 310–12

problems: adaptive problems, 59–74, 81, 97, 131; agreeing on, 109–16; caused by competing goals, 175,

179–81, 180f, 181f, 224; framing, 57–67, 121, 124–5, 171–3, 310–11; issue management, 124t; "in the room," 157–61, 172–3, 306–7; solving, 73–4, 76, 80–1, 310–11; technical problems, 3–7, 59, 66, 102–4

processes, reflective, 167–8, 195t, 212–13, 234–49, 256–7

program evaluation, 25, 30, 168, 256, 328n23

projective identification, 139

projects: charters, 120–4, 128, 132; deliverables, 94, 122t, 129, 224–34; journals, 142, 232; meetings, 168; organization, 123t, 321n15; post-mortem, 256–7

psychological safety: confidentiality and, 114; creating, 184–5, 194t, 207–8, 220, 327n1; striking a balance, 86, 139–40, 304–5

qualitative methods, 153, 323n11

Qualitative Research & Evaluation Methods (Patton), 323n11

realistic evaluation, 25–6, 256, 328n23. *See also* evaluating

reasoning. *See* human reasoning

red zone, 135

Reflective Practitioner, The (Schön), 73

reflective processes, 167–8, 195t, 212–13, 234–49, 256–7

refreezing, 91, 92, 320n1 (chap. 4)

relational pauses, 326n23

representativeness heuristic, 49

Requests for Proposal (RFPs), 111, 112, 222–4

responsive behaviors, 70–1

risk mitigation, 123t

Rogers, Carl, 305

Rogers, Everett, 240
Ross, L., 51, 205, 299–300

scapegoating. *See* blaming
Schein, Edgar, 14–15, 304–5, 309–10, 322n17
Schön, Donald, *The Reflective Practitioner*, 73, 279, 311
Schwarz, Roger, 328n17
Senge, Peter, 19
sensemaking sessions. *See* feedback sessions
shared intentionality, 110
Sibony, O., 224
Smith, Cedric, 329n4
social change. *See* change, planned
social facts, 316n6
social structure: blocking change, 84–5; defined, 18–19, 318n8; levels of, 70t, 73t; modeling, 76–80, 176–8, 300–2. *See also* system patterns
social world. *See* human systems
Staats, B., 73, 78
stakeholders. *See* system members
Stanovich, Keith, 298
stealing intellectual property, 264–6, 291–2
Steiner, George, 291
Stimson, Lewis, 329n4
Stouten, J., 89
strategies for change, 37–41, 42f, 43, 45–6, 59–60
structuring. *See* social structure
subject-object theory, 136, 323n5
surveys, 152–3
System 1 cognition, 279–80
system leaders: approaches of, 3–6, 33–6, 239, 282–8; beliefs of, 4–5, 295; coercing change, 61–3, 263–4,

282–6; compared to doctors, 12–13; getting credit or blame, 114, 199–200, 326n10, 326n12; thinking about change, 11–13; using power, 44–5. *See also* change agents
system members: checking in with, 239–41, 244–6; disclosures from, 135–6, 323n4; discovering solutions, 157, 189, 191, 205–6, 237; feedback sessions with, 191–3, 194t, 195–207; flawed reasoning of, 48, 55; focus groups with, 152, 155, 156; gaining trust of, 126–8; interviewing, 115–16, 152–6; involvement in change process, 129–31, 187, 191–3, 210, 239–41, 244–6; knowledge distributed among, 35–6, 126–7; living the solution, 126; as part of the problem, 158–61, 186–7; as playing roles, 164, 203. *See also* clients
system patterns: blocking change, 68–9, 83–4, 137; disrupting, 157–61, 172–3, 241–2, 306–7; dysfunctional patterns, 51–2, 179–82, 199–200, 242–3; as linked to structure, 83–5, 137; looked at as a thing, 40, 136, 218–19, 323n5; mapping (*see* problem mapping); modeling, 70t, 76–80, 176–8, 300–2; pattern causality, 41–2, 307–8, 316n9, 320n21; stability of, 18–19. *See also* social structure
systems. *See* human systems
systems thinking, 19, 287, 307

taking sides. *See* collusion
tales from the field. *See* case histories
Taylor, Frederick, 284

teams, core, 123t, 187, 210, 250,
    321n15
technical change. *See* change,
    authoritative
technical problems, 3–7, 59, 66,
    102–4. *See also* change,
    authoritative
Theories E, O, X, and Y, 3–5, 295
theories of action: defined, 15–16,
    54–5; guiding change, 297–8, 306;
    theories-in-use and, 175, 314n5,
    322n16
theories of change, 3–5, 37–42, 295
theories-in-use, 175, 314n5, 322n16
theory of leadership, 239
thinking. *See* human reasoning
Tilley, N., 328n23

transitional objects, 327n1
trolley problem, 272
Tversky, Amos, 49
undiscussables, 136, 137
unfreezing, 91–2, 320n1 (chap. 4)

von Moltke, H.G., 29, 315n17

Waddell, Craig, 33
water recycling, 63–4
Watzlawick, P., 309, 317n14
WIIFM ("What's in it for
    me?") phenomenon,
    37
Winnicott, D.W., 327n1

Zaffron, S., 79, 298, 302

Lightning Source UK Ltd.
Milton Keynes UK
UKHW010624061121
393462UK00003B/28/J